AF441814

THE COMPLETE SALESPERSON

THE COMPLETE SALESPERSON

A recipe for success in direct selling which explains what you will need to believe, to think, to do, and to feel, in order to achieve a successful sales career.

Rosemary Moore

Hale & Iremonger

Typeset, printed & bound by
Southwood Press Pty Limited
80–92 Chapel Street, Marrickville, NSW

For the publisher
Hale & Iremonger Pty Limited
GPO Box 2552, Sydney, NSW

National Library of Australia Catalogue Card no. and
ISBN 0 86806 278 2

PREFACE

We are all salespeople.
Somewhere, sometime, each of us needs to persuade others to
our way of thinking.

The boy on the street corner sells newspapers . . .
The teacher and the preacher sell knowledge . . .
The high school graduate sells his potential . . .
The doctor sells his skills . . .
The consultant sells his service . . .

We are custodians of our world while we live, responsible to,
and responsible for, the generations to follow . . .

The future of our planet may one day depend on the ability
of just one person . . . to persuade.

It has happened before!

Persuasion is a large part of selling,
and it is valuable for each of us to consider
how we might become more proficient in its use.

DEDICATION

This book is dedicated to the three major influences in my sales career
Margaret Christensen
Diana Rose
Peter Dinsdale
whose contribution to the sales industry has spread beyond the shores
of Australasia, affecting the actions and attitudes of thousands
of salespeople
. . . and into whose footprints
I have tried, for years, to fit my feet.

This book acknowledges a deep indebtedness
to the talent and tolerance of
Judy Hardy of the United States of America,
who bravely accepted the task of copy-editing and translating
the manuscript into an understandable language and spelling
for the salespeople of Canada and America,

and to the computer expertise, patience and support of
my son, Nicholas,
without which
The Complete Salesperson
would have remained forever incomplete.

PROLOGUE

The restaurant was shaded from the sun's heat by the overhanging build-
ings, but I knew that the trainees for the sales training class I was about
to run would arrive hot and tired, as the streets were stifling. I wanted to
reward them with a friendly welcome, so I sat over my iced coffee
memorizing their names. Three young people came and sat at an
adjacent table, and their conversation invaded my concentration.

'How did your interview go, Tom?'

'No good . . . there were eight others waiting for interviews. I don't
think I'll get the job; it didn't sound like much anyway.'

'You never know, you might be lucky.'

'Look, Betty, it's hopeless. I've tried for three months now . . .'

'Well, I've been offered a sales job . . . it sounds all right and I can
work in my own time.' The girl sounded optimistic.

'Commission selling? Oh, I've done all that . . . you can always get
a sales job . . . that's no good.'

'John,' she turned to the second boy, 'didn't you do selling for a
while?'

'No, I was warned off before I started.'

'What happened?'

'They showed me some products and told me I had to close.'

'Close what? What's that?'

'This closing business, I couldn't get the gist of it, Betty, . . . I
wouldn't get into selling if I were you.'

As their words penetrated my conscious thought, I was reminded of
the parable of the sower, which Jesus told the crowd listening by the lake.

'A farmer went out to sow his seed. As he was scattering the seed, some fell along the path and the birds came and ate it up; some fell on rocky places where it did not have much soil. It sprang up quickly because the soil was shallow, but when the sun came up the plants were scorched and they withered because they had no roots. Other seed fell among thorns, which grew up and choked the plants. Still other seed fell on good soil where it produced a crop, a hundred, sixty or thirty times what was sown . . .'

It seemed to me that John had been a victim of the birds, Tom had withered for lack of roots, and Betty was being choked by thorns . . . I looked across at the three young people. How sad it was that the great profession of salesmanship is itself sold so disparagingly! On impulse I picked up my list and crossed to their table. Placing my business card on the table I explained, 'Forgive me for interrupting but I couldn't help hearing your conversation. I'm a sales manager and I believe I can help you. My office is on the third floor. If you will come up at 5:00 o'clock, I will tell you a story which could change your lives.' John, Betty and Tom came at 5:00 o'clock, and this book in essence is the story I told them.

The nineteenth-century British statesman, William Gladstone, once said,

'Man himself is the crowning wonder of creation; the study of his nature is the noblest study the world affords.'

This book studies two very important people

A SALESPERSON AND HIS CUSTOMER!

ANALYSIS OF A SALESPERSON

SECTION 1 (p.25)
Chapters

SECTION 2 (p.65)
Chapters

ANALYSIS OF A CUSTOMER (p.262)

CONTENTS

SECTION 1   ANALYSIS OF A SALESPERSON

SECTION 2

ANALYSIS OF A CUSTOMER

EXPLANATION

The English language lacks a word meaning 'he or she' and 'him or her'.
It offers only 'them' and 'their', which, to my understanding, mean
'he and she' 'his and her'. I ask you, therefore,
to consider 'he' and 'him' as representative of both men and women.
I ask the women to understand
that this decision was made in the interests of brevity,
— and forgive!

INTRODUCTION

In the beginning I would like you to meet my two friends and fellow travelers, Pozi and Neg. I was introduced to them as Positive and Negative, but when I got to know them well it seemed natural to give them more friendly names.

I met Neg first; he was my constant companion during my first doubt-filled year as a salesperson. It was comforting to listen to the re-assuring advice which he willingly gave. He carried a bag containing a mixture of excuses and problems which he happily shared, and he kept a supply of carpets under which he encouraged me to hide anything bothersome. Our friends make us feel secure by taking away feelings of guilt and shame, and creating comfort zones of self esteem. Neg did this for me. Everywhere I went Neg came along, but looking back we never went very far . . . around the kitchen table, around the house and garden, . . . and of course we shared many cups of coffee. We never ventured out much because when we did Neg would point out the advantages of going home, so in the end there didn't seem much sense in making the effort to go out.

One day I made my first sale and Pozi came to congratulate me. Right away he showed me how I could achieve something with my life. He made me feel excited, and I asked him to stay awhile so we could become acquainted. He did! Then he started taking me out, and I began going places I'd never dreamed of visiting before. It was a bit frightening at first, so I tucked Neg into my pocket just in case I needed him; but Pozi was so convincing that I found I preferred listening to him, even though he kept suggesting I do things I knew perfectly well I couldn't do. Neg had said so, and Neg so often proved to be right.

Both Pozi and Neg were wonderful story tellers and I loved to listen, but somehow Pozi could make me believe that he could write me into one of his inspiring stories, but Neg's heroes were not at all like me.

When I became a salesperson, in a sense, I went on a journey. Pozi led me out by the hand, gave me a flashlight, a map and running shoes; but Neg insisted on coming too, as he said that the average salesperson always needed him sooner or later, and he was sure I was average.

Eventually Pozi became the major influence in my life, and I began to see Neg as he really was, pathetic somehow. When he realized his influence was lost, he changed his clothes, wore a mask, and adopted a new approach, which he likes to do sometimes, but I still could recognize him.

In the end I made it to the top of my mountain, thanks to Pozi, and when I gaze down into the valley below I can sometimes just see Neg in the distance, dashing about talking to everyone who will listen, dissuading them from attempting the mountain climb.

To whom will you listen . . . Neg . . . or Pozi?

Section One

Chapter One

INTELLECTUALLY

1.1 The intellect's contribution to the success of a salesperson

One of the most significant differences between mankind and other animals is humanity's ability to reason. Any study of the components of a salesperson must acknowledge the contribution made by this faculty. A successful salesperson applies his intellect to every aspect of his career. This must be his starting point because, although influenced by other facets of his composition, it is with his intellectual or mental faculty that his decisions are made.

His emotional component may argue that it would like a certain action taken.

His spiritual component may argue that it should be taken.

His creative component may argue that it can be taken.

His financial component may argue that it can afford to be taken.

But if his intellectual component has decided that it won't be taken, then taken it will not be!

So, if his intellectual faculty is to make a decision, it must be presented with logical reasons, facts and benefits, upon which a decision can be based.

The brain of a human being is a marvelous creation. Computers are constantly in the process of developing more advanced skills, but the brain will never be superseded. What comes out of a computer depends on what goes in, but the human brain holds within itself the capacity to imagine and create. A computer will always be earthbound, but the human spirit knows no bounds.

The greatest physicist of recent times, Albert Einstein, first made the world aware that, during an average lifetime, only one tenth of our intellectual capacity is used, so a salesperson who must live on the results of his efforts should devise ways of developing his mental abilities to ensure they serve him effectively.

1.2 How you can help

At this point, if you are a salesperson you might ask yourself,

'How can I do this? What steps can I take to develop my intellect?'

First, give your intellectual faculty plenty of valuable stimulation. The output of an intellect depends on the input it receives. Small minds express themselves through incessant chatter about self or other people. Average minds are preoccupied with things; for men usually cars, boats, or sports, for women usually clothes, children, or social activity. Progressive minds reveal themselves through talk about ideas, change, improvement and growth in their lives and in community contribution. Feed your mind with new ideas through exposure to learning experiences and seminars, books, tapes, records. Ask achievers for their success formulae. To copy is to compliment: imitation is the sincerest form of flattery.

Set goals which stretch your potential, accept short and long term tasks which challenge. Give your intellect lots of sales material, phone numbers, names, addresses, dates and times to memorize; decisions to make; problems to solve. A reliable memory is a great asset to a salesperson. Face your intellectual component with the reality of your achievements, and compliment it with high expectations. The less you ask of your intellect, the less it will be capable of achieving.

1.3 Making positive decisions

I like to imagine that we harbor two consultants within our brain which reliably provide us with the benefit of different opinions. Each of these consultants attempts to advise and direct our actions, with our interests as its propelling force. One tends to protect our immediate comfort and the other, with greater vision, plans for our future betterment. If you are not practiced at decision making, two opinions can leave you undecided, and indecision invariably translates into lack of activity — when it is action you need!

The first action you attempt in response to a positive decision, (perhaps to get out your door) may be countermanded by an inner voice which presents the logical reason the intellect needs to form a negative decision.

'I must write that letter first.'

'Those phone calls are important.'

'Another cup of coffee will sustain me . . .'

Salespeople who lose listen to the voice which recommends a comfort zone, a no-risk, no-effort environment.

As long ago as the eighteenth century, the German poet Heinrich Heine wrote:

'The men of action are, after all, only the unconscious intruments of the men of thought.'

The salesperson's constant aim should be to become a conscious instrument of his own thought.

SUCCESS IN LIFE DOES NOT STEM FROM A SINGLE MAJOR CORRECT DECISION AT A GIVEN POINT IN TIME: IT GROWS AS THE RESULT OF HABITUAL MINOR RIGHT DECISIONS ON A DAILY BASIS.

Too often the work environment asks you to make one important decision, such as a career choice, and then offers few other decision making opportunities, perhaps for many years. A successful sales career results from constant decision making, even if many of these decisions would seem unimportant if taken out of the framework of a sales environment.

If you are to succeed you must listen to the voice that drives you into the cold when you'd rather be warm; to work when you'd rather rest; to discipline in all its forms when you'd rather be undisciplined. This is the price of success in salesmanship, and it's cash up front, no time payments here . . . and when you are successful you will look back on the price you paid as measurable in small coins.

The first step to achievement is to accept the responsibility of developing your intellectual faculty to its maximum potential.

The second step is to commit that potential to the attainment of goals.

Then, with growing confidence, you will reach out to give and receive the manifold benefits of a successful sales career.

Chapter Two

PHYSICALLY

2.1 The need for stamina

Salespeople need stamina! Not for us is the cosy security of four walls and a typewriter, — if a life is lived within four walls the best of experience is shut out!

As a salesperson, you make your own world in an environment that has no walls, no ceiling and few boundaries; but stamina is vital as you are required constantly to move, to lift, to exert, sometimes in demanding bursts, sometimes in prolonged drives.

The journalist Mignon McLaughlin wrote,

> 'Our strength is often composed of the weakness we're damned if we're going to show!'

Successful salespeople demonstrate this truth — sometimes daily!

2.2 Healthy attitudes

My philosophy on health has always been simplicity itself — *forget it!*

Dr. O. Carl Simonton, M.D., director of the Cancer Counseling and Research Center in Fort Worth, Texas, wrote in *Getting Well Again*,

> 'The results of our approach to cancer treatment made us confident of this conclusion — a positive mental attitude participation can influence the onset of disease, the outcome of treatment and quality of life.'

The author Mark Twain gave a light-hearted version of this attitude when he said,

'Part of the secret of success in life is to eat what you like and let the food fight it out inside!'

Eat when you're hungry, drink when you're thirsty, but seldom to your full capacity! Consume quality food, not excess quantities of food (it costs the same in the long run), and drink lots of water. Eat energy generating meals and eat slowly. In this way you will give your appetite a chance to feel satisfied before you consider that second helping of pudding. If you eat quickly, you don't allow time for the effect of your food to do battle with your appetite, consequently it will busy itself asking for more. If you vigorously gratify it, half an hour later you can experience the discomfort of having eaten more than you needed!

Overweight salespeople need to diet. Face the fact that you are allowing that vital little machine, which is your body, to operate under stress. It must carry more weight wherever it goes, and the components upon which you depend can be placed in jeopardy. Many people give more thought to and invest more money in maintaining their car in good running order than their bodies!

The most commonsensical diet I know is *eat less*; it is simple, communicative and effective. Check your progress with a constant reminder. Mount the bathroom scales daily, they never pay false compliments. But don't be like the lady who declared she weighed herself every day . . . and when asked what she weighed, replied,

'I don't know because I can't wear my glasses when on the scales in case they add to my weight!'

Slogans are helpful in mental discipline, so commit these words to memory, and apply them to every gastronomical temptation.

'It will be one minute in my mouth, one hour in my stomach, and a lifetime on my hips!'

2.3   Unhealthy attitudes

I believe too many people have formed a psychological dependence on pills and medicine, and these can be more addictive than is commonly realized.

Don't be a pill-popper! Don't take pills with the 'I'll try this' attitude. Too often medicines are given the credit which rightly belongs to time. Be really 'sold' on its necessity before you agree to subject your body to its influence.

Stretch your potential; the mind can overcome physical problems, if it is not allowed to form the habit of outside dependence.

Generally, non-achievers have higher medical costs than achievers.

> IT IS NOT SO MUCH THE SYMPTOMS OF ILLNESS THAT RESULT IN FAILURE, BUT THAT FAILURE RESULTS IN THE SYMPTOMS OF ILLNESS.

Research has shown that 85 percent of all patients crowding doctors' offices are experiencing psychosomatic disorders. Those who wait for an ache or pain to direct their activity and dominate their thinking will not wait in vain.

The mind should direct the body; not the body the mind.

Accept the responsibility of directing your thoughts into result-oriented activity, and your body will welcome this rightful leadership. You will find, in many cases, it will make the necessary adjustments and follow!

2.4   What you can do to help

You have approximately six hundred muscles in your body — each one needs daily exercise. Does that sound difficult? It isn't. All body motion involves muscles and they develop through use and challenge. Stretch . . ., dance to music — pull the curtains and play a cassette. Climb the stairs two at a time, run when you would walk. Use the steps rather than the elevator, break sitting or standing sessions with movement. Exercise while waiting for a kettle to boil, or the photocopier to warm up; it's an intelligent investment of otherwise wasted time!

There is no need to make exercise a fetish, a chore or a time waster. Choose a sport — tennis, golf, squash, or simply walk, jog, or swim, which also provides you with mental stimulation and fun. You need less sleep than is commonly believed, *but be warned* — if you hoot with the owls at night, you can't expect to soar with the eagles in the morning!

2.5   Inspirational attitudes

We feel privileged in Zondervan of Australasia to count among our sales agents Julie Lambert of South Australia. Julie, born with cerebral palsy, was institutionalized at an early age. Her refusal to allow this devastating physical handicap to stop her becoming an achiever has inspired all who know her. Her speech is affected, her movements are uncontrollable, and she has never known the luxury of walking, and yet she has masterminded a Church for the Handicapped. She is the editor of a magazine called 'Praise Him Anyway', and is a sales agent for the Book of Life, Zondervan's family Bible programme.

Another of our salespeople commented,

> 'I used to be a failure but when I thought about Julie Lambert I decided to make greater demands on my own ability to cope with life.'

By her example, Julie Lambert shows us how much can be done, with so little, by refusing to accept the handicap of so much. My life's experience has never included serious illness, but I have a deep respect for people who fill leading sales roles, despite ill-health or handicaps. These people's achievements cannot be measured as only personal; their examples inspire us all to cope better with the challenges of the sales environment. Their lives set before us the victory of the human spirit over its physical component. Who can read these inspiring words . . .

> 'I CRIED, BECAUSE I HAD NO SHOES,
> UNTIL I MET A MAN WHO HAD NO FEET'

. . . without realigning his attitude? Salespeople need to give their physical component a high priority. But, since our physical, mental, emotional and spiritual conditions are connected, we must avoid nurturing one and neglecting another.

2.6 Balanced strength is the key

If a salesperson does not strengthen himself mentally, he will be a ready listener to the voice that recommends a lower goal.

If a salesperson does not strengthen himself spiritually, he will happily harken to the voice which persuades him God has other work for him.

If a salesperson does not strengthen himself emotionally, he will fall easy prey to the voice that offers a comfort zone.

If a salesperson does not strengthen his character and align his commitments to the ethical, fear will take a disproportionate grip of his life's direction.

If a salesperson does not strengthen himself physically, the wind will blow him from the marketplace.

A salesperson should accept the responsibility and act to keep his body warm, rested, fed, exercised and at a top performance level on a regular basis . . . and then tell it — 'GO AND MOVE THE WORLD!'

Chapter Three

SPIRITUALLY

3.1 The benefit of faith

Christian salespeople do not need a sales book to suggest that life, without a reverence for God, would be without ultimate purpose. However, for the many hundreds of achieving and non-achieving salespeople who face the environment without faith, I would like simply to emphasize the importance of faith in the life of a salesperson.

There has never been a challenge that isn't more readily overcome by faith, nor a door which isn't more widely opened by love. Love serves; salespeople need to serve.

No one can deny that Christianity is an active force for peace in the world today; but it does not stop at nations. It offers an inner peace to everyone who seeks and finds God. Sadly, Christianity is perceived by many as the 'don't do' doctrine put forward in parts of the Old Testament, and summarized by the Ten Commandments in Exodus. Through a veil of negativity the focus seems to be on restriction, resignation, condemnation, submission, relinquishment, humility, perdition and surrender.

But in the New Testament the life and words of Jesus Christ stand in marked contrast to this interpretation of Christianity. He replaced negatives with positives, despair with hope, condemnation with forgiveness, and fear with love.

In John 15:12 we read the one commandment Jesus Christ gave the world,

> 'This is my commandment, that you love one another, as I have loved you.'

What especially great advice for a salesperson!

And the French artist Vincent Van Gogh left us a combination of words as arresting as one of his paintings when he wrote:

'I always think that the best way to know God is to love many things.'

3.2   His example

Because Jesus Christ took His product so effectively to the people of His time over a billion Christians acknowledge Him today. His product and His teaching offer justice towards all people and humility to God. He preached mercy and brotherhood, and taught the love of God.

Salespeople can readily identify with the experiences of Jesus' life. Was he not involved in explaining, teaching, demonstrating, and handling excuses?

Did He not suffer rejection, and sometimes fail to convince the prospect of His product's value to them?

Are there not parallels between the encouragement, teaching and motivation received by the Disciples from Jesus, and the work done in sales organizations?

Did He not faithfully persevere with His work, despite criticism, fatigue and stress?

We can learn much about communication from His use of parables to emphasize His message. Successful salespeople constantly use stories with which their prospects can relate: relevant stories can be powerfully persuasive.

A salesperson who has found faith need never travel alone. A wise and loving counselor goes with you as you face each door and confront every challenge. If you have no faith, commit yourself to acquiring a knowledge of the teachings of the Bible. It is especially inspirational for salespeople, and among its pages faith may be revealed to you.

Faith should not be a lifeline, but rather a springboard.

Faith should not be an insurance policy, but rather a policy of assurance.

In 1896 Charles Sheldon wrote a book called *In His Steps*, which was reprinted by the Zondervan Corporation. Every salesperson would find beneficial the simple suggestions for attitude in daily life found in its pages.

It tells the story of Dr. Henry Maxwell, Pastor of the First Church of Raymond in America, who struggled with the idea that Christian discipleship demanded more than mental assent. He suggested that every attitude and action in life should be prefaced with the question, 'What would Jesus do in this situation if He were me?'

The application of this simple question to the many challenging, and sometimes complex situations faced in a sales environment, brings into sharp focus a positive and practical solution.

It is my conviction that all salespeople would be fortified by a belief and faith in God. Those who do not know this benefit would, in all probability, grant that the characters of the greatest among us are enriched by the acknowledgement of a divine power greater than ourselves, and a gratitude for our opportunities; and that the characters of the humblest among us are comforted and strengthened by the knowledge of God's love.

I believe Jesus Christ was the greatest direct salesman who ever lived, — *get to know Him!*

GOD'S GIFT TO EACH OF US IS OUR POTENTIAL.
WHAT WE BECOME IS OUR GIFT TO GOD.

Chapter Four

EMOTIONALLY

4.1 Emotion and conditioned thinking

The Swiss psychologist, Carl Gustav Jung, once said:

> 'Emotion is the chief source of all becoming conscious. There can
> be no transforming of darkness into light, and of apathy into move-
> ment, without emotion.'

How true, but more probably you will have heard people talk of
emotions in a disparaging manner. You may have been warned against
making emotional decisions. Women especially are accused of reacting
emotionally to a situation. Public opinion has been conditioned to
believing that a judicious decision cannot result if emotion has been an
influencing factor.

In my opinion, men are just as emotional as women, but customs and
the attitudes of our times decree that it is unmanly to acknowledge or express emotion, except in traditional channels. From birth, society conditions our thinking to ensure we grow up qualified to fill acceptable
roles.

Why do we give our girls dolls and our boys guns?

It is not because of inherited preferences.

No, it is simply our turn to perpetuate the conditioned thinking to
which we were subjected.

A knowledge of conditioned thinking and how emotions are influenced helps a salesperson understand and handle 'people' situations,
because emotion is feeling, and all salespeople need to 'feel' for, with, and
on behalf of — their prospects.

4.2   A knowledge and understanding of emotions

A knowledge of emotion and how it affects a sales demonstration and influences buying decisions should be part of on-going sales training. There are many and strongly contrasting emotions.

Here are some of the most activating:

ecstasy	love	jealousy	pride	envy
apprehension	guilt	relief	hate	anxiety
disillusionment	shame	compassion	fear	grief
resentment	remorse	rage	desire	fury
jubilation	pity	hope	joy	terror

Fear is one of the most influential emotions, but love is more powerful still. Fear manifests itself into all sorts of buying reasons, as does love. Fear is like waves in the sea, fast to rise and fall, but love is more like the waters of a lake, constant, reliable, provident.

During a sales demonstration a salesperson can make of fear what he can, quickly, before it recedes. But to make of love what he can, he will need to bring the product to the water's edge, and with sincerity, value and explanation enter and disturb the often deep water of the prospect's needs.

It is important for a salesperson to identify emotions because of their influence on buying decisions, but all resultant action should filter through his integrity before being introduced to a sales demonstration.

Genuine concern for the customer's interest is the first priority of quality salesmanship.

4.3   Emotion's counterpoint — logic

Logic deals with reasons — reasons for or against buying — and should not be confused with emotions which deal with feelings.

> LOGIC GIVES A REASON TO BUY, BUT EMOTION GIVES THE POWER TO ACT.

Some common logical buying reasons are:
1. Feature benefits
2. Changed attitudes
3. Security
4. Altered circumstances
5. Specific functions

6. Price
7. Time/Lack of time
8. Convenience
9. Health
10. Necessity

The degree to which logic and emotion are involved in a demonstration depends on:

1. The kind of product
2. The salesperson's character and techniques
3. The prospect's character, convictions and reactional tendencies.

4.4 Striking the balance

During a sales presentation, logic and emotion battle for supremacy, although the nature of some products precludes logical involvement, and the nature of others precludes emotional intervention.

Normally, however, both are involved to varying degrees when buying decisions are made, and a salesperson should enlist the support of both. This is achieved by supplying the prospect with facts, features, benefits, appeal and explanation, which satisfy his emotional and logical expectations of the product's potential.

Here is an example of the balance:

The salesperson says,

'Mrs. Jasper, I can give you 40 percent off the listed price of this beautiful lounge suite . . . and the manufacturer's not making any more of this particular quality material. This is a real bargain which won't be repeated, and you must admit that somehow it makes you feel "on a cloud" the way it cushions you so gently when you sit down to rest . . .'

Logic and emotion are both taken into account in these statements.

Logical objection can be 'swamped' by a flood of emotion, but it does not drown . . . it can keep bobbing back, and if the salesperson makes a mistake, or adopts an unwelcome attitude of which the prospect disapproves, logic will rise and overshadow emotion, and the sale is lost.

The successful salesperson understands a balance must be achieved. Too much of either can result in a cancelled sale, or a discontented customer.

4.5   **The influence of emotion**

Emotions persuade, and many products are sold as a result of this influence.

A mother purchases an encyclopedia; she wants her children to achieve at school. Love can be the influencing emotion.

A father selects an insurance policy; fear can be the influencing emotion.

A neighbor chooses a new car; shame of the old one can be the influencing emotion.

A family decides on a larger home; envy of another's can be the influencing emotion.

A boy buys a bunch of daffodils for a girl; hope can be the influencing emotion.

If insufficient consideration is given to emotional needs, a purchase can result which is later regretted.

Robert Jones was an example of this when he went shopping for his twelve year old daughter's birthday present. Since he was away on business and missed the actual day he was anxious to compensate for his absence by returning with a special gift. He decided on a pretty pink dress. He had purposely checked her measurements prior to his departure, so size wasn't a problem (logical anticipation). The shop assistant was most helpful, and he described his preference for material which would wear well (logic again). He selected a plain skirt so his wife would not have difficulty with ironing pleats (logic). Despite his thoughtfulness, Robert Jones was never destined to see his daughter wear the dress, since when she saw it, she dissolved into tears saying,

'*Pink!* Everyone knows pink is sissy, and that only babies wear pink.'

No amount of logical persuasion ('but your mother has a pink suit . . .') could change her opinion. The sale so logically planned and executed ended in a decision later regretted.

So it was with Harriet Burton. She made a different mistake, but a more costly one. In her own words, she just 'fell in love' with a deep, fluffy cream carpet, so soft and luxurious in quality that she simply could not resist (emotion). But her husband pointed out it was impractical for their beach home. Their four children and dogs would run sand into it every day, and the higher price meant they would have to forego furniture.

Fortunately Harriet Burton was able to cancel, but she lost her deposit.

The successful salesperson knows that the only customer he wants and needs is a contented, satisfied one!

4.6 Emotions in a sales demonstration

Every salesperson should be influenced by emotion, but during a demonstration it should not govern what you say or how you act.
You are there to display the product, not your feelings!
In a single demonstration a salesperson can be called upon to contend with many emotions. Among these can be hope for the sale, fear of mishandling the closes, compassion for the prospect, and relief at the outcome, all felt by him. At the same time, he can be called upon to contend with the customer's fear of a wrong decision, love of children, desire for improvement, or resentment of truth. Each demonstration arouses different emotions. A salesperson needs to be something of a psychologist. An emotional reaction of kindness or sympathy should never prompt you to offer to assist with payment of the product, but rather should manifest itself as perceivable evidence of genuine care and concern.

Excessive emotional reaction of irritation or impatience in the face of a disappointment is unprofessional. Jubilation in the face of a decision to buy can cause your prospect to react by thinking,

> Didn't he expect to make the sale? I wonder why. Perhaps it's not as good as I thought . . . we'd better think again . . .

Be friendly, happy and relaxed, but keep excitement and enthusiasm for later. Share them with your family, the other salespeople in the office, or your manager. Every salesperson benefits from seeing and feeling the propelling forces of these splendid emotions.

Never denigrate emotions. They are a salesperson's friends. Most people reach the peak of their human experience through emotion. Instead you should fear lack of emotion.

The Jewish Auschwitz internee, Elie Wiesel, writing from tragic experience, warns the world:

> 'I have seen children thrown into flames, alive, so I have learned the fragility of the human condition. I have learned the dangers of indifference, the crime of indifference. For the opposite of love, I have learned, is not hate, but indifference.'

Chapter Five

FINANCIALLY

It is the love of money, not money itself, which the Bible states is the root of all evil. There is a difference. We should have a respect for the significance of money in human achievement.

Many of man's greatest creations have been inspired by the desire to make money. When George Frederick Handel was desperate for money, he shut himself away for three weeks, and emerged with the complete score of the *Messiah*.

He acknowledged that money had been his motivator!

A financially insecure salesperson should make a commitment to financial independence, and work tirelessly to provide for those dependent upon him. A financially secure salesperson should accept the responsibility of investing his money in a growth direction.

Good stewardship starts with an attitude of accountability.

I have lived with money and I have lived without it. As a salesperson you will experience both, and this experience provides you with an opportunity to accredit the effect of money on your life with greater accuracy. Those who have never had it, and those who have never been without it, tend to lay disproportionate praise or blame on the possession of money.

It is when you have known both that you are in a position to assess its contribution to the quality of your life.

5.2 It's up to you

No financial ceiling is ever placed on a commission salesperson. You are paid what you are worth. You employ yourself, and can give yourself a raise at any time, simply by:

1. working more effectively
2. working longer hours

For this reason, salespeople in many companies have access to wealth, but at the same time, through lack of knowledge or training, make poor investments and lose their security.

The salesperson is back to base one!

If this has been your experience console yourself with the realization that

> IF YOU MADE A MISTAKE AND YOU LEARNED FROM IT,
> YOU NEVER MADE A MISTAKE!

Though it offers no guarantees, money can bring peace, comfort, leisure, pride, satisfaction, and happiness, but it also can attract responsibility, complex and continuous decision-making, anxiety, stress, perhaps jealousy, envy or blame. Salespeople are especially vulnerable to the ravages of fortune. They can be and often are in a position of affluence one moment, and financial calamity the next, due to ignorance, extenuating circumstances or environmental inexperience.

5.3   Your need for sound financial planning

In Shakespeare's play *Hamlet*, Polonius gave advice every salesperson could valuably heed.

> 'Never a borrower nor a lender be:
> for loan oft loses both itself and friend.'

Gratitude for money lent all too often ceases the moment it is given.

Most salespeople have a need for sound advice in the area of financial planning.

There are two ways of accumulating money:

1. Either you go out and work to increase its inflow or
2. you work to block the areas of outflow.

Notice they both involve work! Financial security and peace of mind result from a lifestyle that ensures a greater inflow than outflow, with a built-in balance for personal needs. If each month a family provider can go out with the knowledge that he is making steady progress towards long term financial goals such as house, car, and children's education, doubts cease to punctuate his attitude. His performance improves.

Every salesperson benefits from a responsible awareness of the family's income and expenditure. When a cash flow imbalance exists in your situation, the application of this little sentence to every buying decision will clarify the real need. Stand honestly before the product under consideration for purchase, and ask yourself,

'Do I need it, or do I just want it?'
and if you are still undecided, ask yourself,

'What is the worst thing that can happen if I don't buy this?' and,

'What is the worst thing that can happen if I do buy this?'
You will find that the purchase under consideration often will be left on the shelf!

When my husband and I first married we halved our bills with those questions.

A successful salesperson is his own security. You can transplant a good salesperson and he always has a meal ticket because the world is so short of good salespeople. However he must live a tomorrow-conscious life or eventually undermine his sense of achievement, self-respect and peace of mind.

5.4   The 'today salesperson' versus the 'tomorrow salesperson'

Another angle is to remind yourself that it is not just one dollar that you're making a decision on here, it is what that dollar could conceivably become if it is not exchanged for an object or an occasion before it has a chance to grow. A single dollar invested at the low rate of 10 percent at compound interest over one hundred years becomes $13,780! Now, even taking the changing financial environment into account, you must wonder what your grandchild might have achieved with the dollar you just frittered away!

Awareness of these things will encourage a salesperson to make long term decisions.

When you earn a sales bonus try to avoid the attitude that immediately converts the cash into short term pleasure. Make an extra payment on something owed, or select an extra income producing investment. This will help alleviate the difficulty of a fluctuating income.

Don't trade peace of mind for an extravagant memory and a future regret.

Every salesperson, part-time homemaker, or full time professional should make it a commitment to learn about investments by subscribing to financial newspapers and magazines. Investment opportunities abound; stocks, shares, trusts, real estate, art, stamps, antiques and jewelry all offer growth potential, or you may prefer to eliminate mortgages or bank loans ahead of time. A knowledge of the investment markets presents an exciting alternative to the temptation of buying that new garment, and gives you a sense of progress.

Too often a salesperson who is impressed by apparent wealth seeks to drape himself in the trappings of wealth.

I remember field training once with a young aspiring salesman. As we set forth from my home we came abreast of traffic lights and he immediately drew my attention to two cars opposite:

> 'See that magnificent Mercedes,' he chatted happily, 'and see that Volkswagen next to it?'
>
> 'Why yes,' I replied.
>
> 'Well, I'm going to be wealthy and drive a Mercedes when I get going in sales,' he said. 'You'll never catch me behind the wheel of a Volkswagen'.
>
> I looked at the two cars and recognized the drivers of both cars and I replied to my new salesman:
>
> 'Well, Charley, if you want to *be* wealthy rather than *appear to be* wealthy, you'd better buy the Volkswagen. Of those two drivers opposite the one in the Mercedes went into receivership last week, and the other is one of the wealthiest men in Sydney.'
>
> Charley had some thinking to do.

A salesperson who invests in the trappings of wealth without its substance, is making a decision for short term gratification rather than long term benefit. If you are concerned to impress people, and every salesperson should be, plan to do so through the quality of your contribution in everything with which you are associated. Set yourself worthy, moral, ethical and professional standards of performance, then look after them on a daily basis and they will look after you on a lifetime basis.

I don't mean to advocate that all salespeople should forgo luxuries. If you worked for them and earned them, and can pay for them, you are entitled to them. But too many salespeople imagine the security and respect they seek is found behind the wheel of an expensive car or something similar, when the very thing they seek is jeopardized by an over-commitment to a finance company with little long term benefit.

Some people find financial commitments motivating; they know they have to go to sell because they must make the payments. If this works for you, so be it, but I believe this is because you have not yet become a decision-maker and prefer circumstances to make your decisions for you. You have yet to learn to think of money's long term benefits, and still measure success in terms of material possessions.

I have known and loved salespeople for many years and believe they deserve the best of life's riches, not apparent riches and ulcers!

5.5 The 'haves', the 'have-nots', and the 'yet-to-haves'

Another financial aspect a salesperson should consider is his attitude to those with more money than he possesses, and his attitude to those with less.

As it says in Proverbs 23:7

'For as a man thinketh, so is he.'

A person with little money can be subjected to unwarranted patronage, and manipulated by the unscrupulous, but a person with money can be exploited by those he has trusted, and even tried to help. Actions and attitudes are easily rationalized, then forgotten, by those concerned only with self interest. A salesperson's responsibility is his attitude to both. Always be ready to initiate, not just respond to an opening offer of friendship whatever the circumstances.

I have never found more virtue in poverty than in prosperity. If anything, it has been my experience that among the many salespeople with whom I have associated, the successful sales manager almost always deserves his success. He has risen while helping others rise. Generally he has achieved his success by overcoming his weaknesses, while the unsuccessful has nurtured his weaknesses. The attitude and lifestyle of an achiever is a constant inspiration to those who aim to follow. He stands high among his colleagues like a beloved statue in the village square, while the unsuccessful are packed and gone before the morning, leaving only shadows.

Guard your financial component; it's associated with responsibility, accountability, leadership, power, influence and a commitment to loyalties. It's all about getting, having and giving. Keep the mix right and be an important person, serving importantly, in the all-important profession of salesmanship.

Carry with you these succinct words of the Scottish theologian, James Moffat:

'A man's treatment of money is the most decisive test of his character — how he makes it, and how he spends it.'

Chapter Six

SOCIALLY

The Importance of Friendship

Few would deny that man is a gregarious creature, or that the average salesperson is an embodiment of this observation! Salespeople need people. They need to take time to enjoy people of similar and diverse interests, and they also need times of solitude.

THE BEST WAY TO HAVE A FRIEND IS TO BE ONE!

. . . and when you find a valued friendship, keep it under constant maintenance. It's precious.

A balance should be struck between private and business goals, and if for you the two are synonymous, then take a clear look at your port of disembarkation. The trip may be enjoyable, but you need to be sure you're traveling with friends towards a carefully considered destination of your choice and not being swept along engulfed by the tide of circumstance!

6.2 You're always 'at work'

Unlike other professions, a salesperson never completely leaves his job behind, even on social occasions. Lunches, dinners, coffee breaks, barbecues, parties, church gatherings, school activities, places people wait, hotel lounges, swimming pools, gymnasiums, bars, even airports, can develop into social occasions.

Regard yourself as an ambassador of your product, and may your belief be believable, and your pride discernible, wherever you are.

6.3   Make the most of social occasions

On social occasions a salesperson should have six aims:
1.   To enjoy himself and to contribute to the enjoyment of others.
2.   To plant a seed of interest, and make an appointment where tasteful and timely.
3.   To explain as little as possible in the course of achieving an appointment, and to ensure that enthusiasm is not allowed to carry the conversation beyond the prospect's interest peak.
4.   To change the subject completely, or to allow another to do so, as soon as an appointment is made, or clearly cannot be made.
5.   To not make the mistake of trying to interest an unlikely prospect, or a likely prospect in an inappropriate manner.
6.   To realize that the most profitable course of action in which a salesperson can engage at any social function is likely to be the activity of listening.

Remember the four *dont's* of good listening at all times:
1.   Don't daydream
2.   Don't jump to conclusions
3.   Don't interrupt
4.   Don't contradict

THE PROSPECT DOESN'T CARE HOW MUCH YOU KNOW,
UNTIL HE KNOWS HOW MUCH YOU CARE.

6.4   The salesmother's dilemma

It could be said that Eve was the world's first salesperson! She 'sold' Adam the apple. Adam listened to his partner, and men and women have influenced each other ever since.

A woman has natural sales instincts and the sales industry offers her an arena where dormant talent can blossom into achievement; and a forum where she can receive recognition for that achievement. Often this stands in marked contrast to her home environment, where she receives little recognition, and most of her effort is taken for granted. She must find the balance which maximizes the benefits and minimizes the disadvantages.

6.5   **The status quo of the working mother's challenge**

When a mother receives payment for work:

1. The family has access to a higher income. This provides it with important and permanent benefits.
    (i)   The risk may come if too much pocket money or expensive activity gives the children an unrealistic idea of money's value and availability.
    (ii) The risk may come if solutions to problems are 'bought' instead of being worked out on a shared basis.
    (iii) The risk may come if too many expensive toys, equipment, etc., are allowed to restrict or eliminate the development of creativity, imagination, and the skills of improvisation.

    Awareness, and appropriate counteraction, maximizes the benefit and minimizes the risk.

2. A working mother becomes a more interesting person. Exposure to varied work and social experiences, the development of skills, and acquisition of knowledge, result in sounder judgement and better proportioned values.
    (i)   The risk may come if she's seldom home for the family to experience and benefit from these changes; a less interesting mother may have been better than no mother!

    Wise working parents are aware of the risks and work to bring the benefits into the home.

3. The family of a working mother tends to become self-reliant and independent. Personal experience of the results of poor decision-making tends to improve the quality of subsequent decisions! Of necessity family members have to shoulder a greater share of household chores, which is usually a habit-forming benefit.
    (i)   The risk may come when one member inherits a disproportionate share of the household work load, to the detriment of his/her personal goals, perhaps homework or sports training, or in the father's case his work environment. Resentment can result and jealousy can grow.

    Wise working parents anticipate and take preventative action rather than curative action at a later date.

4. To be exposed to other people is educational for children at all ages. To visit with another family, or to feel the influence of

Grandma and Grandpa, or a babysitter, gives children early people experience.

(i)   The risk does not lie in lack of love (love is not necessarily best expressed by constant presence); it is lack of discipline. Only parents care enough to exert the physical and emotional effort involved in providing children with the discipline they vitally require for their own eventual success.

A spoiled child is a handicapped child.

Wise working parents recognize this and on arriving home to an embattled babysitter, don't reward the miscreant child with dinner at his favorite restaurant! They conscientiously provide the balance, love and discipline.

6.6   Guilt gets nowhere!

If you, as a salesperson, feel guilty at work or on a social occasion because you are not home with the family — and guilty when you're with the family, because you are not out making your sales quota — then you haven't yet achieved that important balance from which permanent and worthwhile success springs. A salesperson, either mother or father, can experience feelings of guilt without justification.

One mother I know, in this situation, decided to evaluate her use of time. She committed herself to spending two hours of concentrated time a day with the family. She found this 'quality' time spent reading, listening, playing games and developing skills with the children, resulted in closer relationships and deeper understanding. Previously, when she had taken days off to be at home with them, everyone 'did their own thing' in the vicinity of each other, and the benefit was imaginary. *Quality time* substituted for *Quantity time* proved to be the answer. The role of 'just being there' can be filled by any caring, conscientious adult.

Evaluate quantity time against quality time in your family. It should enable you to give more and receive more from both your home and work environments.

6.7   Plan to make your social occasions significant and memorable

As the family grows older, and the children leave home, working parents can be forgiven for thinking more of their own pleasures and achievements. Although you need be home less often, family social times should be treated as very precious. The role of parenting is an on-going process of 'letting go' from the first time a child takes a step until adulthood, and the dangers come when parents let go too soon, or hang on too long.

Social gatherings should become occasions when families value one another and their friends, and for salespeople they can be ways to enlist family help, and reach out for new prospects. The success of a social occasion is not dependent on a lot of money; planning and preparation are the two most important ingredients.

Recently I listened to two saleswomen, whose sons were turning twenty-one, discussing their celebration plans.

Said one:

> 'We are having just a family dinner at the Steak House Restaurant for John; we gave him the choice of party or a trip and I must say I was relieved when he chose the trip.'

Said the other:

> 'Bruce wanted a trip too, but he has accepted a lot of hospitality over the years, and we felt we should mark the occasion by welcoming his friends to our home and showing them we are grateful for the friendship they've given Bruce. The house really isn't big enough for a party, so Bruce and Fred plan to put a dance-floor together from some boards in the garden, and we believe they'll have a fun night. Bruce needs to learn to give as well as to receive, and to have the experience of running a party.'

As a listener I applauded the second speaker, and could well understand why she was a top district manager in her sales field.

Every human being, but especially every salesperson, should take time to socialize and he will find his griefs lessen, and his joys increase.

Jawaharlal Nehru, Indian nationalist, summed up the need for people to socialize when he said:

> 'Wisdom and foresight would demonstrate that, in the long run, the best way of profiting oneself is to profit society as a whole, of which one is a member.'

Chapter Seven

CREATIVELY

7.1 The importance of creativity

The first action (verb) in the Bible is 'created.' Nothing important took place until heaven and earth were 'created'.

> 'Why is it so important for a salesperson to be creative? Surely, selling is largely repetitive.'

This question, so often asked, suggests the answer.

It's because a salesperson's routine can be repetitive that it needs to be creative, or it reduces him to the level of an answering machine. Learning a spiel, doing things by rote, is neither challenging nor satisfying. However, every salesperson should memorize the company's basic sales demonstration. It will have been tried, tested and proven, and creativity applied without understanding can detract from its impact. Changes, additions and omissions are often appropriate and valuable, but must contribute to a sales result.

Bearing this in mind, regard the sales arena as an empty art gallery, and see your job as not only to hang the pictures (do the demonstration), but to paint the pictures. The choice of paint is yours (you decide which piece of sales material to produce, and when) and every statement, each action, can be likened to a stroke of your brush! Your personality should infiltrate the company's recommended demonstration, and your hands should bring it to its peak of effectiveness. No two demonstrations, nor two original paintings, ever can be the same.

CREATIVITY INVOLVES THE EXPERIMENTATION WITH NEW IDEAS, WHICH ARE THE OFFSPRING OF INSPIRED INTUITION.

It enables you to find a door in a blank wall, to open it without a key, to find the ingredients of opportunity and develop them into a valuable reality. Most people are capable of originality once they have disentangled themselves from conditioned learning or traditional argument. These tyrannies stultify imagination.

It was the American advertising executive, David Ogilvy, who wrote:

> 'The creative process requires more than reason. Most original thinking isn't even verbal. It requires a groping experimentation with ideas, governed by intuitive hunches initiated by the unconscious.'

As a salesperson, you should think creatively about every aspect of your work: the preparation, the approach, qualifying, the demonstration, excuses and closing; but probably the area of greatest potential benefit is prospecting.

Salespeople who are afflicted by feelings of:

'I don't know where to start . . .' or

'I've seen everyone, there's nowhere to go . . .'

. . . need to think creatively to get started!

Lateral thinking

If addressing a problem or circumstance squarely does not result in a solution, lateral thinking can prove a creative problem solver and an idea generator.

1. Move away from the situation in a lateral direction; distance can give it a different perspective.
2. Approach the problem or circumstance from a new angle and the solution can clarify.
3. Isolate the problem or circumstance; disentangled from side issues solutions can break through!
4. Apply suggestions to the challenge and prepare for ideas to stir.

A creative thought can unleash a rush of excited activity which obliterates obstacles and makes an idea work. The enthusiasm generated propels the idea forward from imagination to reality.

A CREATIVE THINKER APPLIES IMAGINATION TO REALITY,
AN UNCREATIVE THINKER APPLIES REALITY TO IMAGINATION.

Uncreative thinkers are not initiators, so if you want to get out and going, initiate your own success through creative thought.

The mind of a creative thinker fragments easily. It hits a challenge and breaks into many pieces which ricochet in every direction seeking solutions. The mind of an uncreative thinker remains faithful to its known way. Hitting a challenge, it applies a familiar solution. If this fails, it is blocked by the challenge.

Here's a hypothetical example:

Suppose the reality was:

> . . . a company was short of a quarterly target and one week remained.

The creative thinker, (not necessarily purely optimistic) announces,

> 'I have a suggestion, if we book display space in the local shopping center, we'd get enough quality leads to ensure our target is met.'

The uncreative thinker, (not necessarily purely pessimistic) answers,

> 'The display center manager told me just last week that he isn't taking any more bookings until Christmas. We'd waste time trying.'

The creative thinker replies,

> 'Well, we could try an incentive bonus for our part time sales force; that would give them encouragement to go out.'

The uncreative thinker reasons,

> 'It happens to be the school holidays and our part time sales force, being mothers, won't work during holidays. No, there's nothing for it, we must go out and try ourselves.'

The creative thinker finds the solution,

> 'Just a minute, I've got an idea. Let's arrange a company working picnic on Saturday, parents welcome holiday activity. While one of us organizes games for the children, the others can arrange field training for the representatives. Out of two hundred, at least forty would come, and in three hours they'll each do at least two demonstrations. For every four demonstrations the company averages one sale, so by organizing a hundred demonstrations we should have twenty-five sales. We'll go way over target!'

The uncreative thinker responds,

> 'I believe you could have a good idea there. Now, let's look at the mechanics of the plan, — phone calls, food, cars . . . and the children could have a peanut hunt . . .'

Reality and imagination interlock to find not just a solution, but to activate the follow-through.

Interestingly, although new challenges and solutions are invariably suggested by creative thinkers, it is often the uncreative thinker whose attention to detail and awareness of the issues involved who more efficiently follows through with an idea's execution.

Salespeople should be aware of the need for both talents. A salesperson with no ideas and nowhere to go is heading for failure, and a salesperson who cannot follow through and organize ideas into a reality is headed in the same direction.

All those involved in team work, who strive for common goals need creative input, and all ideas however contentious should be given consideration.

In the words of the Rev. Gordon Moyes, Superintendent of The Wesley Central Mission, Sydney, Australia,

> 'I don't want anyone on my Board who thinks the same way I do, because in that case one of us is superfluous!'

7.2 First steps towards unleashing creativity

Go forth into the sales environment . . .

1. Recognize the need for creativity in every aspect of your work.
2. Determine to develop your own creativity by reading, asking, listening, looking, and by refusing to accept the fact that you can't think creatively. Search for ideas and solutions by exploring your own potential, and thus open doors which previously have been closed.
3. Experiment, and be prepared to take risks. Compare the benefit of success with the consequences of failure. Make adjustments, keep flexible.
4. Realize the need for well-planned action to follow through and consolidate ideas.

It is within your power to unlock your creativity which perhaps up to now has never felt the need to unfold its wings.

Achieve this — *and fly!*

Chapter Eight

CHARACTERISTICALLY

Within every newborn baby lie seeds of greatness and seeds of failure.

Who or what decides which seed will grow?

What makes one person courageous and another cowardly?

What makes one person selfish and another unselfish?

How much say does anyone have in the choice of the qualities of character which develop within him?

The decisions of life which are made for him, and later by him, determine which seeds grow.

Some seeds find themselves in dry ground, which restricts their growth. Some seeds are trampled on, and their growth is permanently affected. Some seeds grow so profusely that they need to be pruned back; others are stifled. Some are grafted and depend forever on the root of another. Still others become parasites whose existence saps the strength from others. Some seeds grow straight and tall and provide shade for many all the days of their lives. All have inherited genes, but the environment has the developmental influence.

Is it not the same with the development of character?

Salespeople should consider their character's growth, because their success depends on it.

Elbert Hubbard clarified the degree to which we control our own character, when he wrote,

'Character is the result of two things, mental attitude, and the way we spend our time.'

Think about that. They are profound words.

Recently, I noticed a little plant in my garden. It was self sown, dropped by circumstance in a spot where, so choked by bushes, it could never feel the sun's warmth. It didn't shrivel and die. Instead it grew an unnaturally long, frail stalk, and finally burst through the foliage and found a place in the sun. I transplanted it to a position of eminence in the garden because it had shown such determination to survive, and succeed!

People are the same. Within each of us are seeds of courage and cowardice, honesty and dishonesty, failure and success, and we decide, wittingly or unwittingly, which plants we will allow to grow there.

Salespeople cope with these feelings all the time, and for that reason you will find successful salespeople have a strength of character with which they respond to and overcome challenges.

> CHARACTER HAS BEEN DEFINED AS THE RESOLVE TO KEEP GOING, LONG AFTER THE DESIRE TO DO SO HAS PASSED.

Too often salespeople give up at the first recession of enthusiasm, and when altered circumstances rekindle enthusiasm they are no longer in the market place to catch its impetus, and ride with it to success.

8.2 The seven characteristics most associated with success

Here is my list of the seven seeds you need to cultivate in order to become successful in the sales arena, and without which, in all probability, you will not survive.

1. COURAGE

    Without a courageous attempt, you won't get out your door to start your sales career.

    The French philosopher, Jacques Maritain, wrote,

    'The coward flies backward away from new things, a man of courage flies forward into the midst of new things.'

    Which is true of you? Will you react to your first discouraging experience by abandoning the sales environment? Or will you tighten your determination and return to the fray?

2. PERSISTENCE

    Courage gets you out the door, but without persistence you will not stay long enough to learn. Courage stands by you when you are knocked down in the market place, but persistence picks you up and gets you going again.

These beautiful words, written in support of persistence by the thirteenth President of the United States, Calvin Coolidge, have been long favourites of mine:

'Nothing in the world can take the place of persistence.
Talent will not;
Nothing is more common than unsuccessful men of talent.
Genius will not;
Unregarded genius is almost a proverb.
Education will not;
The world is full of educated derelicts.
Persistence and determination alone are omnipotent.'

3.   EMPATHY

This is the quality or process of entering fully, through imagination, into another's motives or feelings.

This native American proverb communicates clearly the meaning of empathy:

'To understand a man you must walk a mile in his moccasins.'

A salesperson is shielded from offending his prospect by a sense of empathy. It enables him to establish a rewarding and lasting relationship with his prospect. Sensitivity enables him to ascertain his prospect's real needs and aspirations, so that he is able to tailor his product to meet those needs, and reach those aspirations.

Every salesperson should empathize; it is one of the easiest things to do, but one of the hardest things to teach.

4.   INTEGRITY

Integrity is its own justification. It is a basic character requirement for all good salespeople. Unlike courage, it is not a quality which can be assumed from time to time, or be present in fluctuating degrees. Its constant and reassuring presence should be an inseparable part of your innermost being. Integrity is sensed by a prospect and a salesperson who has a scant regard for accuracy soon finds his integrity is questioned. When you hold a justifiable belief in your product you have no need to indulge in exaggerated claims, or fanciful facts. No sale is worth a scratch on your integrity.

As a salesperson you are not judged only by your presentation and the reputation of your company's product. Your personal reputation often arrives before you, and stays, or at least departs, long after you do!

Your reputation is your public relations representative. It travels around, not necessarily with you, sometimes with one of your customers, across hundreds, even thousands of miles, on your behalf. But sometime, somewhere, your reputation comes home — perhaps to check if you have introduced any modifications! You have to live with it. You'd better like it! You have to be very *strong* and *wrong* to live comfortably with dishonesty. It can be done . . . but if this is your inclination, I hope you never work in a sales environment.

5.   SELF-DISCIPLINE

A salesperson must strive for his 'place in the sun', it won't be handed to him.

An international market research company interviewed hundreds of achievers, representative of many professions, among them education, church, business, entertainment, politics, sports. The search was specifically for the qualities which make people successful. Many different qualities of character were found to be present in achievers, but there was one, and only one, common to each achiever — *self-discipline!*

> SUCCESSFUL PEOPLE ARE THE ONES WHO CAN MAKE THEM-
> SELVES DO THE THINGS UNSUCCESSFUL PEOPLE CANNOT MAKE
> THEMSELVES DO.

The day you realize:
> 'If you want to be successful, get up one hour earlier than unsuccessful people'
> . . . you will have picked up the key to success. Whether you put it in the door and turn it is up to you!

6.   HUMOR

This is an important ingredient of a successful salesperson's make-up. If you fall in a crevasse, or lose your footing mountain climbing, or simply slip in a puddle because your eyes were on the stars . . . a sense of humor can save you. It will put the situation in proper perspective, and send you regenerated on your way.

As the nineteenth century English clergyman, Thomas Higginson, so aptly expressed it,
> 'There is no defence against adverse fortune which is, on the whole, so effectual as a habitual sense of humor.'

A salesperson whose attitude is inclined to be humorous will survive long after others fail. Humor shields a positive attitude, it cushions every hurt. People who have the ability to laugh with others, and at themselves, have a huge advantage. Like a lifeline in heavy seas, their sense of humor rescues them when they might otherwise have drowned.

7.   VERSATILITY

I believe a poor little failed salesperson has a lot in common with a piece of chewing gum. Its flavor fades as its shape is constantly changed by the biting forces of the environment, and finally it's stuck somewhere, never to move again!

Every prospect, every demonstration, every situation differs, and a successful salesperson adjusts quickly and imperturbably to ensure an atmosphere of comfort and acceptance for his prospect.

Salesmanship is leadership and the salesperson must lead the thinking and the action. If the prospect changes direction, the salesperson has to be sufficiently versatile to jump into a leading position again, instead of falling behind.

A SALESPERSON MUST ADJUST TO THE PROSPECT,
AND NOT EXPECT THE PROSPECT TO ADJUST TO HIM.

This is the epitome of versatility in a sales environment.
Every salesperson needs to be aware that:

NOTHING IN LIFE IS CONSTANT — BUT CHANGE.

Instead of being flattened by circumstances, a salesperson should adapt, capitalize and, if need be, initiate — *change*.

8.3   The seven characteristics most associated with failure

Now let's look at the seven qualities of character, any one of which can guarantee the failure of a sales career. Too often we lay the blame for failure on outside factors, when in truth they lie within us.

1.   FEAR

Fear is the major cause of failure in salespeople. Its crippling influence is the root cause of so much non-achievement and non-activity. Fear-filled salespeople stand at a crossroad; they either quell their fears . . . *or go!*

Fear is not the dominant force it is so often portrayed as being. Cowardice attends fear, and a display of very little courage, even a brave endeavor, can banish both. We cannot eradicate fear entirely. For survival purposes, fear will be present always in our subconscious, but salespeople must not allow its influence to direct their thinking and actions, or they inevitably will lessen their success potential in the sales environment.

The truth of this old Moorish proverb has ensured its survival to the present day:

'He who fears something gives it power over him.'

Make a list of the things you fear and determine not to allow them to have power over you.

What does a salesperson fear?

Salespeople fear their environments, some of which are:

In the work place: doors, receptions, secretaries, demonstrations, the telephone, rejection, excuses, closing, decisions, and their own perceived weaknesses.

In the home environment: criticism, insecurity, lack of respect and support, patronage, wrongful time application, and empty-handed home comings.

These fears manifest themselves in sentences such as:

'What will so-and-so think if I do this?' (fear of critical opinion)

'I don't think I'm a sales type of person.' (fear of non-acceptance)

'I couldn't do it.' (fear of failure)

'I'll never convince anyone.' (fear of adding to an already low self-esteem)

'I want a job with a set wage.' (fear of insecurity)

'What will the prospect say to me?' (fear of rejection)

'I couldn't stand up and speak at the sales meeting.' (fear of challenge)

'But what if it doesn't happen that way?' (fear of the unknown)

'I'll have to ask my husband/wife.' (fear of disapproval)

Last century the American author, Christian Bovee, wrote:

'There is great beauty in going through life fearlessly. Half our fears are baseless, and the other half discreditable.'

So many people are beset with minor fears that it is a marvel they stagger out of bed and into the daylight.

Salespeople are different; they must be, to survive.

2. COWARDICE

Cowardice is the child of fear and this insidious quality isn't only present when we fail to leap off the cliff to rescue the drowning child . . . it creeps into seemingly unchallenging situations, a difficult phone call never made, needed support never given, misappropriated credit, or recognition withheld. These can be a direct result of the influence of cowardice.

The American author Cora White Harris gave us good advice when she wrote:

> 'The bravest thing you can do when you are *not* brave is to profess courage and act accordingly.'

Try it and see! In so doing you'll prune cowardice back, or weed it out of your garden altogether. Courage will be choked no longer, and can start to thrive.

3. LAZINESS

The effect of this quality on failure is easily understood, as it tarnishes all forms of human endeavor. People who have allowed a habit of sloth to become a lifestyle can be temporarily rescued by talent, but ultimate failure awaits. If you feel you have permitted this seed to germinate, you can eradicate it in four steps:

(i)   Calculate the value of a time investment in result associated work, per hour, per day, per year.

(ii)   Acknowledge laziness and assess its influence on your achievement level.

(iii) Make a decision to break the habit.

(iv)   Commit yourself to an active program and follow through.

4. UNTEACHABILITY

This characteristic may not affect your initial success. Natural talent and enthusiasm can assure a degree of success, but sooner or later your progress will be severely checked.

If you are not teachable, you cannot learn from mistakes, and you cannot be taught to improve. Repetition will hammer away at you, until its influence is felt, but repetition is a costly teacher. Every demonstration, every excuse, every close, every field training day, every failure should be a step up the stairway to success and promotion, but if you are unable to benefit from these experiences, or to retain what you have learned, you are destined to stay on the ground floor and watch the 'teachable' pass you by.

5.   IRRESOLUTION

The uncommitted salesperson, he who is not fully committed to his product and its benefits, his company and his goals, will fall under the influence of the first temptation he meets. Just as smog spreads over our cities, so does apathy pervade our attitudes.

If you feel irresolute in your commitment to your sales job, take time to think it through and do something about its cause. You may not have sufficient belief in your product, or your company, or your goals; you may need to change them. But something must change; failure will be inevitable if irresolution is allowed simply to become part of your character.

Start by taking a realistic look at the consequences of possible failure and by making decisions, action oriented decisions, (not just a rearrangement of prejudice after consultation with someone else). Commitment and resolution will result.

6.   PESSIMISM

A pessimist prostitutes life. I know of no characteristic for which I have less patience.

The poet, Ella Wheeler Wilcox wrote:
'This is the unpardonable sin; to talk discouragingly to human souls hungering for hope.'

Negative influences, attitudes and statements can run rife in a sales environment. They are implanted, often unwittingly, by the failures, the about-to-be failures and by fear itself, and they are infectious!

If you feel you've caught the virus and it starts penetrating your commitment and undermining your confidence in your ability or work environment, take stock of the cause and effect, and initiate remedial action.

Here's what you can do:
(i)   Talk to a positive person.
(ii)   Listen to sales tapes; read positive teaching literature; remind yourself of your favorite motivational slogans.
(iii)   Take action to experience a positive sales day; in other words, if you cannot think positively, you can at least act positively, and very soon the new experience will eclipse the old!

(iv)   Remind yourself that your attitude is your personal responsibility.

Eradicate pessimism from your thoughts with these words:

A pessimist takes the abundance of life, and finds only needs,
A pessimist walks in a garden of flowers, and notices weeds,
A pessimist lifts his face to the sun, and cries for the rain,
A pessimist takes good health as his right, and feels only pain,
A pessimist mingles lost among saints to seek out a sin,
He runs the greatest race of his life, *never to win!*

7.   DISHONESTY

A salesperson who lacks honesty can only work with short-term goals; he realizes he must move on in the morning to avoid facing consequences. A dishonest salesperson grabs whatever he can, however he can, and whenever he can, usually motivated by self-interest and sustained by meanness.

A salesperson, to be successful, must take joy and pride in serving. He must serve his customer, his prospect, his company, his family, and other important loyalties on a permanent basis.

If dishonesty prompts him to extract more than his due from a customer, a colleague, his company, or his family, life will extract more than its due from him, in its own time. Failure shades his every move.

NOTHING, ABSOLUTELY NOTHING, IS AS ADVANTAGEOUS TO A SALESPERSON AS A CHARACTER OF DISCERNIBLE QUALITY.

Section Two

Chapter Nine

PROFESSIONALLY

9.1 Salesmanship

This book tells the story of what I have learned over many years of selling. It includes a recipe for success which explains what you will need to do, to think, to feel and to believe in order to achieve a successful sales career. A live persuasive human being is still the best way to sell anything; and neither modern technology nor mail order companies will ever render the salesperson redundant.

If you were going to take a university/college degree or diploma, you would need to study several subjects and pass examinations before qualifying to take up employment in your chosen field. These subjects usually include both the practical and theoretical aspects.

Approach the profession of salesmanship with the same attitude. It is no different, except that it doesn't happen in a classroom. It happens in life, and you will fail or succeed just the same on the knowledge you have and your ability to apply that knowledge.

The most important aspects of selling

My favorite definition of selling has always been,

THE TRANSFERENCE OF FEELING

What you feel for your product, you need to transfer to your prospect . . . and, in order to achieve this, you are going to need to study the following subjects:

1. Attitude

It is important not just to have a positive attitude, but to study mental attitude and understand its effect on performance. Psychology tries to explain why people think, act and feel as they do, and it is easy to see how an understanding of this subject would benefit a salesperson.

2. The product and its demonstration

All sales people must have a belief in, a knowledge of, and enthusiasm for their product, and realize that sales orders are achieved through a process of multiple 'mini sales,' as the 'product of the moment' changes constantly.

3. Prospecting

You must learn the different methods and techniques of prospecting. If you don't, your hours worked will be less effective.

4. Approaches

You need experience in approaching all kinds of people in differing circumstances in appropriate ways.

5. Qualifying

You need to qualify your prospects, and to develop the ability to discern how, why, when, and when not, to give a demonstration.

6. Closing

You must learn to close. If you don't, you will work twice as hard for half the result. The difference between a demonstrator and a salesperson is, one has learned to close!

7. Handling excuses and objections

Excuses and objections are a normal part of selling, but it is necessary to be able to distinguish between the two, and to be able to anticipate their introduction. Also, you must learn when to acknowledge but ignore them, and when and how to answer them to the customer's satisfaction.

8. Failure and rejection

You must experience failure and rejection.

You need to fail, because failure is the greatest teacher of all, and you benefit from being taught well.

You need to handle rejection positively.

Sales people, on average, achieve fewer successful sales demonstrations than unsuccessful demonstrations. Logically, therefore, they are dealing with failure and rejection for the majority of their time. Many factors influence the demonstration to sale ratio, and it is your responsibility to know your company's average and to work on increasing your own.

You need to learn not to take rejection personally, nor to pretend it doesn't happen, but simply to cope professionally.

9. Time management

You need to value, plan and maximize time.

10. Goals

You must set, accept, respect, chase and achieve goals.

11. Grievances and controversy

You can expect grievances and controversy, both genuine and imaginary, to be part of the sales environment, somewhere, sometime. They are responsible for the termination of many promising sales careers. A knowledge and understanding of these two influential realities both as they affect you and others can be crucial.

12. Decision making

The ability to make correct and timely decisions is a major contributor to a successful career in sales.

13. Sex

You can benefit from an understanding of the role your sex plays in a sales demonstration.

14. Body language

The ability to interpret body language can be advantageous to a salesperson.

15. Pressure selling

A knowledge of pressure selling techniques, and a customer's perception of them, will help you avoid the pitfalls and protect your reputation.

16. Equilibrium in winning and losing

Successful salespeople develop a balance, whether winning or losing or just hanging in there! They stay competitive! They maintain an imperturbable dignity, a reflection of their pride in the profession of salesmanship.

Sales management

When you are familiar with the problems and challenges of salesmanship, your interest may turn towards sales management. For some people, a purely sales environment suits best their ambitions and aptitudes, but for others, sales management is the most fulfilling reward of a sales career, that of helping others help themselves.

> EVERY SALESPERSON NEEDS TO LOOK BOTH AT THE KIND OF MANAGEMENT HE NEEDS TO RECEIVE IN ORDER TO REACH HIS PEAK OF POTENTIAL, AND THE KIND OF MANAGER HE NEEDS TO BECOME, IN ORDER THAT OTHERS MAY DEPEND ON HIM FOR THE DEVELOPMENT OF THEIR POTENTIAL.

A sales career is all about giving and receiving, and success can hinge on the right recipe!

9.2 ATTITUDE

9.2.1 The Influence of Attitude

Would you believe that there lies within each of us a power which can start a sales career, accelerate it, continue or terminate it? A force which determines success or failure, and can at any time change either?

It's attitude.

You might consider that a sales career would begin with a product, or a strong need, either to work for money or recognition, or to serve importantly. Each of these can influence attitude, but your attitude is forming and selecting a viewpoint from the day you are born. Seldom is an attitude capable of a complete reversal. However, many people have the advantage of a flexible attitude, or an open mind, and a minority have the right attitude in the first place. Without a positive attitude you will not become a successful salesperson.

Attitude comes first it is a major contributor in any field of endeavour.

Your attitude to the success potential of the job, and your product's acceptance in the marketplace; your attitude to your success potential within the company structure, and the conviction that it can meet your needs; your attitude to the importance of the job that you do for others, and your confidence in the company's ability to create an environment in which you can be successful, these attitudes are of paramount importance.

9.2.2 Success Starts With Attitude

Attitude inevitably influences a salesperson's choice of product; you need a product in which you can fervently believe. Attitude will help you assess the marketplace and your likely competitors. Attitude will play a leading role in the selection of a company, and help you select one which has the interests of its sales people at heart, and in whose policies and ethics you feel you can trust. Faith in these factors will affect your success because your attitude is the foundation on which you will grow.

9.2.3 Attitude Analysis

The World Book dictionary defines attitude as *a way of thinking, acting and*

FACTORS WHICH DETERMINE SUCCESS

feeling. Of the three I believe *feeling* is the most relevant in the sales environment. How you feel affects what you think and how you act.

Amateurs tend to make decisions as a result of their feelings. They are guided and often controlled by their feelings. Professional people tend to control their feelings and make decisions bearing their feelings in mind, but able at all times to consider other factors.

Experience plays a large part in the difference, but all sales people have to begin, and all beginners are amateurs. New salespeople can draw reassurance from the fact that buyers, too, are amateurs! Amateur customers. Certainly in once-or-twice in a lifetime purchases. They haven't been in that situation before. Direct sellers are dealing with amateurs most of the time.

> RESOLUTE PEOPLE, PEOPLE WHO HAVE GOALS AND AN UNSHAKEABLE DETERMINATION TO ACHIEVE THEM, CHANGE THEIR ATTITUDE TO ACHIEVE THEIR GOALS.

> THE NON-ACHIEVER CHANGES HIS GOALS TO FIT MORE COMFORTABLY AROUND HIS ATTITUDE.

Which are you? Do you have a goal, or a dream?
A dream is just an out-of-focus goal!

9.2.4   A Successful Salesperson Has a Goal-Oriented Attitude

> IF PROBLEMS OR DIFFICULTIES PRESENT THEMSELVES TO YOU, DO YOU LOWER, CHANGE, OR BACK OFF YOUR GOAL TO PROVIDE A MORE COMFORTABLE ZONE, AND PROTECT THAT BACK-OFF WITH EXCUSES AND JUSTIFICATION?

> OR

> DO YOU FOCUS ON YOUR GOAL AND CHANGE YOUR ATTITUDE?

Success is directly related to goal consciousness.
Don't let your dream dissolve or blow away.
Keep feeling it, reinforce it, make sure it's still there.

> HOLD FAST TO DREAMS, FOR IF DREAMS DIE
> BEFORE YOUR WORK IN LIFE HAS BEEN COMPLETE,
> FAITH IN ANGUISHED DOUBT IS HEARD TO CRY,
> AND HOPE TURNS OUT THE LAMP BEFORE YOUR FEET.

Change your attitude instead.

Successful sales people feel things strongly, they are emotional people. This is both a strength and a danger zone. I've never met a top salesperson who is not emotional, and I don't want to, but I have met many sales people who have let their feelings affect their attitude negatively, instead of disciplining their feelings to strengthen their attitudes positively.

Emotions or feelings are God-given, just as much as our arms and legs, and if you have no feelings for your product, your company, or your prospect, you cannot be a successful salesperson.

9.2.5   Take Steps to Ensure You Start With a Positive Attitude.

FIRST DECIDE TO BE A SALESPERSON, AND THEN DECIDE TO BE A GOOD ONE.
THEY ARE SEPARATE DECISIONS.
THE WORLD IS FULL OF PEOPLE WHO MADE ONLY THE FIRST ONE.

Make your decision momentous and irreversible, not a wishy washy maybe, or a pussyfooting perhaps!

Now face facts. Think through logically the best and worst of the experiences you will have to face, and try to identify squarely your likely strengths and weaknesses in this environment. Take steps to make necessary adjustments, and be prepared to challenge some basic, entrenched assumptions. Open your mind to learning via meetings, seminars, tapes, books, and ask questions of achievers.

Nurture your attitude, it's your baby!

Give it the diet it needs to grow strong.

FROM THE BEGINNING, ACCEPT THE RESPONSIBILITY OF YOUR OWN ATTITUDE.

Ask for help from your manager, but walk beside him without holding his hand. Remember, you're a team member and your job is to build your mental attitude, not pull your manager's down.

Approach the job logically but make sure your emotions come along too! Think of your attitude as a part of your sales equipment. You would not go out, I hope, with dilapidated sales material. Approach your attitude in the same way. Make sure it's crisp and exciting, and something your prospect would like to reach out and touch.

LEARN SOMETHING NEW ABOUT YOUR PRODUCT EVERY DAY.

This enhances your attitude. Even if you know it well, reinforce in your mind the benefits of ownership. Have a love affair with your product and what it can do for people.

Love has proven again and again that it *can* conquer the world!

9.2.6   What to Guard Against

A successful salesperson actively protects his positive attitude against the negative influences that aim to render it less effective.

How can you identify these?

One of the most lethal is destructive comment.

Why do people make destructive comments?

> PEOPLE MAKE DESTRUCTIVE COMMENTS UNDER THE
> INFLUENCE OF FEAR.

If they love you, it may be fear that you will fail, or more selfishly, fear that you may be a success, and a widening gap develop between you.

If they do not know you, and they are in the sales environment themselves, they may fear your competition.

If they do not know you, and they are not in the sales environment, they may fear the success you describe may hold a solution for their problems, and they fear being moved into a decision-making situation. You do not need to identify the reason, but every salesperson needs to be resilient in the wake of destructive comment. It is non-progressive: both those who indulge in it and those who allow it to be effective either stay put or travel downhill.

Did you ever hear the story of the crabs on the seashore? It illustrates this point.

A little boy was playing on the beach. He caught a crab and put it in a bucket on the sand. The bucket had high sides but they presented the crab with no problem. It just turned sideways and ran up the side and over the top to freedom. But when the boy caught a number of crabs and placed them in the same bucket, he noticed that every time one tried to escape over the top, one of the others pulled him back. So he left them to fight it out, and in the morning when he returned he found to his surprise that they had all perished. The freedom which had been readily available for each of them was denied them all.

Will you allow destructive criticism to cripple your attitude, and pull you back from success?

This is why new salespeople sometimes outsell experienced salespeople!

No one has ever told them it can't be done!

They just go out and do it, before anyone has a chance to pull them back.

9.2.7   How to Protect Your Attitude Against Discouraging Comment

People, even those who love you, will pull you back as you move to try something new. You will hear,

'Surely you don't want to be a salesman?' or

'I could never do that' or

'I think it's awful the way some people try to make money out of their friends' or

'The only people who go into selling are the ones who can't do anything else'

... or something destructively critical about your product or its price, or your presentation, or your company, or invasion of privacy.

Remember, your job is to nurture your mental attitude. It's your future success. Don't let it shrivel and perish there; retrieve it with positive response or constructive action.

Let's look at it again.

The critic stated,

'You're not going to be a salesman? I could never do that.'

Just try quietly saying,

'I agree, I don't think you could, either.'

That leaves them wondering what you can do that they cannot do!

Now your mental attitude is on top again.

If someone accuses you of making money from your friends (and that can be hurtful) climb back up and say,

'I don't see it that way. I believe in the benefits of my product and consider that I would be doing my friends a disservice by not giving them the opportunity of knowing about it. How can anyone learn to recognize good value if they don't know what's available to help them? My friends have been grateful for the information I was able to give them.'

Honest and appropriate defence tools are always available; reach out and apply them.

When you are told that no one sells anything if he can do anything else, just ask gently and with dignity,

> 'Are you speaking just for yourself, or for everyone? Increasing numbers of people are electing to be salespeople today. Some because they believe in a product, and others because people traditionally have been attracted to high-income jobs, and sales people are among the highest paid in the world. The facts just don't support your statement. Besides, every country depends on its sales people, because whenever a salesperson sells a product he strikes a blow at unemployment. He creates and consolidates jobs for those employed in the product's production. I feel proud of contributing to our country's economy.'

And perhaps as you grow more confident, with a twinkle in your eye, you might add,

> 'And what are you doing these days?'

> I DON'T WANT TO SUGGEST THAT A GLIB OR DEFENSIVE RETORT IS APPROPRIATE.
> BUT A DOSE OF HONESTY AND SINCERITY, MIXED TOGETHER WITH A DASH OF THE COURAGE OF YOUR OWN CONVICTIONS, CAN BE AN INSTANT CURE FOR AN ATTITUDE REQUIRING IMMEDIATE MEDICAL ATTENTION.

If a critic denigrates your product, smile and say,

> 'It's easy to see you haven't had a good demonstration'

and give him a choice of appointments with flair and confidence.

> A SALESPERSON IS IN THE BUSINESS OF INFLUENCING PEOPLE'S THINKING. *How about starting with yourself?*

Take care to shield your attitude from destructive comments, and learn to recognize and understand the real reason they are made. Just calmly answer from the reservoir of strength from which a person of sincere convictions can always draw.

YOU WILL MAKE DESTRUCTIVE COMMENTS TO YOURSELF!

But worse than attack from without, your mental attitude can actually be subjected to assault from within! You may find it hard to believe, but YOU will attack it.

A little inner voice will say,

> 'I'm not sure I'm a salesman type,' or

'I wasn't smart at school, I couldn't learn all that,' or
'What will my mother think,' or
'Whatever will my neighbour say,' or
'Will the children suffer if I do something like that? There must be an easier job.'

DON'T SABOTAGE YOUR OWN MENTAL ATTITUDE.

Recognition of the process will help lay it to rest.

PROSPECTS WILL PUT YOUR POSITIVE ATTITUDE AT RISK!

Sometimes prospects' excuses affect your mental attitude. Just decide not to let that happen to you. A salesperson should be alert to the danger of being influenced by a customer's excuse, and recognize with an inner smile that it is your job to do the influencing!

GIVE YOUR ATTITUDE STAYING POWER.

Be careful not to over-protect your attitude. Don't shield it and grow a hothouse flower.

It should be shielded only from injury, not combat!

Attitude must be strong enough to stand against the wind, not just be sheltered from it.

Your attitude needs to be exposed to strengthening, building experiences.

It is possible for a salesperson to maintain a positive attitude and never go out and do the job at all; but you will never be an achiever, and barely a contributor, only a hanger-on.

YOUR ATTITUDE, ALTHOUGH INTACT, WILL REST IN A HIGH RISK AREA, ENVELOPED BY INSECURITY, INEXPERIENCE AND UNDER-DEVELOPED TALENT.

9.2.8   Character is at the Base of Attitude

In order to become a topnotch salesperson, it is necessary to have, or develop, particular qualities of character. These qualities ensure that your attitude is fed a constant positive inflow which maintains it at a level which generates successful activity. Strong characters hold strong beliefs, and you must have an attitude of belief in your product, and possess a reliable product knowledge.

Belief is a powerful attitude.

A SALESPERSON WITH A SUCCESS PATTERN HARBORS WITHIN
HIMSELF A STRONG BELIEF IN THE BENEFITS OF HIS PRODUCT
OR CAUSE.
HE BELIEVES HIS PRODUCT HOLDS A KEY CAPABLE OF DETONAT-
ING A POWERFUL EXPLOSION OF BENEFITS IN THE AREA OF THE
CUSTOMER'S NEED.

Work is the winner: character demands a commitment to work.
Never undertake a challenge without the resolution to work to achieve
it.

SUCCESS IS THE ACHIEVEMENT OF WHAT YOU WORK TO
ACCOMPLISH.

You might ask,
'How do I develop qualities of character associated with success if I
feel I do not possess them in abundance?'
They can be developed by practicing* them. I have seen a sales career
not just change people's lives, but dramatically change people.
Dr. Gilbert Beers in *The Book of Life* encourages us with this powerful
prayer:
'Remind me Lord, that my daily conduct determines my character.
As I do, so shall I become.'
What we think, do and work at largely determine our characteristics,
and these can change and grow.
An optimistic attitude and a willingness to work are winning partners.
Peter Dinsdale, who became the Managing Director of Zondervan of
Australasia, exemplifies this combination. No matter what the day
brings forth, problems become shadows when Peter arrives as he focuses
only on solutions. Everywhere he goes people reach out to borrow a little
of the strength his enthusiasm radiates.

9.2.9   Develop an Attitude of Respect for Discipline

Successful salespeople acknowledge the inseparable association between
success and discipline.
Think of discipline in the manner the English poet Edmund Spenser
did when he wrote:
'A stern discipline pervades all nature,
Which is a little cruel, that it may be very kind.'

---

* American spelling has been used throughout this book.

An attitude of respect for the role of discipline in your life will get you out your door promptly when you'd rather stay. It is truly said that the hardest door to go through is your own! Discipline will turn off the television when you'd rather watch; will resist that extra cake or untimely invitation; will confront a difficult people situation which you'd rather avoid.

Your regrets will be few, and your benefits manifold!

Discipline yourself to your goals. Be prepared to be tested. Too many sales people float through life like flotsam and jetsam on the tide. Sometimes the water rises, sometimes it falls. They just float along, without contributing much, depending on others, having little say in their life's direction.

9.2.10   **Pay Yourself a Compliment in Life — Aim High**

If you don't, maybe no one else will ever be justified in having high expectations for you. . . . Besides, if you have tried to do something and failed, you are vastly better off than if you tried to do nothing and succeeded!

> SUCCESSFUL SALESPEOPLE MAKE THINGS HAPPEN.
> THEIR INFLUENCE IS FELT BY THOSE TO WHOM THINGS HAPPEN,
> AND CONSTANTLY SURPRISES THOSE AROUND WHOM THINGS
> HAPPEN!

Sir Henry Laing, Chief Executive of United Biscuits in the United Kingdom, once asked a taxi driver in Paris whether pedestrians were given the right of way at street crossings.

The driver replied,

'In France, the right of way is taken, never given.'

This may not sound very courteous, but it is an entrepreneurial attitude!

> ACHIEVERS LOOK INWARD FOR THE ANSWERS TO THEIR
> PROBLEMS, AND ONLY LOOK OUTSIDE OF THEMSELVES IF THE
> ANSWERS TO THEIR QUESTIONS CANNOT BE FOUND THERE.
> WITHIN THEM IS AN INNER AND GROWING STRENGTH OF
> SELF-RELIANCE.

When a salesperson faces the challenges of salesmanship and finds it doesn't immediately surround him with success, he reacts in one of two ways. Either he blames the product, the price, the company, the training, the manager, the weather, the marketplace or something else — *anything other than himself*; or he comes back wanting to learn, with suggestions or with questions.

How can he either change himself or the environment?

In each case his attitude is his steering wheel.

9.2.11   The Inspiration of Example

The greatest sales manager I ever knew, Diana Rose, told me she made only five sales in her first year of working full time.

'Oh, how dreadful,' I groaned. 'I would have given up. What kept you going?'

Her reply typified a great sales person's attitude. She said,

> 'I BELIEVED MY PRODUCT WAS THE BEST ON THE MARKET; THAT DIDN'T NEED TO CHANGE. I KNEW THE PUBLIC HAD A GREAT NEED FOR IT, NOTHING WOULD CHANGE THAT. IF SOMETHING WAS WRONG, IT WAS ME, IN THE MIDDLE, AND ME I COULD CHANGE IF I STUCK TO IT!'

And she became one of the top personal sellers in the company. She faced the facts, with the right attitude.

9.2.12   The Enthusiastic Attitude

At this point I would like to include what constitutes, at least in part, a warning. In my long experience in sales, I have seen many new people fling themselves into a sales career armed only with enthusiasm. This is a beautiful attitude and a great contributor to achievement. However the importance of actively looking after an enthusiastic attitude, and of taking steps to ensure that it springs from knowledge and not naivete, cannot be overemphasized. It is so vulnerable.

I would liken those naturally enthusiastic people to a bulb that bursts forth with roots and shoots even in the darkest corner of a cupboard. If you are one of these, value your attitude — water it, feed it, expose it to the sunshine, repot it sometimes. Plant it where it can take firm roots.

But if you are one of those people who need to develop it, then you are like the bulb that can't get going unless put in the right environment. You are just as likely to be a winner, but you need to create the right environment where your attitude can take strong roots and grow and blossom.

Everything else you can learn.

For myself, I envied those who sprouted in the dark corners. My attitude held me back at the beginning of my sales career. I had to find the right environment to succeed. I was destructively critical of most things, and lacked faith in my own ability to succeed in the job. My attitude hampered my progress. I was a slave to my fears, — fear of being criticised, fear of admiring the unadmirable, fear of taking a retrograde step. I had been taught that sales people were suspect, and shrank from being numbered among them.

I was lucky enough to have a supportive husband and managers who slowly untied the ropes that bound me, which changed my mental attitude and set me free to achieve.

> YOU MUST SET YOUR ATTITUDE FREE!

But I had to help myself too. I remember saying, 'I'll never be a salesperson; there must be something else I can do.'

It was the cry from the battle-weary so often heard from new salespeople.

My manager, Diana Rose, recognized the cry, and her responsive words set me free:

> 'IF YOU CAN LEARN TO KNOCK ON A DOOR AND MAKE A SALE, THERE'S NOTHING IN THE WORLD YOU CANNOT DO.'

Her words inspired me to tackle again the difficulties of the sales environment. I lost my courage when I allowed it to drain away, but I found it again in those words. Carry them with you as you face the challenges of a sales career.

Winston Churchill acknowledged the importance of courage in our lives, when he wrote:

> 'Courage is rightly esteemed the first of human qualities, because it is the quality that guarantees all others.'

9.2.13   A Message of Responsibility

This is the message that I pass on to those of you who face the challenges of the sales arena:

> YOUR ATTITUDE IS YOUR RESPONSIBILITY.
> IT IS THE WINGS ON WHICH YOU WILL FLY,
> OR THE CHAINS THAT WILL BIND YOU DOWN.

Get to know yourself; take stock of your attitude. Face the true facts about what you are looking for as you take up each new challenge.

Are you among those who want to be paid without actually wanting to work? Something for nothing?

It's a common enough attitude today.

ARE YOU WILLING TO LISTEN AND LEARN, AND THEN PUT WHAT YOU LEARN INTO PRACTICE, OR ARE YOU ONLY PREPARED TO LISTEN AND LEARN? **THERE'S A DIFFERENCE**.

DO YOU HAVE THE CAPACITY TO CHANGE YOUR ATTITUDE TO REINFORCE YOUR GOALS, OR WILL YOUR GOALS AND DREAMS *SMASH* AGAINST A WALL OF HARDENED ATTITUDES?

Take time to collate your answers. Attitudes are seldom changed overnight; but if you can put a crack in a hardened or preconditioned attitude, you can end up with all the advantages of an open mind.

In the beginning just realize the importance of attitude, and be prepared to absorb and practice what you learn, and experience will teach you. It will help you graduate in the most exciting profession of them all — the sales profession — the business of influencing people's thinking. The rewards are unlimited. No one can ever put a ceiling on you. Once you learn to be a successful salesperson, you dictate your own level of achievement.

It was from a dear friend, National Mutual Insurance salesman 'Hebby' Heberlein, that I first witnessed that attitude was more than words. It is a bearing. Until the day he died, 'Hebby' carried an aura of 'pride of salesmanship,' which elevated his profession and made you feel glad to be with him even before he had spoken. It radiated from an attitude of conviction. He was proud of what he did, and a mark of quality permeated all his dealings.

Likewise John Fielder of Sydney, who sold hundreds of sets of the World Book Encyclopedia in Australia, never told you he *sold* a set, but that he'd *placed* a set in a home; his attitude reflected his pride. A single word told the story.

As a successful salesperson, take pride in each small achievement, realise you are an important part of an important team — your company's team. Your product will provide you with the motivation, the mission and the challenge. Your company will provide you with the opportunity, the training and learning tools.

YOU MUST CONTRIBUTE THE ACTION OF LISTENING AND FOLLOW THROUGH WITH THE ACTION OF DOING.

Alone, each contribution can be ineffective. Decide that your contribution will never be the weak link in the chain. Determine to serve valuably.

ATTITUDE IS WHERE YOUR SALES CAREER MUST START, AND IT WILL LARGELY DETERMINE THE ACHIEVEMENT LEVEL AT WHICH YOU WILL FINISH.

Forget yourself, your feelings, your problems, and concentrate on *finding* the positive or, if need be, *creating* the positive in every situation.

This little poem puts it in a nutshell:

ATTITUDE

As two little boys on the river bank lay
They watched their reflections below.
John laughed, as the water played games with his eyes,
And changed the shape of his nose . . .
And his attitude changed in a world that was new,
While Christopher — lay in a doze.

'I want to see what my face can see
And go where my face can go.
There'll be stately galleons, steamships and boats,
And fishes and starfish and whales,
And battleships bigger than houses by far,
And yachts with the wind in their sails.'
And turning he nudged the friend by his side,
'Now tell me what your face can see.'
And the rippling face looked back at the boy
And he answered, *'I only see me!'*

9.3   THE PRODUCT AND ITS DEMONSTRATION

9.3.1   The Importance of 'Know' and 'Know-how'

All salespeople must have a belief in, a knowledge of, and an enthusiasm for their basic product, and realize that sales orders are achieved through a process of multiple 'mini-sales,' as the 'product of the moment' changes frequently.

A salesperson needs to demonstrate creatively, from a sincere conviction and not from a learned spiel, although he should take time to build a bank of memorized presentation sentences on which he can draw, and establish an increasing knowledge of his product upon which he can rely.

Success also depends on competent handling of sales material, and the ability to present it to the prospect with maximum impact.

9.3.2   The Birth of Realization

June 1st, 1979 — the most significant day in my sales career. Looking back, it was the day I split the *sales atom* . . . and what an explosion occurred in my mind. . . . *How radioactive I felt!*

I was scheduled to field train three people each for three hours, which is usually too short a period to be of permanent benefit. Watching each trainee demonstrate in such quick succession emphasized the contrasts of approach, style and personality each contributed. Ron brought a quiet concern and perceivable control to each stage of the demonstration. It resulted in a sale. Louis demonstrated a greater product knowledge, and explained in more detail the benefits of ownership, but the sale somehow evaded him. Ruth was a new sales agent, but her sincerity and enthusiasm, and the fact that she had obviously 'done her homework,' compensated for her lack of experience; but she too lost a sale I felt had been obtainable.

Customers vary as much as salespeople, but it was the fact that each of the three prospects brought to the demonstration the same degree of 'likelihood to buy' that enabled me to make a comparative analysis of the factors that influenced the sales result.

Driving homeward through a deluge in the darkness, watching the headlight-lit raindrops splatter against the windscreen, a single fact suddenly burst through the drift of conscious questioning. The answer seemed to explode in my mind, releasing a rush of energy.

THE 'PRODUCT OF THE MOMENT' CAN MAKE OR BREAK THE FINAL RESULT EACH IS A SALE IN ITSELF

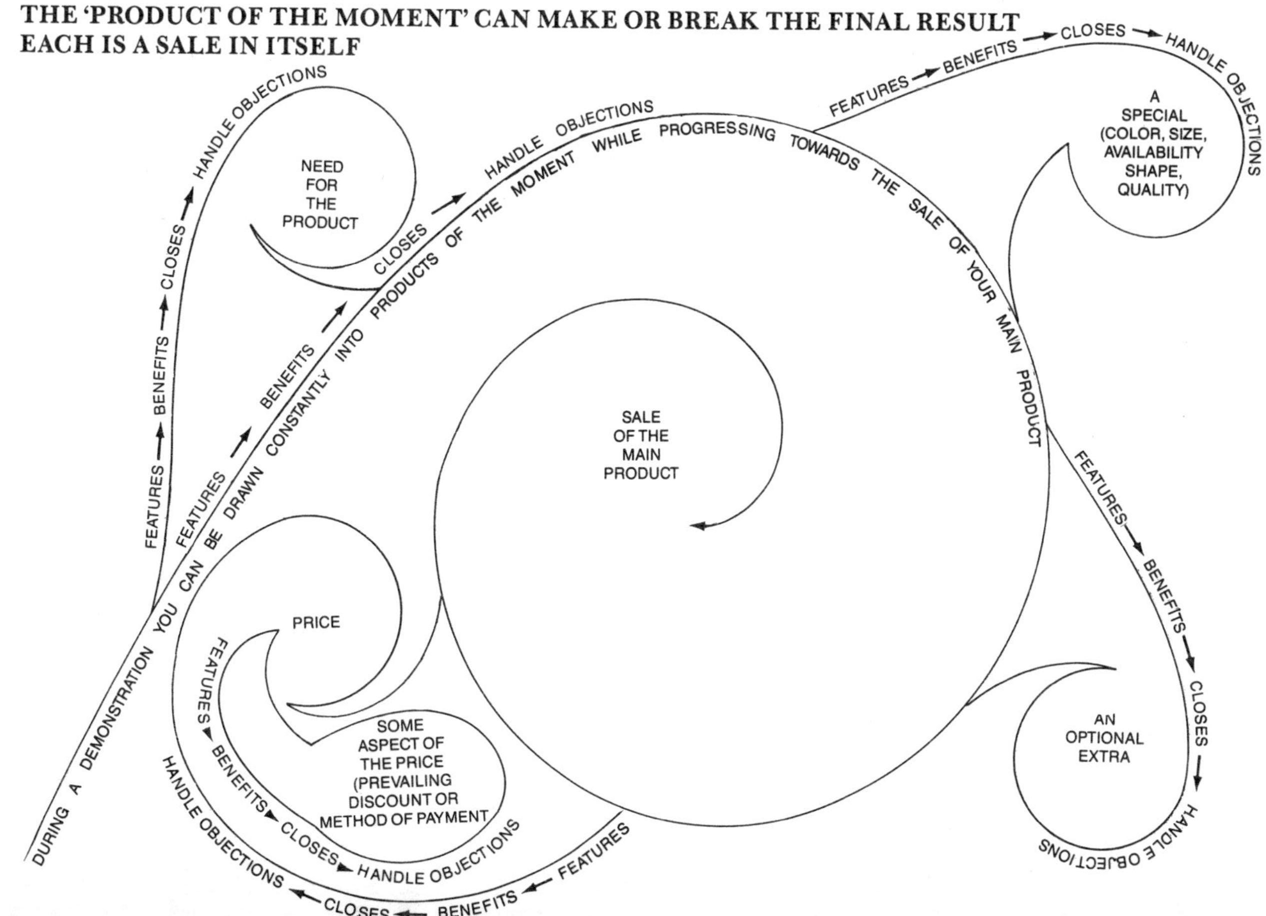

The product changes! The product changes!
Ron hadn't been selling his basic product all the time. The product changes, not the sales process.

Previously I had been convinced that fundamentally, selling was a case of representing an unchanging product, varying the presentation according to the customer and circumstances. Now, suddenly, I saw that it was the sales process which must remain unchanging, and it was the product which constantly changed.

9.3.3   The 'Action' of Selling

The action of selling basically involves the salesperson in five functions.
1.   He explains the features of his product or service
2.   He communicates the benefits
3.   He closes the sale
4.   He handles the objections
5.   He writes up an order or continues with the demonstration

These five functions need to be applied to constantly changing multiple little *'products of the moment.'*

9.3.4   The Importance of Recognising 'The Product of the Moment'

These products might be,
   on the phone — the appointment;
   at the door — the interview;
   inside the home or office — the 'need' for the product;
   during the demonstration — some special feature of the basic product, or the price, the color, the style, the function, the convenience.

These are all individual sales, each one important in itself and contributing to a positive buying decision of the basic product.

I now understood that Louis and Ruth, concentrating inflexibly on the product as they saw it, had paid insufficient attention to each important little sale during the demonstration, and when they closed and reached for the order pad, the sale disintegrated. It had no substance.

THE FIRST STEP TO SUCCESSFUL SELLING IS TO RECOGNIZE THE PRODUCT OF THE MOMENT!

When you attempt to sell something you explain the features and benefits to the prospect, but before the prospect accepts your product he must accept you, he must accept the demonstration, he must accept the time, he must accept the place. There are lots of minor sales the salesperson must make before he arrives at his product.

You only *sell* your basic product when the minor 'sales' have been accomplished to the customer's satisfaction. As you proceed into the demonstration, be prepared at any time to change product, in response to a reaction, comment or query from the customer. Allow him to select the minor products as you progress, at his pace, explaining the features, describing the benefits, closing and handling objections at each stage.

9.3.5   The Wrong Product at the Wrong Moment Invites Calamity

The salesperson who confronts a bewildered housewife on her doorstep with an analysis of his basic product's virtues is selling the wrong product.

The salesperson who harasses a callback or a reluctant prospect for a decision *is neglecting to sell the 'product of the moment'* — *HIMSELF!*

The salesperson who inundates the busy secretary with a barrage of technical information *is selling the wrong product.*

The phone prospector who extols the details of his basic product on the phone *has selected the wrong 'product of the moment', and certainly the wrong time and place.*

The demonstrator who continues to explain the product's features when the customer has asked the price, *is selling the wrong product.* He should take time to *sell* the price.

The salesperson who persists with an explanation of the product's features when the customer has enquired about the benefits in his particular situation, *is again selling the wrong product.* He should move quickly to his new product and *sell* that, while the prospect's interest is at its height.

> A CUSTOMER IS NEVER MORE RECEPTIVE TO PERSUASION THAN AT THE MOMENT HE ASKS A QUESTION.

9.3.6   Selling a 'Mini' Product En Route to The Basic Product

When you phone a prospect, your product is the appointment. Start your sales presentation with the FACTS and FEATURES, which could include:

1. You will call at a convenient time
2. The appointment takes about half an hour
3. There is no cost involved, and no obligation
4. No alternative way of knowing about the product exists
5. All the family is encouraged to attend

Proceed with the BENEFITS (which can be 'sold' in conjunction with the features or afterwards) and which could include:

1. The prospect need not travel to the appointment — *a convenience benefit.*
2. All the family can be present at the time — *another opinion benefit.*
3. The time involved is minimal — *a time benefit.*
4. In the comfort of his home, and at a time of his choice, he can receive a full, interesting explanation — *a knowledge benefit.*

Then close the sale:

1. 'Would Saturday afternoon or Tuesday evening be more convenient?'
2. 'Which would you prefer, a morning or afternoon appointment?'
3. 'Would you rather I call at the office, or at your home?'

Then handle the objections, among which might be:

1. I'm not interested.
2. My husband/wife is away.
3. We don't need anything extra at the moment.
4. We can't afford anything.
5. I've got no time.

9.3.7　The Product Changes But the Stages of the Sale Remain Constant

The price, too, needs to the 'sold' not just 'told'.

When the price is introduced treat it as an individual sale; honour it as a salesperson should respect his product. Don't slither across it in fright!

Explain its features, which might include:

1. The actual cost figure
2. The figure including optional extras
3. The time period of the invoice
4. The interest rate
5. The prevailing discounts

BUILD TO THE ALL-IMPORTANT 'YES' BY ELICITING A LOT OF LITTLE YESES by means of TRIAL CLOSE

Follow this with the benefits, which vary according to the product, but may be:

1. Good value
2. Highly priced because it guarantees quality
3. About to rise
4. Subject to a prevailing discount

Close the sale, perhaps with:

> 'Would you prefer to include the optional extra with your order? Or would you rather receive the product on its own?'

Then handle the objections, and/or write up the order!

Even within the price demonstration, multiple little 'sales' emerge!

Each method of payment is a separate mini sale within itself. A successful salesperson is able to fully inform his prospect of the features of a credit card method of purchase, cash, time payment, or cash on delivery or invoice. He is able to communicate the different benefits of each method, but he places emphasis on the benefits of the one for which he feels the prospect has a preference. He knows when to allow the prospect to select the next mini sale, or when it is in the interests of the sale's outcome to introduce a new mini sale himself. He closes with a choice of payment methods:

> 'How would you like to handle this Mr James? Would you prefer to pay cash, or would one of our easy budget plans suit you better at this time?'

These mini sales are often the choice of the prospect. He leads by asking the price, the optional extras, the function, the delivery date, the size, the color, the reliability, the resale value . . . there are dozens of introductions to mini sales, and an aware salesperson recognizes the opportunity they represent — *and takes it!*

This precious discovery, *this revelation* . . . opened up for me a whole new understanding of the business of selling, and if you grasp and implement the concept, *it can do so for you.*

9.3.8 The Preparation

The preparation of a demonstration has significant influence on its outcome.

Prior to your arrival check three things:

1. Select your clothes with care. Many salespeople choose to wear clothes most acceptable to the sociological area in which they plan

THE PRODUCT'S VALUE IS MEASURED IN THE PROSPECT'S MIND

STEP BY STEP

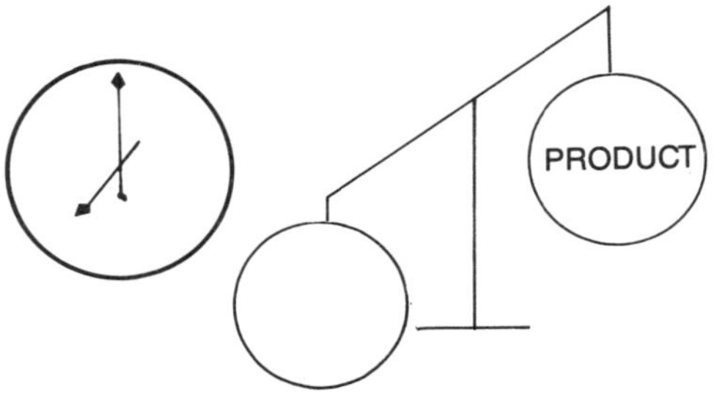

1 APPROACH
2 QUALIFY
3 THE NEED FOR THE PRODUCT
4 COMMENCE THE PRESENTATION

MONEY OUTWEIGHS VALUE

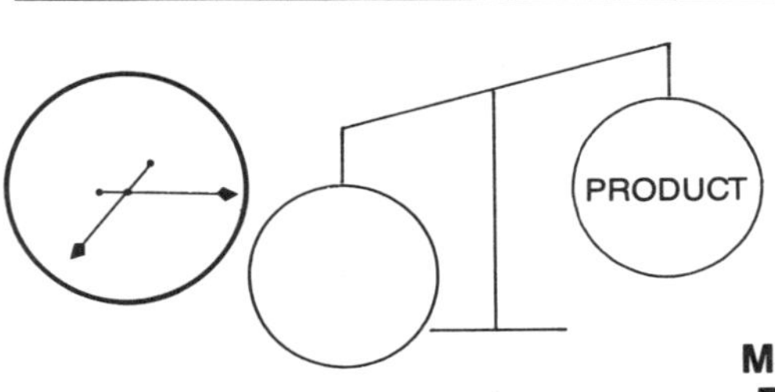

1 CONTINUE PRESENTATION OF
   FACTS
   FIGURES
   FEATURES
   BENEFITS
2 1ST CLOSING QUESTION

**MONEY STILL OUTWEIGHS VALUE
BUT THE PRODUCT HAS GAINED
WEIGHT**

1 CONTINUE PRESENTATION
   WITH MORE
   NEED
   USE
   VALUE
2 2ND CLOSING QUESTION

**MONEY AND VALUE
IN LEVEL BALANCE**

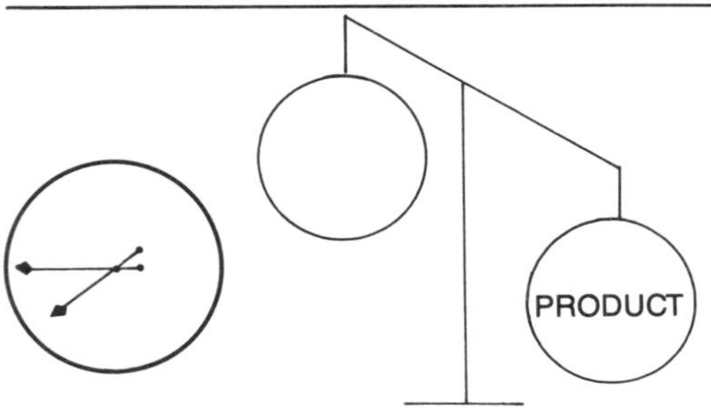

1 MORE VALUE
2 3RD CLOSING QUESTION

**PRODUCT'S VALUE
OUTWEIGHS MONEY**

to work, others prefer to 'dress for their product.' Personally I prefer to see a salesperson's clothes reflect the pride he feels in the product he represents. Professional dress and clean shoes which project a businesslike approach are appropriate, unless the heat makes this impractical. Ella Wheeler Wilcox could have been advising salespeople when she wrote:

> 'There is new strength, repose of mind, and inspiration in fresh apparel.'

2. Check your sales material. It's embarrassing when a customer wants to buy to find your have no order forms! Never carry scruffy sales material. The customer may relate this to the product.
3. Recall your memorized phraseology, endorsements and testimonials. The opinion of experts, educators, institutions, research departments, government authorities, known and respected customers, etc., accurately quoted, are more influential than a salesperson's say-so!

9.3.9 The Presentation

The basic objective of a sales demonstration is to instill in the prospect a desire for ownership of the product.

Your posture should reflect the importance of the occasion. Trust and confidence need to be established and maintained, while the features and benefits are communicated. Your fundamental job is to match the product with the needs and interests of the prospect. Desire for ownership waxes and wanes and the challenge of a demonstration is to present the product so as to arouse, sustain and lift the interest to a peak where the prospect perceives that the product's value outweights the cost and the sale can be negotiated. From beginning to end the presentation must be a dialogue, not a soliloquy! It needs to be valid, personal, believable, and enthusiastically presented. The time period must fulfil the prospect's decision-making needs: to continue the demonstration beyond the prospect's interest point endangers the result and can place the salesperson in a position of having *sold the product, then bought it back*!

The introduction of the order pad should be casual, not momentous: bring it out at the slightest opportunity even if only to explain some figures. Use a pen, rather than a finger, to indicate points of interest on the sales material; it's more professional. The sequence of the demonstration should be punctuated with closing questions. Trial closes or clincher questions serve to accustom the prospect to the idea of owning the product. In response to trial closes the prospect gives multiple minor 'yeses' which help establish an environment of agreement where the major important 'yes' can more readily germinate. Full choice closing questions give the salesperson control and provide valuable assistance with buying decisions.

To achieve maximum impact you have a choice of tools. You select how, when, and in what order to present your sales material. You choose your voice inflection and its modulation. Less controllable, but choices nevertheless, are your gestures and movements, your facial expressions and length of eye contact, the times of silence and periods of persuasion. You decide on your closing questions, and the method of handling an objection.

Initially most of these will be instinctive while you concentrate on achieving a smooth flow through the sales material, but eventually experience and confidence enable you to rely on your subconscious to perform the mechanics of the demonstration, and release your attention to identify the right choice of tool to use at the most effective time.

Another contributor to the outcome of a sales presentation is the level of eye contact at which you choose to deliver your message. The nature of your product or its sales material can preclude any variation in presentation, but when your product's explanation involves a visual demonstration you have many choices. You will find that the creation of a 'buying environment' occurs most readily when the salesperson's eye level is lower than his prospect's. When facts and figures demand close scrutiny the same level of eye contact may be a necessity, but a position of height over the prospect's eye level is seldom advisable. The prospect tends to be more guarded and less relaxed when he is obliged to 'look up' at the salesperson. Friendship and care are nurtured and generated more readily from non-dictatorial postures. If it doesn't present a physical problem, consider sitting on the carpet; this projects the attitude of service that most salespeople seek to establish. Sit on your feet, don't straddle your legs all over the floor where they may detract from the sales material. Office presentations necessitate eye-to-eye contact, but avoid placing yourself in the position where you are perceived to stand and dictate the demonstration.

Experiment and assess for yourself how different eye contact levels can contribute to the buying environment you strive to create . . . and when you move to rise, a natural opening occurs to introduce a closing question.

>'How do you normally handle something like this Mr Brown? Do you prefer cash or would one of our easy purchase plans suit you better at this time?'

Tackle your first demonstration as soon as possible after class training; don't decide to look through your material first for too long. Make your mistakes in front of a prospect — *their consequences are more memorable that way!*

A salesperson who approaches the marketplace with a sincere desire to serve, and who practices his demonstration regularly in front of a prospect, will very soon be able to perform a persuasive presentation.

9.3.10 Negotiating Deals

People buy things for many reasons, but most fall into one, or a combination of the following categories:

1. Pride of ownership
2. Anticipated profit
3. Anticipated pleasure
4. Desire for security, or fear of its loss
5. Desire for change — improvement, efficiency, convenience
6. Necessity

Often a prospect expresses a buying reason other than his real motive, so the ability to identify the actual buying motive/s becomes important for a salesperson.

The two most influential factors in the negotiation of deals are timing and emphasis.

When the salesperson is in a position to change his product's price, or introduce a premium, or add an extra benefit, the right timing and correct emphasis can be as influential as the benefit itself! Poor timing and misplaced emphasis can terminate a sales opportunity. Care should be taken to maintain trust, which can be at risk when deals are negotiated.

The sensitive moment, when the benefits of ownership are being weighed against the product's price and usefulness in the prospect's mind, is the time to add weight to the force of your argument. Consider the buying motives carefully, and decide when and which added benefit to mention. If you present every advantage of ownership to the prospect, as soon as you are physically able, the liklihood is that one benefit will detract from the impact of another. Benefits interspersed with the features and introduced at interest peaks tend to be more persuasive. A special concession, a personal advantage, an extra benefit presented at a moment of decision can become the deciding factor.

Timing is of prime importance: *emphasis* is second.

Emphasis is the special force a salesperson can choose to apply in order to increase the effectiveness of his persuasion. It is a mixture of sincere conviction and important urgency. Meaningful emphasis is associated with statements of gentle clarity as much as increased volume and repetition. Resist the impulse to tip all the benefits over the prospect like a bucket of water in an attempt to drown any objection. When this happens emphasis becomes the first casualty — objections usually prove waterproof!

Salespeople need to develop an awareness of the contribution made by both timing and emphasis throughout a sales demonstration, but especially when deals are being negotiated.

9.3.11 Cancellations

A salesperson, beginner or professional, should never be discouraged by a sales cancellation. Disappointed, yes! but discouraged, no! You lose your commission, so your pocket is inevitably affected, but your self esteem should not be.

Take action!

Call back physically if practical, identify the cause, and do everything possible to reinstate the order. Personal contact is important. If the customer's decision is irreversible, sow the seeds of friendship, and stress the need, use and value of the product, making a future sale more likely. If agreeable, set a callback date, even years ahead. Ask for referrals — the prospect may be sorry for the inconvenience he has caused, and welcome a chance to compensate you. If finance is the cancellation's root cause, and the prospect qualifies, consider offering him a job opportunity.

Cancellations are most often received by two categories of salespeople — *the best and the least experienced*! First class salespeople with their expertise, product knowledge and people skills, often are able to procure agreement to sales in the face of deep-rooted objections, when a less able salesperson would have failed to influence the prospect's thinking. Later, when the customer no longer feels the salesperson's persuasion as strongly, or a third person contributes a reverse influence, the objections re-emerge and a cancellation results. These should be regarded as normal averages in a sales environment. Lack of cancellations is not necessarily a matter of congratulation; you may be only an order-taker representing a highly saleable product!

Cancellations are also received by salespeople whose product, performance and statements seem questionable, either during the demonstration (when the prospect signs the sales agreement in order to terminate the demonstration, knowing he can easily cancel) or, in retrospect. If a beginner has not done his homework adequately, ignorance can combine with inexperience, resulting in a partly deserved cancellation; at other times cancellations can be thoroughly undeserved. Customers are not renowned for making charitable judgements in areas of doubt, so if you conclude that something you said or did, or should have said or done, contributed to the cancellation, do what you can to retrieve the situation, then simply determine to learn from the experience and do better next time!

The calibre of a salesperson's potential is often revealed during the aftermath of a cancellation, or as can happen, after a string of cancellations . . .

Does he give up . . . . *or go out again determined to achieve his sales goals?*

9.4　PROSPECTING

9.4.1　The Importance Of Attitude To Prospecting

We have seen how mental attitude affects every aspect of a sales career, but it is particularly important that the activity of prospecting be approached with a positive and creative attitude.

Would you believe that prospecting is an instinctive attitude, and that a successful salesperson does it eighteen hours a day?

When I was a young girl growing up in the country, we used to go rabbiting. We chased the rabbits on our ponies, and when they ran into burrows, we would dismount and dig them out with a spade. As we dug, we found the burrows divided into two passages, over and over again, and we used to try to guess which tunnel the rabbit had chosen to run down. Sometimes we found the rabbit quickly, other times we dug all day. Prospecting is like rabbiting — as you follow one lead you come across others. You have to decide which one to follow up, which burrow has the rabbit at the end of it, or which lead is most likely to result in a sale.

9.4.2　The Eight Main Sources of Prospects

Basically, there are eight main areas of prospecting.
1.　Friends and acquaintances.
2.　Referrals, or leads suggested to us by other people.
3.　Leads from newspapers, magazines, trade bulletins, circulars, church or phone directories and mailing lists offer starting points. Even television and radio can provide a constant flow of fresh prospects. These are leads that we find or ferret out for ourselves.
4.　Cold calling — the adventure of just knocking on a door, or calling without appointment at a home or place of work.
5.　Service calls — the time set aside by the salesperson to call back after the product has been delivered or installed to explain its use, and serve and satisfy the customer.
6.　Display centers, agricultural shows, trade centers, conventions, conferences, shopping centers, church and school programs, swimming pool centers, railway station platforms, or any public area where you can take space and expose your product to its marketplace.

7.   Telephone prospecting
8.   Product advertising

Some salespeople confidently tackle all eight simultaneously! Professional sales people at least must know how to tap each source. Other sales people concentrate in the prospecting environment where they feel most comfortable, either from choice, or from lack of confidence or special circumstances. Neither is right or wrong — selling is an individual creative profession. However the higher you climb the company ladder, the greater the need for you to learn every aspect of the business. Eventually you'll be teaching others. and a new prospecting method can provide important and timely motivation.

9.4.3   Friends And Acquaintances

Friends are natural starting points but they are not always the easy first sale a new agent sometimes expects. A timely warning can be valuable . . . Don't pounce on your friends; don't announce you're coming to sell them something. You'll frighten them into reverse gear.

> WHEN PEOPLE ARE FRIGHTENED, INBUILT DEFENCE MECHANISMS PROMPT THEM TO THINK THE WORST, NOT THE BEST.

This approach prompts them to think you are presuming on their friendship for your own benefit, without regard for their best interests.

> THE ESSENCE OF GOOD SALESMANSHIP IS COURTESY AND CONSIDERATION FOR OTHER PEOPLE'S FEELINGS IN ALL SITUATIONS.

Sir Fulke Greville, first Baron Brooke, once said:
'As charity covers a multitude of sins before God, so does politeness before men.'

Approach the task of prospecting with sensitivity.
How do Tom and Mary feel if you dash up and say,
'I have a new agency, you just have to be my first customer!'
Unless you represent a low ticket item, the chances are they will reject even the demonstration.
Aim to be professional in all aspects of the business. Prospecting and the approach are a matter of study and practice. A sloppy attitude to your approach, — 'These are my friends, anything goes here. They'll understand me,' — neither compliments the job, the product, nor your prospect. Rather try saying, 'Good morning Tom and Betty. I've been thinking about you. May I come and see you both? I've started a new job

and my company has introduced me to their exciting range of products. I'd value your opinion and I need to practice my demonstration as well, and you'll be really helping me. Would Thursday or Saturday afternoon be convenient for you?'

Now, if Tom and Betty say, 'Why, certainly, we'd love to see you,' — just be there!

But if they reply, 'Oh, just a minute, we're not buying anything at the moment' answer with,

> 'Look, I understand how you feel, please don't think I'm about to push something on you. Our friendship is too important to me for that. I think you know I would never want to show you something if I didn't believe it was a benefit to you, but I would blame myself if you were looking for something like this for your family, either now or in the future, and I hadn't taken the trouble to let you know it was available. Would it be convenient if I called either on Thursday evening or Friday afternoon and gave you a quick look?'

If Betty and Tom agree, . . . you have your prospect, but if they say something like, 'Now, just a minute, how much is it?'

> . . . you can tell them that you have a number of products, and the price depends on the various combinations. Explain that it's a visual presentation, and really needs to be seen for an overall assessment to be made. Choose words which are relevant to your product's presentation.

Then say something like,

> 'Would you be home on Monday evening, or Saturday afternoon? Do either of those times suit you?'

If they agree, you have your prospect. But if they comment,

> 'Exactly what is it you represent?'

then answer,

> 'It's hard to explain. It's really something you need to see. Could I drop in for just a minute? It will only take five minutes for you to know, if you'd like to see more.'

> IF FURTHER QUESTIONS INDICATE THAT YOUR PROSPECTS INSIST ON HAVING A FULL DESCRIPTION AND KNOWING THE PRICE IMMEDIATELY, THEN YOU MUST TELL THEM, OR RISK LOSING THE OPEN, FRIENDLY RELATIONSHIP A SALESPERSON SHOULD ESTABLISH AND MAINTAIN WITH HIS PROSPECTS.

However, realize that declaring a price before value is seen or anticipated decreases interest, and avoided or cancelled appointments often follow. If you give too much information, every method of payment, color, size, shape, function, or attempt to describe the features and benefits, you will be less effective without the sales tools to support your statements, so resist the temptation to do it until the time is right!

A MAJOR RISK AREA OF PROSPECTING IS THE SNAP JUDGEMENTS PEOPLE MAKE ON WHAT THEY IMAGINE THINGS TO BE.

All too often, friends anticipate, that they may not want your product, and that it could be embarrassing to refuse you, as a friend. A less painful method, perhaps, would be to avoid the situation altogether. As a result, they give excuses about an appointment.

When setting up an appointment describe as little as possible, being careful not to convey the feeling that you are holding back information.

DOUBT SOWS FEELINGS OF MISTRUST,
GOOD SALES PEOPLE SOW FEELINGS OF TRUST.

DEFINITION OF A SUCCESSFUL SALESPERSON

A successful salesperson is one who correctly assesses what a prospect needs to hear, see and feel, to be activated to buy.

The first stage of purchase is to agree to an appointment!
If, at this point you are thinking,
'Oh, I couldn't do that, I'll just tell my friends I'm coming.'
. . . you will not necessarily be unsuccessful, but selling is a business of averages, — and the averages will be against you.

I've always believed that friends are entitled to the same courtesy, consideration and professional approach that you would extend to a stranger, and you may be surprised and possibly learn a painful lesson if you assume a sale with a casual *selling* performance to good friends. They can react with a casual *buying* performance too!

If you are calling on friends without an appointment, explain before entering their home that you have called today on business, and mention your company's name — not half way through a cup of coffee. The reason for this is that you may have visited the one in a hundred who resents your calling as a friend and then giving a demonstration. He may interpret your visit as an assumption on a friendship, or even misrepresentation.

SELLING IS ALL ABOUT ANTICIPATING PEOPLE'S FEELINGS AND REACTIONS.

Give your friends a full private demonstration. Too many sales people mention their agency to friends and hope something will come of it — perhaps give them a sample or a brochure and expect it to do the job.

THE BEST WAY TO SELL MOST PRODUCTS IS TO DEMONSTRATE THEM PERSON TO PERSON. A HALF-HEARTED DEMONSTRATION, A CASUAL DESCRIPTION, A WEAK COMMITMENT, CARRY THEIR OWN RESULTS AND REWARDS.

9.4.4   Averages Constantly Prove Themselves Right

Unless you sell low ticket items or party plan products, don't agree to group demonstrations, for friends or others.

Most products sell an average of one in four in the $500-$2000 price range. Logically therefore, if you demonstrate to a group of eight, you will have an average of two buyers, but you will also have six non-buyers present!

If two purchase there and then, how may the other six feel? Think about that. A little uncomfortable perhaps that they apparently didn't share a belief in the truths you exposed during your demonstration, nor could support the worthy convictions you expressed about your product? Perhaps just a little guilty?

So what might they do to prevent this happening?

Yes, make remarks or adopt attitudes and expressions which may dissuade the other two from buying.

Two against six — who is likely to be more influential? You know the answer, so only arrange personal, single demonstrations with prospects.

EXTEND YOUR CUSTOMER THE COMPLIMENT OF YOUR CON-CENTRATED ATTENTION AND INTEREST IN THEIR NEEDS.

9.4.5   The Think Four Formula for Success in Prospecting

The 'Think Four' formula works particularly well with friends, even though it does apply to every avenue of prospecting.

Every time you meet someone, he presents you with four prospecting opportunities:
1.   He may buy.
2.   He may know someone who will buy.

3.   He may like a job opportunity.
4.   He may know someone who would like a job opportunity.

Maximize every opportunity, and carry these four in your mind when you meet and mingle with people. Ask courteous questions in that order. Try first for a sales appointment. If that succeeds, leave the other three until after the demonstration, or at the service call.

If he won't agree to an appointment, proceed immediately to ask for sales leads, or enquire if he'd like a job opportunity or has a friend who would welcome some extra work.

A new salesperson might ask,

'Why should I introduce new people to the company? I might lose sales.'

Most companies reward people who recruit other salespeople to their ranks, and once you become a manager you usually benefit financially as well. Strive to become a manager from the beginning, — you'll be paid more, and have faith that what is good for the company inevitably benefits the salespeople.

A product which includes a mission among its benefits needs little other justification for recruitment.

OUR WORLD IS BURDENED WITH AN UNEMPLOYMENT PROBLEM. HELPING OTHERS TOWARDS AN OPPORTUNITY THAT WILL ADD NEW BREADTH AND DEPTH TO THEIR LIVES IS A RESPONSIBILITY WE ALL SHARE.

9.4.6   **Referral Prospecting**

THE KEY IS TO ASK, SIMPLY ASK — ASK, ASK, ASK!

Ask for help in finding sales leads or in finding people who would like to join the company. Ask for help of those from whom you have bought — the butcher, the milkman, the garage mechanic, the seamstress, the plumber, your doctor, your dentist They are obliged to give you a hearing if you gave them one! Ask companies to refer other companies.

DO NOT ASK PEOPLE IF THEY KNOW ANYONE WHO WOULD BE INTERESTED IN BUYING YOUR PRODUCT.

This involves them in making a decision in advance, on behalf of a friend. Rather explain that many people who would benefit from knowing about your product have never had the chance of seeing it.

ASK IF THEY COULD HELP YOU BY SUGGESTING PEOPLE WHO
PERHAPS WOULD LIKE TO KNOW ABOUT THE AVAILABILITY OF
YOUR PRODUCT.

You might also ask if they know someone who would like the opportunity of some part-time or full-time work. People react willingly to extending opportunity to their friends; but if you ask them to make a judgement or assess their likelihood to buy or work, they will back off the responsibility.

9.4.7 Prospecting From Publications

If you represent a home product, another reservoir of leads, and a splendid source of prospects are church magazines, company bulletins, directories, newspapers, circulars, scout and school magazines. Look in the engagement, marriage and birth columns in a newspaper. Trace the people through the telephone book. These sources represent a continuous and fresh flow of prospects. Lottery winners (they are usually advertised) make good prospects. They should be in a buying mood.

Leads collected may not always be near at hand. When planning to visit new territory, write or phone, letting the prospects know that you are visiting their area. Explain that your visit represents a real and rare opportunity for them to learn the benefits of your products, if it does! Put a sense of urgency into your message, disclosing the minimum of information on the phone. In the case of a letter, word it in such a way that a reply is not expected, such as,

> 'I'll be visiting Cobar on Tuesday, October 4th, and will call during the afternoon to see you. If this is not convenient, would you be good enough to leave a message with . . .' and so on.

In this way, action is only required of the prospect to stop you from coming, and not to have you come.

Most people prefer not to take action. They will take the easiest course. We all do.

9.4.8 Cold Call Prospecting

The achieving salesperson develops the skill of creating prospecting opportunities wherever he finds himself!

Recently, I overheard a saleslady prospecting in the cake shop, and it was a pleasure to listen to an expert.

It went like this:

'Good morning, you look busy today. Is it always as busy in your shop or has the cold weather made everyone hungry?'

The woman behind the counter replied,

'Oh, I'm rushed off my feet most days.'

'Do you like your job?'

'Yes, it's all right, I suppose, but I must say it's starting to bore me. I've been here so long I'm beginning to feel like a buttered bun myself!'

'Well, I represent an opportunity you may well benefit from knowing about. Let me have your telephone number at home. I'll phone and give you some more details when you've got time to talk, and even if you're not interested yourself, you may be able to help a friend.'

She must be successful salesperson, I thought to myself. She has correctly assessed that the cake shop assistant might like a new interest, but that this was not the time or place to tell her about it. She identified the 'product of the moment!'

When she phoned, very likely she would have found the prospect a good source of sales or recruiting leads. It's unlikely that she would have been totally uninterested or she wouldn't have given her phone number.

You will find it a great sense of achievement to sell or recruit someone into your job opportunity from a chance acquaintance.

The 'Think Four' formula investigates every burrow for the rabbit! It is applicable at school or social functions, supermarket shopping lines, bus and train stops, in airplanes, or at seminars — anywhere people stand or sit still. It is effective calling on homes too.

When you are cold calling, making new approaches, watch out for 'For Sale' notices. They tell you that the owners are about to receive a lump sum, or have already received a lump sum, and are receptive to a product they might not otherwise have been in a position to afford.

9.4.9 Service Call Prospecting

There are products for which it is uneconomic or inappropriate to provide a service call, but generally the customer, the customer's company or family, the salesperson, and the salesperson's company all benefit from a service call after the product has been delivered.

Personally it is my favorite prospecting area, and I did not prospect at the point of sale unless I was not going to be able to follow up with a service call. The moment of sale is a time of trust and friendship, and the first beneficiary is the salesperson. In most cases the customer will not experience the benefit of ownership until later. The moment you have been given something is never the time to ask for more! You have just been given an order, and the customer's trust; if a salesperson immediately starts asking for names of friends before the ink is dry on the order, it can be demeaning. If you have the alternate opportunity of the service call, it has the double advantage of being more conducive to results, and of carrying no risk to your relationship with the customer.

At the time of the service call the customer is the first beneficiary, and if you fill or exceed his expectations of your call, he feels grateful to you for your time and attention.

What an ideal time to ask for help of him.

Treat a service call as an important occasion. *It is!*

Arrange the day and hour by phone, and stress the benefit of having everyone present who will be using the product. The time for prospecting comes at the end of the explanation, just before you leave, and when the customer's satisfaction is at its height. Then ask for names of people who 'might be interested in knowing about the product.' (Never ask for suggestions of names of people who would want to buy, or have, or invest.) Take out a note pad and pen, and be ready to write.

Psychologically, I have found that if you sow a need and project an expectancy into grateful soil, it germinates. If you casually ask for referrals as you move to depart as if it was unimportant, the customer responds in kind. Treat the time you allocate to prospecting as important; put a lot of thought and effort into it, *and so will your customer!*

Address each person present by name when asking for referrals:

'Bobby, do you have a friend who . . .?' (relate to the product's benefits).

'Mary, what about you, could you help me . . .?'

'Perhaps you could suggest someone who would benefit from knowing about . . .'

'Now, Mr. Brown, I can't leave you out, can you help me with someone you know who . . .?'

Include everyone, even visitors; suggest a school, church or scout photograph, or an address book as a memory jogger. Sometimes, to give everyone a laugh, I would lastly turn to the family dog or tomcat, and ask him whom he visited. Occasionally the children gave me a new batch of names! Everybody likes to have a smile.

In an office ask as many people as empathy permits, but only at the level of understanding the product demands. Never forget to thank, for any name, phone number, address, description, recommendation, or just word of encouragement. Remember, prospecting doesn't stop when you depart. If possible always ask permission to leave your name and phone number on the product, and in their directory alphabetically under the product's name, with yours in brackets. They may forget your name, but they remember the product. Ask them to phone you if, in the future, someone expresses interest. If the laws of your land and company allow, offer an incentive or gift. I have always been a great believer in flower power, and if an old customer rang to introduce me to a new customer, I would call to thank them with a bunch of violets, or something seasonal.

Helga Schulze of Wollongong initiated a creative and effective prospecting method from a service call. Meticulous and caring about everything she does, Helga keeps a record of her hundreds of service calls with the World Book Encyclopedia by photographing each family group around the product. Later she shares this album with prospects and offers this extra inducement to buy — they will become the next group in her book! She has also found the photographs prompt referrals to other family groups.

9.4.10 Public Display Centers

Display centers offer a great variety of opportunities for product exposure for family-related products. Shows, trade fairs, conference centers, and school open days offer short term occasions when people are in buying moods: shopping centers and other permanent places usually provide ready prospecting lists. Organize an attention-grabbing feature, a free draw, a give-away competition or a quiz. Work actively and professionally, gathering sales and recruiting leads. Make appointments where possible, but leave the door open if an actual appointment is refused, but interest is evident.

Make openings:

'Well it's been nice talking to you, but I can see you can't spare much time just now. If I'm in your area sometime, may I have your permission to drop in and give you a better understanding of it, — when you have more time?'

An assumptive attitude is vital to 'over the counter' selling; expect to sell and act accordingly. Close early and be ready to ricochet to an appointment at the sniff of a firm objection, — better a second chance than a lost opportunity! Develop the product knowledge and skill of demonstrating with maximum impact in minimum time. Contain irrelevant chatter within the boundary of perceivable courtesy and care, but not beyond it, and make every passer-by an open door.

Many times I have witnessed two people together on a display stand. One will come off with lots of leads, the other few.

> THE DIFFERENCE IS A CREATIVE, GOAL-ORIENTED ATTITUDE, PUT TO WORK TO FIND OPPORTUNITIES WHERE THEY DO NOT APPEAR TO EXIST.

9.4.11   Telephone Prospecting

Telephone prospecting is probably the most sophisticated method of prospecting. It offers the advantages of time and travel, but it is a high risk area, and a personal visit is more likely to be successful.

General rules for telephone use:
1. Before you start brace yourself to accept a challenge to your potential and decide to enjoy and learn from the experience whatever the outcome.
2. Select a telephone where interruptions won't occur.
3. Plan your objectives and have a written message in front of you which achieves maximum communication with minimum wordage. Beneath this draw columns headed Name, Telephone No., Address, Appointment time and Helpful Information.
4. Use the prospect's name up front, and frequently during the conversation.
5. Give your name and your company's name and follow with the reason for your call.
6. Speak slowly and articulate clearly — and welcome an opportunity to listen at any stage.
7. Use a Christian name only if the prospect uses yours first.
8. Demonstrate politeness by punctuating your call with expressions of gratitude, and phrases such as 'I hope it's not an inconvenience', 'may I ask' and 'I understand how you feel.'
9. Be friendly — but not unprofessional. Be courteous — but not obsequious. Be relevant — but not inflexible. Be humorous — but not flippant. Accept discourtesy with unfailing grace.
10. Allow the prospect to hang up first.

Success in phone prospecting depends largely on the salesperson's resilience, tenacity and empathy. Courtesy, too, is a high priority.

Identify your 'product of the moment'.
Normally the only sale a phone prospector should attempt is the appointment; any advance on that is achieved at risk. The 'product of the moment' is the appointment. Many salespeople do more harm than good to their cause on the phone: they close doors, rather than open them.

> SPEAK OF THE BENEFITS OF THE APPOINTMENT
> RATHER THAN THE BENEFITS OF THE PRODUCT.

If the prospect draws you into a main product description proceed with reluctance and brevity, and hurry back to your 'product of the moment' — the appointment!

Put forward the features and benefits of an appointment, close by giving a choice of times or places, and handle any objection with speed and tact.

> LIMIT YOUR CONVERSATION TO THE MINIMUM,
> AND HANG UP AS SOON AS COURTESY PERMITS.

Describe as little as possible, and end as soon as you make the sale — *the appointment.*

Avoid giving your prospect the impression that you are coming a long way, at inconvenience to yourself. He will tend to back off the responsibility of your time and travel. Rather explain that you will be in the area, and it will be no trouble to call in for a few minutes.

Plan your phone prospecting in one geographic area at a time, to conserve time and travel costs.

Telephone approaches resemble door approaches, but instead of finishing with,

> 'May I come in?'

you say,

> 'Would Friday morning, or Tuesday afternoon be more convenient?'

Phone prospecting demands a versatility of mind, as it relies entirely on two of your sales tools — your tone of voice and your choice of words. Your sales material cannot provide you with a back-up; the prospect sees nothing, and a picture speaks a thousand words, all in support of your cause! During a phone conversation the communication of empathy and sincerity depends purely on what you say. How you look and how you act cannot lend support. When these are absent, the prospect may conclude they are non-existent! Occasionally you will experience rejection. Accept this, regard it as a learning experience. Say to yourself,

'I may have missed that one, but by the law of averages, I am one step nearer an appointment.'

Often the best you can hope for is that you do not irritate the prospect, and be aware at all times that failure in this prospecting area can harm your company's name, or your personal reputation, because lost ground is hardest to regain on a phone. Knowledge of this fact should not act as a deterrent, but consciousness of risk encourages judicious caution.

When you master this, the most challenging of prospecting methods, a new world opens up to you; a world of quick results for the time invested. Successful salespeople constantly stretch to increase their skills, and extend their horizons.

9.4.12 Advertisement Prospecting

It has been written that 80 percent of all advertising fails; it has been said that only those seeking tax deductions should advertise. These statements may be true in the short term, but long term advertising does pay.

Before placing product advertising, advice should be sought from anyone experienced with advertising your particular product. Careful consideration needs to be given to the type and layout, cost, media, position, emphasis, timing, wording, and even the significance of repetition.

Too often new salespeople perceive advertising as a lifebuoy which will save them from drowning, when, had they taken time to master the strokes, or make the effort to kick harder in the water, they could have learned to swim themselves!

9.4.13 Record Keeping of Prospecting Leads

How can you organize these accruing leads, to capitalize on the opportunity each one represents, and to eliminate time waste?

These two popular ways, which have stood the test of time, are among the simplest.

1. A book.
2. A card system.

Both have advantages, but the main aim is to have easy access to accurate and up-to-date information on every lead you have. Time invested on a regular basis keeping it this way guarantees the salesperson the support he needs.

Too often leads are left on scraps of paper, in car glove compartments, handbags, or abandoned around a phone area. Adding the day's prospecting leads to the record keeping source should be an automatic addition to a day's work.

I used an exercise book, thumb indexed into the eight points of the compass. The city's suburbs covered by each compass point were listed on the thumb indexed page. This took time, but only had to be done once, and proved its worth over and over again. Its home was the car glove compartment, and after a call any resultant lead was transferred immediately from the note-book I always carried in my pocket or hand-bag. Each day I turned the car wheel in the direction of the strongest lead in the book, and then having completed that call, I'd work systematically distancewise away from it.

There are many ways of prospecting, but one thing is sure. When you prospect professionally rather than the 'hit or miss' method, you must select a back-up system of record keeping that suits you. Every name lost is an opportunity lost, an opportunity to think four — to sell, to recruit, and to gather the prospect's selling and hiring leads.

9.4.14   Decide To Succeed At Prospecting

If ever you find yourself thinking,

> 'Oh, this job's too hard, there must be an easier way of earning a
> living,'

immediately go to work on your prospecting list and have a close look at the prospect skills you have developed. Prospecting opportunities surround you, but remember, —

> 'THE BEE WHO GETS THE MOST HONEY DOESN'T
> HANG AROUND THE HIVE!'

Every bus stop, every playground, station, shopping center, doctor's office, gathering, meeting, party, offers a creative opportunity to prospect. Bring the conversation around to your job. It's easy and natural for people to talk about what they're doing, and new experiences they're having. Share your thinking, share your knowledge, and share your excitement.

> DECIDE TO MASTER THE SKILLS, AND CLOCK UP THE EX-
> PERIENCE NECESSARY TO CONTROL THIS VITAL AREA OF
> SALESMANSHIP.

The functions of a salesperson's day all interlock.

A LONG QUALIFIED PROSPECTING LIST AFFECTS YOUR ATTITUDE POSITIVELY; A NONEXISTENT LIST, A 'NOWHERE TO GO' FEELING, WILL AFFECT YOUR ATTITUDE NEGATIVELY.

Prospecting is a state of mind. Regard it as fun, and an exciting challenge.

9.5   APPROACHES

9.5.1   The First Challenge

Many experienced salespeople enjoy approaches because they enjoy meeting people. This aspect of salesmanship is usually the first test of your determination; sadly for some, there never is a second!

This is the time to draw your sword and decide to number among the victors, rather than the vanquished.

Hopefully, you will have worked on achieving a strong positive attitude, and have already a sizeable written prospect list.

> FORM THE HABIT OF WRITING THINGS DOWN;
> THEY ARE MORE LIKELY TO GET DONE.

Ask yourself what exactly it is you are about to approach.

Is it doors, offices, telephones?

No, it is people you are going to approach; realize this, and the doors, waiting rooms, foyers, etc., become less oppressive, and it is unlikely that fear of the unknown will be allowed to dictate the terms of your approach.

People vary in levels of education, availability, temperament, experience, need for your product, ability to pay, and acceptance of salespeople. The salesperson may not even know the prospect's name, and yet is required to 'tailor the demonstration to the customer's needs.' To newcomers to the sales environment, this may seem a pretty daunting task!

In reality it is an exciting challenge to your potential.

The night before you begin, take out your prospect list, decide on your starting point and check your sales kit. Go to your most likely customer first, but not necessarily the second most likely customer next. Your second call should be to the nearest prospect to your most likely customer, unless you take a new direction from something suggested by the first prospect. Time should be a major consideration.

Your daily call list should remain flexible, except for the first call. Don't allow disappointment to change your direction, or shadow your attitude; there's always another door.

SOMETIMES SALESPEOPLE DWELL SO LONG AT A DOOR THAT HAS CLOSED THAT THEY FAIL TO NOTICE ANOTHER ONE HAS OPENED!

While sitting having breakfast, your attitude will be subject to a barrage of reasons why you should postpone or even abandon your original intentions. If you put your finger on something too hot, your brain doesn't wait for you to make a conscious decision to remove it from the source of pain, your subconscious short circuits the system! Your brain gives involuntary instructions to protect you.

So it is when you approach a psychologically unwelcome situation. The brain, programmed not unlike a computer, will act to divert your course of action; thus are success-oriented intentions undermined! Up on to the screen of the computer of your mind, the brain will throw the suggestion of another cup of coffee, another phone call, or other distracting alternatives.

AT THIS POINT THE IRRESOLUTE SALESPERSON FLOUNDERS AND FAILS; THE RESOLUTE SALESPERSON SUMMONS HIS DETERMINATION TO THE SUPPORT OF HIS PLANNED ACTION.

What job doesn't have some unenjoyable aspects attached to it anyway? Successful salespeople recognize those diversionary thoughts, and leave their homes on a planned basis.

The realization that the hardest door to go through is your own will help you go through it!

9.5.2 Gate Approaches

I have always preferred to call 'door' approaches 'gate' approaches, because that is where the job starts — at the gate!

Stand a second, and consciously 'dust-off' your mental attitude.

Many years in direct selling have taught me that most people are more problem-beset than happy. Out in the field you will meet loneliness, anxiety and stress, but you also will find inspiration, satisfaction, and friendship. Successful salespeople learn to handle and often help in each different situation.

When you approach a door, think of it as a new book. Ask yourself whose biography you are going to read today, and perhaps you will write a paragraph in that book! It's intriguing that way, and helps you over the hurdle of the approach.

As you walk down the path, be preoccupied with two tasks:
1. Preparing to project confidence, happiness, and friendship. If apprehension, guilt, or anxiety are your fellow travelers, then the people on whom you are calling won't welcome your visit; they have enough of those things themselves! Concentrate your thoughts on your mission, and how your product can help the prospect. A love and knowledge of your product will give you the wings to fly through doors!
2. Observing possible 'talk points.'
    As you approach the door notice things that you can genuinely admire — flowers, trees, potted plants, paving stones, door handles — they can be 'life-savers.'

When you knock, stand back some distance from the door, for the prospect's sake. Think about his feelings. Your knock may prompt a feeling of apprehension; standing back can be more reassuring and less threatening.

SMILE . . . BE AWARE THAT A FIRST IMPRESSION CAN BE FINAL . . .
WHAT YOU RADIATE IS INFECTIOUS, AND YOU INCREASE YOUR CHANCES OF RECEIVING ONE IN RETURN!

In the beginning, before I learned to enjoy a day in the field, I used to approach a door wishing the hydrangeas would swallow me up, and secretly hoping that the prospect would be out! In this way I could rationalize that the job had failed, and not me. If this is your reaction, remind yourself you have a simple choice. You can be beaten by the door approach, or you can beat it! Minimize the difficulties, and you can come to enjoy the sheer adventure of a day in the field.

Recognize justification.

If you listen to a person who can't or wont handle door approaches describing his reasons, it goes something like this:

'I'm sorry, but I can't do this work. I can't find people home, I just don't think I'm the type. I went out several times but I didn't feel it was me . . .'

What word is he using all the time? It's 'I' isn't it? You just can't help hearing it come through. His problem is his attitude; his only thought is for himself.

SOME PEOPLE DO NOT SUCCEED BECAUSE THEIR WISHBONE IS WHERE THEIR BACKBONE SHOULD BE!

To succeed, you need to think, see and feel beyond yourself. In other words, believe in your product and its benefits, and have the interests of your prospect at heart. This attitude affects every aspect of a sales career, which includes the three basic door approaches.

The three basic gate approaches.

1. The cold call. This is an unsolicited call, the result of an on-the-spot decision.
2. The referral without an appointment. You are given a name and address but call unexpectedly.
3. The referral with an appointment. You arrange the date and time of an appointment prior to your arrival.

9.5.3   **The Ball Game Is Tennis!**

THE SECRET OF SUCCESSFUL DOOR APPROACHES IS KEEPING CONTROL THROUGH THE USE OF QUESTIONS.

Just imagine for a minute that you are going to play a game of tennis. Mrs. Brown opens the door. Speak first, introduce yourself, the person with you (if applicable), and your company.

If the prospect speaks immediately, don't react. Take the initiative and continue as if you had spoken first.

'Good morning, I'm Jane Green of Everyhome Productions, and this is Tom Bayliss, who's with me today.'

(Never introduce levels of management, such as 'This is my supervisor . . .')

You just served the first ball!

What kind of 'tennis' stroke will you receive in return — a hard volley, a baseline shot or a weak lob in the air?

The person who hits the ball out loses, and a champion makes every shot count. Try not to indulge in unnecessary wordage. You have only one objective, to be invited in, and everything said should relate to that objective.

Usually it goes like this:

'What do you want?' or simply 'Yes?'

The prospect's shot has simply kept the ball in play, you won't have to scramble across the court too fast to get this ball back over the net.

'I've been asked by my company to call on families in the area. May I ask you, do you have a family, or have I just been lucky to find you home?'

Think about the question. It includes both likely possibilities, the family and the individual.

You hit a baseline stroke, which ended in the vital question.

EVERYTHING YOU SAY AT THE DOOR SHOULD END IN A QUESTION.

Why? Because whenever we are asked questions our tendency is to answer. If you eliminate questions, and only make statements, your prospect will start asking them, and you can anticipate a tougher time, because you have abdicated the leadership role. You've lost control of the ball, and you'll be dashing all over the court trying to scoop it up and get it back, while the prospect stands at the net whacking it at you! Don't be maneuvered into that position. Questions are the key, not nosy personal ones, just questions related to your only objective at the door — *to be invited in*! The product you are selling at this stage is the interview inside.

LITTLE OF VALUE, EITHER FOR THE SALESPERSON OR THE CUSTOMER, IS ACCOMPLISHED AT THE DOOR.

Your purpose is to be invited in, not to push in. Nothing you say or do should be interpretable as 'pushing in' even in retrospect. The prospect may not actually say 'come in please,' but you move forward when her facial expression and body language tell you that you're welcome.

Now let's return to the ball game.

Following close behind her tendency to answer your question will be her instinct, prompted by curiosity, to ask you a question and take control. You need to be ready to volley with another question, not like machine gun fire, but with genuine interest and friendliness.

If Mrs. Brown replies,

'Oh yes, I do have a family.'

Intercept with something like, . . .

'Oh, how old are the children, may I ask?'

Again your shot was a question; it may not have been a winning stroke, but it kept the ball in play, and you never lose unless you hit it out! She will be busy now getting the ball back over the net to you. She might say,

'We have two, they're seven and ten years old.'

Again, make your stroke purposeful and well placed.

'I'm so glad I found you home. . . . May I come in?'

Notice the question.

If she replies,

'Well, if you don't mind a bit of untidiness . . .'
you've won the ball game, haven't you? You have achieved your objective
of gaining entry. Avoid trying to sell your company's products at the
door. The 'product of the moment' is the interview — inside!

Sometimes your opponent (your customer is an opponent in tennis
terms only) hits a few harder strokes. Mrs. Brown may slip in a few questions herself.

How can you regain the upper hand?

Keep in mind the power of the question. Answer a question with a
question, or at least answer the question and then add a question.

Let's examine this more carefully. Mrs. Brown ignored your question
and gave you one instead.

She said,

'What is this all about?'

Reveal as little as possible at the door; answer with a question and a
smile,

'I can show you in one minute what would take five minutes to
explain. Have you got just a moment?'

Now she might ask,

'Exactly how long will it take?'

'It will only take five minutes for you to know if you'd like to see
more. May I come in for just a moment?'

Only speak the truth. Salespeople of integrity never place themselves
in a position where their words or actions could be interpreted as questionable. If you tell your prospect that you require only five minutes of
her time, and you are invited in as a result, at the end of five minutes just
when she's becoming interested say,

'Mrs. Brown, I told you I would take up only five minutes of your
time — that time has passed. May I show you a little more?'

If she agrees, feel free to stay. These courtesies are opportunities to
communicate the quality of your salesmanship.

To most questions about your purpose or your product at the door,
simply answer with,

'Have you got just a minute? It's really a visual presentation, and
I'd love to show you. May I come in?'

Always end in a question.

She may ask,

'Are you selling something?'

Men ask this question more than woman do, maybe because women enjoy buying things more than men do, and the loss of money is seldom associated in the masculine mind with pleasure. A knowledge of how sex differences can affect reactions enables you to anticipate, and anticipation provides those few extra seconds in which effective words may be selected. You reply simply and truthfully,

> 'Initially, I'm just demonstrating, but if you decide to place an order, . . . well that's up to you. I couldn't deliver anything today (unless you can!), but I'd love to show you. May I come in for a minute?'

This reassures the prospect that any sales decision will be initiated by her. It is a true statement and puts her at ease.

Some prospects are just as good at door tennis as you're going to be, and they have a few hard shots in their repertoire. You might hear,

> 'Look, I wont invite anyone into my home unless I know exactly what it's all about. What do you represent?'

Remember, answer a question with a question. Keep control or she will! How could you answer that with a question?

Here's what I found most effective for a product . . .

> 'Has anyone ever given you the opportunity of seeing Easyhome Production's new range of household products?'

Or for a service . . .

> 'Has anyone ever given you the opportunity of knowing how such and such a service can help you with . . .?'

Your objective at an initial approach is to arouse the prospect's curiosity but give insufficient information for a judgement even to be attempted. Just as once cement has set you cannot change its form, so it is with a customer's judgement at the door. If you give her even a few facts she will blend them with a few preconceived ideas of her own and jump into a judgemental attitude, which you cannot add to or detract from, however wrong you know her conclusion to have been.

> BE AWARE THAT THE BASIC OBJECTIVE OF EVERY RELUCTANT PROSPECT IS TO EXTRACT FROM THE SALESPERSON SUFFICIENT INFORMATION ON WHICH TO BASE A TERMINATING DECISION.

Nobody wants to be sold anything but fortunately lots of people like to buy!

By answering,

> 'Has anyone given you the opportunity of . . .'

you have answered her question, yet kept control. You have supplied the information she wanted, yet steered the conversation in a direction of your choice, as she now needs to reply to your question.

She is likely to say:

'Oh, what's that?' or . . .

'What's it all about?'

She has played the shot you hoped she would. The ball is now directed to your racquet which is poised ready for a familiar favorite stroke, and you reply with the winning sentence, and a friendly smile,

'I can show you without taking up a lot of your time . . . It's very interesting — may I come in for just a few minutes?'

And just as with a tennis stroke you keep moving forward with the follow-through, move forward in expectation of her invitation to come in. She will stop you if it is not convenient.

If the prospect says something like,

'I never allow salespeople in my home.'

Answer, as always, with a courteous question.

'May I ask, have you ever had a bad experience, that you feel that way? Approaching people is my job, and it's important for me to understand what people may feel is discourteous. Could you share it with me?'

Listen to her story sympathetically (if there is one), but usually it's a prejudice based attitude, held by a prospect who has a need to build her self-esteem at the expense of others. It's her problem, not yours. Share a little time with her. She may yet invite you in if you communicate qualities of character attractive to her. Often it is unfounded comment, simply a wild shot she plays!

She may say,

'I'm sorry, I'm not interested.'

Don't allow it to disturb your equilibrium, and your choice of return stroke should depend on her tone of voice. If abrupt, just apologize for troubling her and bringing her to her door, and leave. You can't win them all. Ever heard of a tennis player who won every shot? Just tell yourself that unappreciative people don't deserve your product anyway!

If her tone of voice was gentle, ignore the comment and continue with the next question. Experience will teach you that what people first say at the door often has little relation to their considered opinion.

Another approach, recommended as a counter stroke for a hard initial shot, which may take the form of an aggressive question, is a divertive response. 'What do you want?' or . . . 'I'm not interested . . .' can dissolve in the wake of distractive comment.

When the salesperson draws attention to a subject of interest to the prospect, perhaps an object for which she is likely to feel affection or pride, he has an instantaneous listener.

Comment on something of genuine interest to you. As a garden lover I like to ask about a plant I can't identify, or admire a newly blossoming flower. I always found this easy and natural, because flowers, trees, potted plants, are visible from most doors.

Doormats, doorbells, doorknobs, paving stones, cats, dogs, birds, children, anything belonging to the prospect which catches your interest, can act as a foundation stone on which a friendly relationship can be built. People like to have their possessions genuinely admired, and the prospect who opens the door and sees you down on your knee being friendly to her cat, softens immediately. Whichever door approach you select, be natural and sincere. People can detect insincerity and they welcome confidence (but not overconfidence) at the door.

This approach ensures that you start your relationship with an interest in common, even a friendship established, before you have attempted to explain the reason for your visit.

This is a professional approach, even though it seems amateurish; perhaps that's the reason for its success.
Winston Churchill once said:

> 'If you want something to appear unprepared, prepare it, man, prepare it!'

In other words, do your homework. Give yourself every opportunity to be successful, through practice, analysis, and experimentation.

If a cold call prospect convinces you that you've called at a genuinely inconvenient moment, qualify her customer potential before attempting to secure a future appointment.

Perhaps you have exchanged a few preliminary tennis shots in this way,

> 'Good morning, I'm Joe Blow from Eversham Enterprises, I'm visiting families in the area. May I come in and talk to you for a few minutes?'
>
> 'Well, actually, I'm just going out, I'm baby-sitting at a neighbor's house . . . I'm in an awful rush. Could you come another time?'

Your tendency may be to make an appointment, and sometimes come a long distance to keep it at the arranged time, only to find that she was not a prospect at all, or was already an owner! So, in the case of an on-the-spot appointment, you make an exception to the 'reveal as little as possible at the door' rule, and make sure you do not drive across town on a will-o-the-wisp appointment.

9.5.4   Approaches to Older People

If an elderly person answers your door approach, use that wonderful, gentle phrase, which should be a basic ingredient of every salesperson's vocabulary,

'I wonder, could you help me please?'

Elderly people may feel threatened by a caller, and asking for help is an immediate reassurance. There is a lot of loneliness among old people, so even if they are unlikely prospects, take time to smell their roses! Add a little sunshine to their day; a salesperson should never be too busy to show a kindness. You may be surprised what excellent prospectors elderly people can be; they often turn you in the direction of a sale!

Humor is a great icebreaker at the door. Always keep a smile near the surface of your face, and let laughter be close behind. Differentiate between the glib retort and humor.

'Are you selling something?' should be answered sincerely, not with,

'Oh well, that depends on whether you're buying . . .!'

If, however, you are asked . . .

'Are you a salesperson?'

Don't stammer evasively; respond with perceivable and immediate pride,

'Oh yes, certainly I'm a salesperson, and I'm proud of my product. Have you got just a moment? You'll be glad you spared a few minutes to have a quick look. May I come in?'

The salesperson who answers the 'I'm not interested' door reaction with 'Not interested in what?' is making an attempt, at the expense of his prospect, to restore his own self-esteem after a perceived put down. Successful salespeople have achieved a depth of self-respect which is not dependent on constant and immediate restoration in the face of rejection. They concentrate on building the prospect's feelings of self worth, and forget their own.

The English essayist, William Hazlett, wrote,
> 'It is the most insignificant people who are the most apt to sneer at others. They remain where they are, safe from reprisal and have no hope of rising in their own self-esteem except by lowering their neighbors.'

So meet discouraging response with understanding and answer the hurting people of our world with double courtesy.
> 'I do apologize for having brought you to your door; I can see I've disturbed you at a bad time, I'm so sorry.'

And mean it!

9.5.5   The Responsibility of the Approach

If you decide that all this is slightly intimidating, and are thinking to yourself,
> 'I'll never learn all that, I'll just tell the prospect that I've come to show them my product.'

then you will work long hours for less result, and by not bothering to learn the language, and develop the skills, you will be doing your product, your company, and your prospect, a disservice.

Long ago a saleslady called at my door to sell me the World Book Encyclopedia, a product unfamiliar to me, but one from which my three young boys would have stood to benefit. We were book lovers, in fact I would have bought any encyclopedia from a salesperson who could communicate a benefit for my boys.

To this day I believe my family was deprived of earlier ownership because of an unprofessional approach. She radiated nervousness, and this lack of confidence transferred to me.

> IF YOU, AS THE SALESPERSON, DON'T HAVE CONFIDENCE IN WHAT YOU ARE ABOUT TO DO AND SAY, WHY SHOULD ANYONE ELSE?

She didn't ask a single question, only answered mine, and I soon had enough information to make an assumptive decision against looking at it, and closed the door.

Years later I bought it after a training class to sell it!

It is a sad reality of the sales industry that salespeople are sent out into a challenging environment of confrontation armed with product knowledge only. Approaches are a vitally important part of a salesperson's experience, and he should receive training, read books, practice, analyze, experiment, and persevere, with the understanding that —

> 'AN APPROACH IS NOT AN EXPERIENCE THAT HAPPENS TO THE SALESPERSON, BUT RATHER, THE SALESPERSON HAPPENS TO THE APPROACH.'!

A salesperson owes it to his customer, his company and to himself to be as professional as he can, and with this attitude, he improves and grows all the time, paving the way to success.

9.5.6   Learn The Language

Any study of 'approaches' should include the 'language of the doors.' You may ask,

> 'How can that be? The dictionary gives us the definitions of words. How can they change?'

The dictionary can only give the literal meaning of a word, but emphasis, environment, tone, association, expression, and sentence position can influence and even change a meaning.

For example, the words — life, Bible, insurance, cosmetics, books, health, diet — are all words which in most circumstances conjure up a respectful response. People approve of them. But on the doorstep, they change their meanings, and often evoke a negative response.

The word 'life,' which the Zondervan salesforce of 'The Book of Life,' includes in its title, during a door approach suggests to a lot of people a strange religious cult.

The word 'Book,' which is included in the range of a number of well known companies, can elicit a response of, 'Oh here is someone who's going to try and foist unwanted books on to me!'

The word 'Bible', at a door, can prompt a reaction of, 'Here's some religious zealot flogging Bibles,' — even from Christians who prefer other marketing concepts.

The word 'cosmetics,' can convey something irritatingly trivial to a busy housewife who prefers to allocate her time to more pressing issues.

Conversely, the word 'insurance' can be associated with a heavy time commitment. The public in general would consider they'd have to invest a fair amount of time to listen and understand the benefits of the different insurance plans.

The words 'health' or 'diet' may be thought too personal to discuss with a stranger.

These words, and many others, have a negative meaning at a door which can evoke an immediate and often insurmountable response to the salesperson's approach.

But once across the threshold, these same words are often the very subject the prospect would like to discuss!

What can you do to ensure the customer responds positively to the words you select to use?

Very little, unless you know the prospect, and you can't stand there dumb! . . . so only use words which are likely to evoke a positive response.

Your choice depends very much on your product, but here are some that have more positive associations at a door — family, range, new, program, help — there are many. If your company's name is not known by the prospect, it is positive, as it evokes curiosity, and a curious prospect is interested! 'Family' is a positive word everywhere, except of course where the prospect has no family. 'New' — something new is always welcome; so many lives are mundane. 'Program' or 'range' has the quality at a door of stimulating interest, possibly because they are so undefined. 'Help' is associated with care, and everyone is happy to feel cared about.

Think in terms of customer response to different words, and you will find that your ratio of approaches made to number of demonstrations given improves remarkably.

If you are going to be a successful salesperson you should know that —

WORDS ARE YOUR WORLD,
LEARN TO LIVE IN IT, LEARN THE LANGUAGES.

Be accurate!

Don't select words for frantic short term gain and inevitable long term reputation loss. Deliberately avoid words that you are not prepared to invest the time and trouble to stand behind, nor are in a position to guarantee personally.

For example, instead of:

'Good morning, I'm doing a survey of families in the area,'
protect your accuracy level with:

'I've been asked by my company to call on homes in the area. May I ask, do you have a family, or have I bothered you unecessarily?'

A salesperson must always be accurate; better a sale lost than a reputation lost! Never state or even infer that you are doing a survey, unless you are. Never give your prospect a reason to believe you are not a salesperson, when you are. Never suggest you represent an organization/institution with whom you are not associated.

> HOWEVER THERE IS A BIG DIFFERENCE BETWEEN TELLING A LIE, AND NOT GOING INTO A DESCRIPTION OF YOUR PRODUCT!

Successful salespeople understand the difference, and work to the benefit of everyone.

9.5.7 What Do You Take With You on a Door Approach?

The salesperson has choices.

Nothing is right or wrong, but you need to find what's right for you, and whether there are conditions which from time to time might influence you to change your approach.

There are three main choices:
1. Go empty-handed to the door, except for a notebook and pen.
2. Take a light zippered bag.
3. Carry a briefcase.

Appointment makers tend to give preference to the notebook approach, if they are convinced their time is more effectively invested demonstrating only when the decision makers are foregathered. It has the advantage of presenting a 'no bag, no time involvement' image, which reduces the likelihood of rejection, but it eliminates your chance of being able to accept a spontaneous invitation to enter, as you have nothing to show!

My choice always has been for the zippered bag, because my product and preference was to demonstrate during the day, to women on their own if they were willing to look. I was always prepared to return if necessary, knowing that this method carried the added benefit of the support from the person who had the initial demonstration.

The nature of the sales material sometimes necessitates the use of a briefcase, but the up-front reaction at the door to a briefcase is more likely to be negative, as it carries the suggestion of 'a lot to look at — a lot of time involvement.'

9.5.8 Future Appointments

Successful salespeople are always prepared to return at the customer's convenience.

If for personal reasons you prefer not to return, be careful to express it from the customer's point of view.

Say:
> 'If you would prefer not to have the bother of my returning, I will leave an application proposal/order form with you, and you can mail it to me if and when you wish . . .'

rather than,
> 'To save me coming back, we could write up the order and you could post it . . .'

Either at the approach, or at the end of a demonstration, if your prospect asks you to return, even as much as a year ahead, hand him your pocket diary, and ask HIM to write his name on the day he would like you to return. Don't write it yourself. If he is not genuine about the appointment, you will know now! Make your return approach after, not before, the date so he cannot interpret your call as 'pressure'. Approach the door, introduce yourself and your company, show him the diary and say:
> 'Good morning Mr. Blake, I hope you haven't been waiting for my visit, as it is after the date you selected for my return, but . . .'

You will have a little smile to yourself when his face tells you he'd forgotten he'd invited you to return!

9.5.9   The Return Approach

Sometimes a wife will set up a return appointment for you to show her husband, but when you arrive you are met with,
> 'I'm sorry, but I'm not interested . . .' or,

> 'I'm sorry, but my husband's not interested . . .'

As always, do not allow disappointment to show.

Reply with warmth and friendliness,
> 'I understand Mr. Smythe, Mrs. Smythe explained she could not make a decision unless you were happy about it, but she did invite me back to meet you. It only takes a few minutes, and just seeing this material is interesting. As I've come so far, may I come in for just a minute?'

Having finished with a question, move appropriately forward.

Alternatively, you can choose to leave Mrs. Smythe with a brochure or piece of sales material, and explain that you will need to collect it at the call-back appointment. When Mr. Smythe rejects the appointment, you can ask to come in for the brochure, and once you have gained entry, natural conversation often leads into a demonstration. Many sales are made this way. In some instances customers will eventually thank you for not being deterred by their initial rejection. I remember one lady who had been inconsiderate and unappreciative from the approach to the day she signed the order. Eventually she went to the trouble of writing to thank the salesman for his perseverance, because the World Book Encyclopedia, which she purchased so reluctantly, proved to be such an incredible benefit to her son.

9.5.10   Keep Your Approach Flexible

An approach which is perceived as a stereotyped spiel will never be successful except in isolated incidences.

If a new salesperson asks you,

'What do you say at the door?'

the truly professional salesperson should be able to answer,

'I never know!'

Your prospect's reaction and responses are going to make certain replies more appropriate than others. Would you ask a tennis player what stroke he uses when the ball comes over the net?

There are two people hitting the ball alternately!

Geographic locations, and the sociological differences between towns or suburbs, even the day of the week (people are more relaxed at weekends), or the time of year (people are usually friendlier on holiday), even facial expressions can affect your choice of door approach.

One thing never alters . . . *the salesperson gets nowhere unless he makes approaches*, and the choice is his.

Great people throughout history have knocked on doors of some sort, in some cases a proverbial door. Every door represents an opportunity. You may have heard it said that opportunity knocks, but I have seldom seen it.

> I BELIEVE OPPORTUNITY RUSHES PAST US IN THE DARK,
> AND IF WE ARE ALERT WE WILL FEEL THE WIND,
> AND PUT OUT OUR HAND AND GRASP IT!

A successful salesperson recognises an opportunity, and then he knocks!

9.5.11   Approaches to Referrals

Many successful salespeople never make cold calls.

The nature of their product, or its price, may dictate a different approach, or they become such expert prospectors that they never need to use this approach. But once you have developed the skill of making cold calls, what might otherwise have been challenging becomes easy!

Approaching company directors and decision-making officials requires an ability to make quick and accurate character assessments. Successful people in positions of authority like to find in salespeople the qualities they admire, and of course these can differ. Usually decision-making heads of companies are people of courage, initiative, and have the ability to do their job well. They've often struggled to get where they are, and they value cheerful determination in a salesperson.

Make your approach courteous but purposeful; move, think, and act with confidence.

Commit these words to memory, and draw on them to build confidence:

FEAR FACED FADES!

Decision makers tend to talk a lot, and they like to laugh.

An old salesman once advised me,

'Listen to your customers, they will tell you how to sell them.'

9.5.12   Respect Customers' Confidences and Keep Promises!

When you are in possession of a prospect's name, use it at the approach. It's good manners, and more personal. A light-hearted friendly approach is:

'Good morning, I'm John Small, rumor has it that Richard and Ruth Simpson live here, is it true?'

If the prospect asks how you knew his name, reply,

'Well, I was with Mr. Black of Brownsfield recently, and he suggested that if I was ever in your area, he felt sure that you would like to know about . . . this new product. May I come in for just a minute, and explain?'

If Mr. Black was a customer of yours say so.

It's likely he will reply,

'What is it?'

'Well, I'd love to show you, can you spare a few minutes?'

Never forget to end with a question.

If the person who gave you the referral asked not to be identified, abide by this, and answer,

'I work among families everywhere, and your name would have been suggested by someone who respected you as parents, and who felt you would like to know about this . . . whatever, and how it could benefit your family. Have you got just a minute?'

Move forward expecting to be asked to come in.

If he insists on knowing the name of the person who gave you his name, and in my experience this is rare, answer in this manner:

'Mr. Black, in the course of my work, many people give me referrals to their friends because they believe they would benefit from knowing about our product. Sometimes they ask me not to mention their name for various reasons, and I must respect this because I like my customers to be able to trust me. But how could they trust me if I disregarded a confidence, and how could I ask you to trust me? They were obviously sincere in wanting you to have an opportunity of seeing this material, or they wouldn't have given me your name and suggested I call. May I come in for just a moment?'

Truth is a must always. This answer may risk a slight irritation, but it is more likely that it will convey the presence of integrity to your prospect. Always be mindful of the beautiful words Polonius spoke in Shakespeare's *Hamlet*:

'THIS ABOVE ALL TO THINE OWN SELF BE TRUE,
AND IT MUST FOLLOW AS THE NIGHT THE DAY,
THOU CANST NOT THEN BE FALSE TO ANY MAN.'

Successful salespeople must have high goals, not just of achievement levels, but of behaviour, and a salesperson committed to the truth grows self-respect. The outside sales environment is not always a comfortable one. How much more important then, that he should be comfortable with himself inside!

9.5.13 When the Prospect Approaches the Salesperson!

Over-the-counter selling still involves 'approaches'. Sometimes salespeople select this environment believing the customer carries the responsibility for the dreaded approach. This may be so in a physical sense, but, in my opinion, shops lose millions of dollars a year because of this misconception.

The salesperson who would work to achieve a friendly involvement with the customer and stimulate an interest in the product range needs a result-oriented attitude of empathy, flexibility and sincerity. The conditions in which buying decisions are made differ enormously from customer to customer. The same quality of friendly attention appreciated by one customer can be resented by another who prefers uninterrupted browsing.

The salesperson's objective is to provide tasteful and timely encouragement, which creates the buying environment required and preferred by each customer.

Recently I went in search of a summer dress. On entering a shop I was rushed by an over-enthusiastic shop assistant, who, in response to my request, gushed:

> 'I have the exact dress you will love, which will make you look like a million dollars.'

Startled by the revelation that this was apparently desirable, I followed with foreboding, to be confronted with a scarlet risque garment suited only to a teenager with a flair for the flamboyant. After this debacle I retreated to the privacy of the sidewalk, not searching further, and wishing only to extricate myself from an uncomfortable situation.

The next shop assistant treated my request with,

> 'We've only a few left, they're very much the season's leftovers. All the lovely new fashion colors have gone!'

Disappointment accompanied me to the rack. Already being *sold off* I gave the dresses a cursory glance until I realized I was looking at the very dress I had hoped to find. My encouraging enquiry about size availability was met with,

> 'Oh, there are only small sizes left, I doubt if they'd fit you!'

Mortified that I should appear unable even to attempt to fit a small size, I whispered ashamedly that I would try it, — and slunk into the fitting room. Emerging with my dress, and a buying decision I was greeted with,

> 'You're very lucky, the dress must have been bigger than the label indicated . . .'

Why had she not greeted me with,

> 'Let me show you our range, we have an attractive selection. You may find exactly what you are looking for.'

The reason was, she lacked empathy and made no attempt to see the dresses through my eyes. She had seen 112 dresses on the rack and now there were only 12. She saw only leftovers; I saw 12 new dresses. Clutching my parcel I departed, wondering how many people bought *despite, rather than because of*, the salesperson!

The skilled salesperson senses the type, depth and length of involvement by which the customer is influenced.

How?

He uses sensitive questions, encouraging suggestions and appropriate silences, all with an obliging attitude conveyed by timely attention, and a happy countenance communicated with a smile!

9.5.14   **A Summary**

1. The hardest door to go through is your own, but to be forewarned is to be forearmed. Be prepared for 'call reluctance' and you will overcome it.

2. Your job starts at the gate. Brush up your mental attitude as you approach the door, and make sure you arrive unshackled by fear in any form. Be ready to enter the ball game with friendliness, courtesy, dignity, and genuine interest in your prospect. You only have three seconds to make a first impression, and first impressions can be final!

3. Remember to ask questions empathetically. Answer a question with a question when you can, and answer a question and add a question when necessary. Questions are the key to successful door approaches.

4. Meet discourtesy with double courtesy, not like with like!

5. Practice until the language of approaches becomes a natural extension of your personality. Become so familiar with, 'I'm not buying anything,' 'I'm not interested,' 'What do you want,' 'Are you selling?' and other common first responses, that you begin to think of them as old friends.

6. Give thought and action to the best methods of setting up appointments.

7. Experiment to discover whether you should approach a door with a notebook, a zippered bag, or a briefcase, — and if, when and why you should vary it.

8. Learn to approach doors , but realize that a successful sales career does not depend on cold call approaches.

9. Never underestimate the importance of this aspect of salesmanship-approaches. Ask yourself, how far could anyone working in a people industry, working with people, through people and for people, expect to go, if they could not approach

people? Logic will answer you. Decide, if approaches are your weakness, that you are going to improve them!

Finally, carry with you these words of conviction expressed by the American insurance executive, Walter Lamar Talbot.

In my opinion he says it all . . .

'THE BUSINESS OF SELLING NARROWS DOWN TO ONE THING, JUST ONE THING, — APPROACHING THE PEOPLE. SHOW ME ANY MAN OF ORDINARY ABILITY WHO WILL GO OUT AND EARNESTLY TELL HIS STORY TO FOUR OR FIVE PEOPLE EVERY DAY, AND I WILL SHOW YOU A MAN WHO JUST CANNOT HELP MAKING GOOD.'

9.6   QUALIFYING

9.6.1   Differentiating Between Prospects and Non-Prospects

When you become proficient at prospecting and approaches, you will find yourself increasingly faced with the dilemma,

'Well here I am inside, but is it the best place for me to be?'

Qualifying skills will provide you with the answer. The habit of qualifying a prospect is often a neglected area of selling, probably because the tasks of prospecting, approaching and demonstrating are more readily perceived as essential. But if you constantly demonstrate to non-prospects, your training and good intentions can be to no avail. Add the skills of qualifying to your sales repertoire and you will triple your effectiveness.

Let us look now at the 'What', 'Why', 'When' and 'How' of qualifying.

The World Book Dictionary defines 'qualify' as *to make fit or competent*. In a sales environment, we ask ourselves,

'Is this person a suitable person to have a demonstration? How can I tell if I should spend time here, or whether I should be next door?'

You might argue,

'What does it matter? Surely everyone would benefit from knowing about my product.'

And logically, even if they don't buy, there could be a spin-off that might lead to someone who would buy, or at least spread enthusiastic vibes about the product in the marketplace, which could blossom sometime, somewhere.

This enthusiastic attitude can be a healthy one. The prospect may benefit from knowing about your product; your company may benefit from having the exposure, and you may ultimately benefit in some way. But each of those three — your company, your prospect and you, — will benefit faster and farther by the prospect becoming an owner, so you need to develop the skill of distinguishing a possible customer from an impossible customer. You need to invest your time intelligently. There are four important steps to qualifying and you should apply your eyes, ears, reasoning and sexperience to doing all four at once.

How's that for a challenge?

9.6.2   The Four Qualifying Steps

1.   Look
2.   Listen
3.   Evaluate
4.   Decide

Look

You look around and observe, especially in a home or office environment. Clues stand out at you — photographs, hobby material, flowers, choice of reading material, choice of dollar expenditure — everything in a home paints a picture of those who live there, and their priorities.

Listen

Listen also to what they say and, in reply, ask questions structured around your product, the answers to which will indicate three things:

1.   The likelihood of their needing, or being interested in the product.
2.   The likelihood of their wanting your product.
3.   The likelihood of their being in a position to make a here-and-now decision to purchase.

Evaluate

Commit a series of preplanned questions to memory, the answers to which will supply you with the information you need to evaluate whether your 'suspect' is in fact a 'prospect'.

Decide

Having evaluated their answers, then decide:

1.   Whether to demonstrate then and there.
2.   Whether to set up an appointment at a time convenient for the prospect, or perhaps when another person, (more likely to be a decision maker) is present, or,
3.   Not to demonstrate at all.

This is qualifying, and its benefits are manifold.

9.6.3   Memory Joggers

Some companies train their sales people to memorize single letters or words, to make it easy for them to remember to ask questions about the subjects the letters represent. With World Book, selling educational products, our questions needed to reveal the prospect's thinking in the areas of children, teachers, the parents' responsibility, the child's progress, their homework problems, and available help. So we trained the salesforce to peg their memory on the letters C.T.R.P.P.H. which represented these areas of interest.

The Book of Life is a program to help people know and understand the Bible better, so our memorized letters are C.C.B.D.R.H. These letters act as springboards from which the questions can be launched.

The C stands for Church, and the questions it may prompt can be,

> 'Where do you fellowship?', 'Are you active in the Church?', 'Are you a Sunday School teacher?', 'Are you a Pastor?'

The second C stands for the Children, and that would prompt the salesperson to ask their names, ages, perhaps their Sunday School, and if the prospect considers it important that the children receive Christian teaching.

The B stands for Bible, and the questions prompted there may include what translation they prefer, or if they hold family devotions, or if the children enjoy the Bible stories.

The D stands for Difficult — this prompts the salesperson to ask the prospect if the family finds the Bible difficult to understand, or difficult to apply in daily life, or to make interesting for the children.

R stands for Responsibility. Who reads to the children? Is it a shared responsibility? Does the husband's work prevent him from being involved?

H stands for Help — here the salesperson is encouraged to frame his question in this way,

> 'If there were a way to help you know and understand the Bible better, Mr. & Mrs. Jones, you'd want to know about it, wouldn't you?'

A salesperson should engrave in his memory a set of questions relating to his product, the answers to which enable him to make a decision on whether or not he will proceed with a demonstration.

Many companies provide a qualifying tool to assist their salespeople with this work. Such a tool is usually a need book or brochures, which emphasize the product's need in the marketplace. By sharing this need material with the prospect and inviting his responses, the salesperson is able to assess his customer potential. Normally, your qualifying decision point is reached before you move into the sales material, but if you are still in doubt, proceed with your demonstration. Never be afraid to pull out at any time you decide you are sitting in front of a non-prospect.

9.6.4 Professionals Withdraw, Amateurs Sit and Continue

Success is inseparably tied to result-oriented investment of time.

Inexperienced sales people can be too easily satisfied by the achievement of a demonstration, and therefore do not ask themselves if this is the best investment of their time, training and talent.

It takes courage to make a new decision and change direction in the middle of a demonstration. You need leadership qualities and the ability to make decisions, for it is unquestionably easier to sit and coast. You also need people skills so as not to jeopardize your relationship with your host and hostess. Always think of your prospects as your host and hostess — you are a guest in their home. If you decide you are with a non-prospect, it is better to let them terminate the interview by the use of questions such as,

> 'Do you think that $1000 would be a bit beyond what you would want to spend at this stage?'

Give the highest figure of your products in combination. An unsolicited announcement of the price before the prospect has seen the value or is prepared, usually draws a ready,

> 'Oh, yes, we wouldn't want to spend that amount at the moment.'

And they readily make moves to help you on your way. This gives you a chance to follow with,

> 'I'd like to thank you both for inviting me into your home. I've really enjoyed being with you, but I mustn't take up your time when you no doubt have lots of things you'd rather do.'

Never say things such as,

> 'Well, I'm wasting my time here,' or
> 'I can see that you people don't have the priorities for a product such as this.'

Thought for the feelings of your prospect or non-prospect is the essence of good manners.

COURTESY AND CONSIDERATION FOR OTHER PEOPLE'S FEELINGS ARE THE HALLMARK OF GOOD SALESMANSHIP.

Remember that today's non-prospect often becomes tomorrow's customer!

When you are applying the look, listen, evaluate and decide rule of qualifying, you may be misled by excuses and objections. Excuses or objections do not necessarily indicate a non-prospect. Excuses are a necessary part of the sale.

Often, all the prospect means is,

'I need to see more and think more about what I'm seeing before I make a decision.'

The difference is sometimes obvious, sometimes subtle, but experience will help here tremendously.

Your qualifying or warm-up talk should stimulate interest in your product and bring out the needs of your prospects. Invite your prospects' opinions, ask for their agreement as you qualify throughout the demonstration. Pass smoothly from qualifying to the need sequence, and through the demonstration sales material, not finishing *before the impact is felt*, nor dwelling on it *after the interest has diminished*. A salesperson senses, judges and controls each stage of a sales demonstration.

If you are selling a product which is demonstrated in an office or factory environment, always see the man or woman at the top. Sometimes, companies will delegate you to a non-decision-maker, where you can work twice as hard for less result, and your half-remembered demonstration is relayed to the decision-maker. This seldom results in a sale, and is always detrimental to the result. Take time to sell yourself to the secretary or receptionist. This doesn't mean to distract her with meaningless chatter, although it may be the key to some secretaries, but be sensitive to the kind of approach which she appears to appreciate, and never make the same mistake twice.

Plan your qualifying questions in advance of your visit, and do your homework on the prospect's background. Be flexible. If possible, pay a sincere compliment to an individual or company achievement, or to a decision a prospect has made, rather than to an object in the room.

9.6.5   Qualifying Guidelines

Finally, here is a list of twelve suggested guidelines for use when qualifying:

1. Aim to qualify as soon as you have gained entry, rather than at the door.
2. Find something belonging to the prospect to compliment sincerely.
3. Select the position from which you would like to demonstrate, and ask permission to sit down.

4. Use the prospect's name constantly and accurately. Normally use Christian names only if permission is given, or if the prospect uses your Christian name first, although there are occasions when the spontaneous use of a Christian name is perceived and accepted as offered friendship.
5. Address everybody present by name during your demonstration.
6. Smile and be friendly. Use humor and show genuine interest in your prospects as people.
7. If they want to steer the conversation to topics outside your interest, don't register lack of interest — hear them out.
8. Be warm and friendly to their children and their animals.
9. Listen and value their opinions — never, repeat never, interrupt when the prospect is speaking, even if constantly and at length. Wait for a gap and then speak.
10. Don't smoke.
11. Don't accept food or drink unless an order has been signed.
12. Move through your list of product-related questions as quickly and professionally as courtesy dictates. You have a job to do; *get on and do it*! A salesperson who leads and controls the environment benefits both the customer and himself.

9.6.6 Know the answers to five questions

Lastly, to ensure that you have grasped the basic objectives of qualifying, ask yourself these five questions:

1. *What is qualifying?*
   Qualifying is researching the available data on which a decision to demonstrate, now, later or never, can be based.
2. *Why do we qualify?*
   We qualify to increase our effectivity in the marketplace in our available time.
3. *When do we qualify?*
   We qualify prior to the demonstration, by gathering all the information we can about our prospect before the appointment and then, at the time of the appointment. If we have a choice, preferably not on the doorstep or in an office foyer, but when we are invited inside. In other words, during the introduction or warm-up period, and if necessary continuing into the 'need' sequence, between the approach and the product demonstration.

4. *How do we qualify?*

   We qualify by observing clues through objects, attitude or body language, and through listening and evaluating the prospect's statements and answers to a preplanned set of memorized questions designed to reveal his needs, interests, priorities and likely buying potential. We qualify by deciding on a course of action as a result of this evaluation. This is called the Look, Listen, Evaluate and Decide system.

5. *When do you think you have finished qualifying?*

   The customer can give you added information which may cause you to take a new direction at any time, but you can stop activating the qualifying processes when you are convinced that your prospect needs your product.

IN OTHER WORDS, **THEY ARE QUALIFIED WHEN YOU ARE SOLD ON SELLING THEM!**

THE FIRST STEP TO SUCCESSFUL SALESMANSHIP IS TO FIND OUT IF YOUR PROSPECT WOULD BENEFIT FROM OWNERSHIP OF YOUR PRODUCT, AND THE SECOND STEP IS TO HELP HIM FIND THE BEST WAY TO GET IT.

Qualifying is the first half of that statement — finding out if possibly your prospect will benefit.

In simple terms, qualifying is an intelligent assessment of your prospect's potential to purchase.

9.7 CLOSING

9.7.1 The Salesperson and the Demonstrator

Do you 'sell' your product or just 'tell' about your product? Both demonstrators and salespeople can give excellent product demonstrations but:

SALESPEOPLE CLOSE — DEMONSTRATORS DON'T CLOSE!

In the beginning it's hard to tell them apart. Like ducklings and chickens, they both hatch, look much the same, and run about picking up what they can from the environment, but the day comes when the differences are life-savers.

This reminds me of an experience I once had on a farm where there was much excitement when a hen and a duck both hatched their eggs on the same day. Soon the ducklings and chickens were allowed into the yard, at the bottom of which there was a large pond. It wasn't long before the little group, exploring their new world, arrived at the brink of the water. The mother duck was already afloat calling encouragingly to the young. Fearful at first, the ducklings entered the water. Several little chicks entered the water too, but unable to handle the environment, turned back to scratch in the dirt.

Watching them I thought, salespeople are like chickens and ducklings; only they have a choice, either to turn back and find another environment which offers less challenge and less rewards, or to hang in there and learn to swim.

Master the sales environment and you will not only learn to swim, but you will learn the different strokes, and to dive deeply or to float relaxed in the water.

In other words, you can be in control of your life's direction.

When I was contemplating a sales career, I felt most apprehensive. In my ignorance, I thought all sales people were suspect, and I went along to training class as much from curiosity as anything else. I thought,

'I'll sit at the back and wait for the conning to take place.'

But it didn't happen. I was introduced to the most beautiful set of books, the World Book Encyclopedia, which I immediately wanted for my family. But when the trainer started talking about closing, I sat up and thought, . . . *oh, here it comes, those devious little tricks that make sales people distrusted.*

I heard the trainer say:

 'A CLOSE IS GIVING THE CUSTOMER THE OPPORTUNITY TO BUY.'

and I thought,

How ridiculous! I'm sitting right there, am I not? They can buy when they like, and besides, I'll leave my phone number.

So I closed my mind to closing and wasted two years of my sales career.

9.7.2 Closing Can Be Instinctive

Over two years later it was a very different and somewhat battered salesperson who kept an evening appointment in a Sydney suburb. It was to prove an evening that would change my thinking.

I had evolved from experience some of the lessons I might have learned in class or from books or tapes, had I listened, but I didn't know enough to recognize my need to learn. I made sales occasionally; some buyers just can't help themselves — they're born that way — and I stumbled over my share!

But this night, as I did my demonstration, relying on my instincts only, I could feel conflicting vibes. The intense interest of a buyer was there, but at the same time I could not sense a sale.

When it was time to depart, and without a sale, my prospect thanked me, explaining that he was a professional salesman, but already an owner of my product. He had wanted to listen to my demonstration as he was always interested in other salespeople's techniques and presentations. He commented on the demonstration and thanked me particularly for closing early and often, and not sitting for hours.

My first reaction was to feel insulted. I certainly did not close! Those things belonged to tricksters — just exactly what I didn't want to be. Then doubts crept in. Had I become one of them? But what if I was wrong? I began to wonder. Was I totally ignorant? It was an unpleasant thought and I tried to dismiss it from my mind, but it wouldn't go away. I thought over and over of what he had said. He thanked me for closing — *thanked me*! I had been thinking that closing was something a salesperson did to benefit himself — a manipulation of the customer into a situation which benefited only the salesperson. I had thought it ran contrary to the kind of salesperson I wanted to be. I'd wanted to be proud of what I did, and serve my customers, and never to be associated with devious techniques.

But he thanked me!

THE PROSPECT'S CHOICE CHART

Showing the Influence of a Choice Offering Closing Question on the Progress of a Sales Demonstration

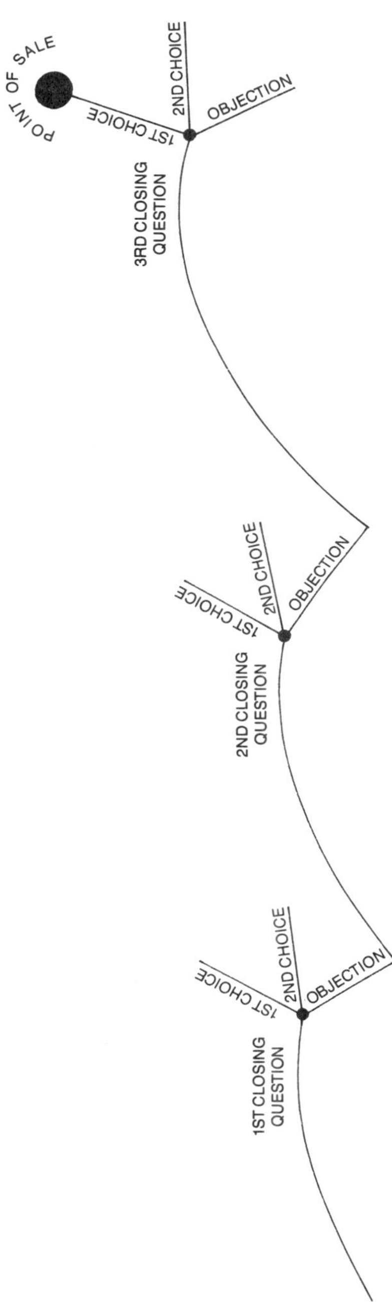

Each time you ask a choice-offering closing question the prospect must select one of your offered choices or declare an excuse or objection. Whichever he selects dictates the demonstration's direction from that point.

It kept ringing in my head.

Finally I decided if I was closing, I'd better learn what it was I was doing! So I went back to class, read everything I could about this mysterious business of closing, asked questions, listened to tapes, and began to understand that closing really showed consideration for the customer. I began to grasp that you could do your job just as effectively, just as comprehensively, just as ethically in three quarters of an hour, as sit awash and out of control for three hours, and that it was in the customer's interests that you should do so.

Have you ever heard anyone say a salesperson visited their house, and sat for hours, and they couldn't get rid of him?

Could that have ever been said of you?

Think back, and realize everyone benefits when the salesperson learns to close. It's a win-win situation. Looking back, I shudder at the memory of some of the long drawn-out demonstrations I inflicted on my prospects.

But I began to get excited too, as clarification dawned.

9.7.3 Reasons For Closing

There are four good reasons why sales people should close.

1. It is a courtesy to the customer to take up as little of his time as possible, yet achieve a full, comprehensive demonstration, leaving him with the knowledge of the features, facts and benefits of your products.

2. Mastery of the art of closing a sale will enable you to double the number of demonstrations in a given period; double the number of people who will know and talk about your products; double the number of prospects who become customers of your product, and, as a well-deserved result, double your income.
    A prospect benefits from having a salesperson who does his job well.

3. Closing gives you control.
    Control gives you confidence.
    Confidence is transferred to the prospect, and a prospect needs and wants to feel confident as he goes through the metamorphosis of becoming a customer.

4. The prospect needs help! As a demonstration progresses, the mind of a prospect is full of thoughts such as,
    'Should I buy this?'
    'Am I being talked into it?'
    'Will I regret this decision?'
    'Should I delay?'
    This is not a comfortable environment, and he needs the salesperson's help to make the decision. Then he can relax and be glad and proud of his new ownership. Without your sales skills he may be deprived of the benefits of ownership. He needs you to be a salesperson, and not just a demonstrator. 'Closing' dictates the difference.

9.7.4   Analysis of a 'Close'

What constitutes a 'close'?

The definition I first learned was too nebulous to provide the help I needed. In order to convert the 'suggestion of closing' into action I needed greater clarification.

If you too need to be activated to 'close', try to grasp this concept in all its simplicity. I believe it will convert you from a demonstrator to a salesperson in a few seconds!

> A 'CLOSE' IS A QUESTION TO WHICH THERE ARE ONLY THREE POSSIBLE REPLIES; TWO LEAD TO SALES, AND THE OTHER LEADS TO AN EXCUSE.

During a demonstration you drop in a closing question which presents the prospect with a choice. In response he must either accept one of your choices, or give an excuse. He only has three choices, although he selects from a large range of words and ways to express his choice.

> IT IS INSPIRATIONAL TO REALIZE THAT THE PROSPECT CANNOT RESPOND WITH A REPLY THAT DOES NOT HELP THE SALES-PERSON!

Remember, the salesperson must ask the closing question, not the prospect, the children, the dog or the cat. *You do it: you initiate the choice question.* You gently drop in your choice-offering question at an appropriate moment, and wait listening for which of the three responses the prospect will select in reply.

If he agrees to one of your offered choices, you move at once to write up the order form.

If he agrees to the other of your offered choices, you move at once to write up the order form.

If he presents you with an excuse, you do not have a sale at that point, but at least you *know* his thinking, which is better than *not knowing* his thinking!

Your closing question should be subtle, sensitive and, above all, timely. This is important because each time you close too soon, you lose a little ground. This may not be serious, but you have to pedal a little faster to catch up, working a little more heavily in the area of need, use and value. Each time you close too late, the impact is lost. So sensitive, timely closing is vital.

9.7.5   The Presentation of a 'Close'

A close should fall softly into a sales environment, blending gently into the scene, having the same arresting quality as a falling rose petal.

> **A 'close' should drop into a sales demonstration with the gentleness of a falling rose petal, and in the stillness that follows, the salesperson should allow the silence to claim a moment of time — from eternity!**

You'll identify more with the process of closing if you think of it as something precious and important.

A CLOSE SHOULD BRING YOU CLOSER TO YOUR PROSPECT AS YOU MOVE WITH A DESIRE TO HELP INTO THE AREA OF HIS NEEDS.

9.7.6   Two Kinds of Closes

There are two kinds of closing questions from which you can select to introduce into your demonstration.

1.   Trial Closes or Half Closes (sometimes known as Clincher Questions)
2.   Full Choice Closes

Both are questions, but only the Full Close offers the prospect a choice.

> I CALL TRIAL CLOSES 'HALF CLOSES' BECAUSE THEY INVOLVE HALF THE EFFORT, AND ACHIEVE HALF THE RESULT.

You might ask, 'Why do we bother with trial closes, when full closes ensure a full result?'

There are benefits.

1. A trial close gives the salesperson greater confidence. New salespeople are usually more comfortable with trial closes, although both amateurs and professionals use them.
2. The salesperson gets an indication of whether it's worth continuing, or whether he's moving in the wrong direction altogether.
3. The opinion of the prospect is invited, and he feels involved, and rapport is built.
4. A trial close allows you to practice a closing question without disturbing the status quo too much. Or you may have decided that a full close was untimely and might result in a backslide from the point of sale. It's a bit like dipping your toe in the water to test the temperature before jumping in. However, you need to be aware that *you are there to disturb the thinking of your prospect*, so don't delay your full close too long!

Why does a trial close fall short?

> A SALE SELDOM RESULTS FROM A TRIAL CLOSE BECAUSE IT DOESN'T OFFER A CHOICE, AND THEREFORE DOESN'T REQUIRE A DECISION FROM THE PROSPECT.

9.7.7   Trial Close Examples

Imagine you're sitting, moving through the demonstration sales material, and the prospect is saying things such as,

'Look at that, that would be useful . . .' or

'Isn't that attractive?' or

'Yes, I can see the benefits of your product . . .'

Comments of appreciation and approval are common, but the prospect seldom will be heard saying,

'I want to buy now. Please get out your order pad and pen.'

It just doesn't happen that way. If you make a decision to introduce a trial close, you might say,

'How do you like what you've seen so far, Mr. Smith?' or

'What do you feel about something like this, Mrs. Blake?'

Now, Mrs. Blake can answer,

'Oh, yes, it's attractive, isn't it?'

and you've really not gained anything except a little confidence, and perhaps increased rapport . You are allowing her to answer you without committing herself in any way.

A FULL CLOSE DEMANDS THAT THE CUSTOMER SHOW HIS HAND, OR DECLARE HIS EXCUSE.

The only place to which he can escape after a full close is to an excuse, but you gain there too, because you benefit from knowing his excuse. You'll never make a sale as long as excuses lie buried inside your prospect. You need excuses out in the open so you have a chance of coping with them.

9.7.8   Full Closes Common to Most Sales Organizations

Now, let's examine some general full closes. Every company has its own. Make sure you know yours.

1.   The cash or budget plan choice closing question, and the minimum regular payment closing question are the two commonest cost-based closes.
2.   The choice of delivery date closing question is available to all salespeople.
3.   The choice of the labels addressed to the children or the family closing question is popular with family oriented products.
4.   The choice of add-on products, or optional extras complimentary to the basic product, is one of the most effective closes.
5.   Choices of size, shape, color, model, locality, pattern, design, edition, or quality all offer closing questions opportunities.

There are hundreds of closes, and as you become experienced, you will enjoy thinking creatively and experimenting with your own closes related to your products.

9.7.9   The Optional Extra Close

Let's take an example from the book industry, using the optional extra close.

Mr. & Mrs. Blake are admiring the sales material which is set out before them. Everyone is involved, interested and attentive. You may have tried a trial close such as,

'Have you ever thought of having something like this for the family Mr. Blake?'

You anticipate and receive a non-committal reply.

'It's interesting.'

Now you are going to introduce a full close. They have no alternative but to answer with one of the three replies to a full close, or variations of those three.

Mr. Blake says,

'Oh yes, it is impressive. I can see it would be useful.'

You close with,

'Well, have you got somewhere to keep it, Mr. Blake?'

Now, Mr. Blake has a choice. He must answer,

'Well, yes, I think it would fit in the sitting room,' or

'No, we haven't really, our bookcases are full.'

Or he can give you an excuse,

'Just a minute, I don't think we could manage it just at the moment. We are putting an extension on the house, and our finances are fully committed. Perhaps next year . . .'

If he says,

'Yes, I think it would fit on the bookrack in the sitting room,'

then you reply,

'Oh, fine, then you can save yourself the cost of a bookrack. I'll make up the order without it.'

Now move without hesitation to write up the order. Don't delay. If he says,

'No, we haven't got a bookrack,'

then assume the sale again and say,

'Well, you might like to include the bookrack. It's custom made to fit and stops the books falling about everywhere. Let me show you a picture of it.' (Any optional extra product can be used instead of the bookrack.)

Describe calmly the optional extra products, and while he decides if he would like to include it, concentrate on a smooth natural flow onto the order pad, realizing that a yes to the bookrack means they are buying the set of books.

If you burst forth with:

'Oh, terrific, that's great, you're buying . . .'

you may find that this dramatic response causes them to change direction, and you can lose a sale.

> APPROACHING A DECISION TO BUY IS LIKE APPROACHING AN UNBROKEN PONY WITH A BRIDLE IN YOUR HANDS — ONE SURPRISING MOVE CAN SEND IT BOLTING IN THE OPPOSITE DIRECTION, AND THEN YOU HAVE TO LET IT RUN AWHILE AND APPROACH IT QUIETLY ALL OVER AGAIN.

Just smoothly and professionally flow from the closing question to the order pad.

9.7.10   The Price Close

The few seconds which follow a completed price description distinguish salespeople from demonstrators!

A product's price needs to be *sold*, not just *told*, and the difference is that after you have told and shown the price in writing, and explained the available choices of payment methods with empathetic communication, you then ask a closing question.

Never introduce or subsequently discuss the price without asking a closing question.

Treat the price of your product(s) as separate sales in themselves; recognize them as the 'products of the moment'. In other words, state the features and facts, communicate the benefits, ask closing choice-offering questions, and handle the excuses not only of the price, but of different aspects of the price. If a customer indicates an interest in a particular method of payment, treat it as a separate sale too. Emphasize its features and benefits, close and be prepared to handle an excuse.

Every salesperson should be prepared mentally to administer the Price Close. Sensitive timing in the introduction of closing questions is related to success. The *right* timing requires instant recognition with some closes, but the *right* timing for the price close can be taught in training class. It follows after the price explanation, and reoccurs whenever the price is under consideration. The signposts are so clearly marked that they offer splendid training ground for new 'closers.'

Example of the price close

Mrs. Jacobs has shown considerable interest in the product. She says,

'Well, I can see it's something we'd value, but how much is it?'

Whenever you introduce the price, *speak slowly and clearly*. Don't make the mistake of rattling it off as if you were ashamed or frightened of it. Explain every detail with perceivable pride and pleasure.

> 'I'm glad you've asked me that, Mrs. Jacobs. We are proud of our price. This product is so easy to own, and you can have it for as little as a few dollars a week, or if you prefer not to be bothered by a regular commitment, the full investment is $----.'

If she asks about interest charges explain them openly and fully, pointing out, if it applies to your product, that early finalization saves interest and, how in this way, *she controls the interest, it does not control her.* Communicate the benefits to the customer of the budget plan, by writing them down, and explain any prevailing discounts, so your customer has no doubts about the benefits.

A successful salesperson now asks a choice-offering question. This is the 'close'.

> 'Which would suit you better Mrs. Jacobs? Would you prefer one of our cash or credit card plans or would one of our easy budget plans be more convenient at this time?'

Mrs. Jacobs has no alternative but to select one of the three replies available to her (or variations of them). She can say,

> 'I prefer cash,' or
> 'I think I'd better settle for a budget plan at the moment,' or
> 'I'd like to discuss it with my husband before I make a decision,' (or some other excuse of her choice).

See the pattern coming through?

9.7.11   Silence is Not Golden — *It is Gold!*

Whenever you have inserted a closing question into a sales demonstration, sit silent and motionless.

> THE FUNDAMENTAL LAW OF SALESMANSHIP IS, AFTER A CLOSE, NEVER SPEAK, AND NEVER MOVE, OR YOU MAY NULLIFY THE WORK YOU HAVE JUST DONE!

To be silent is not enough, you must also be still. You have directed the prospect's thinking into result-oriented channels, allow him to focus and evaluate the new-found facts. Let him think, for even the slightest sound or the smallest movement can disrupt this process.

Each of us has five senses — sight, hearing, touch, taste and smell. All five are alert as long as we are awake, drawing our attention to everything around us. Your prospect is concentrating; your 'closing' question necessitates he make a decision. Try to prevent any one of his senses from distracting him from his decision.

So,

Sight

Don't move, or cause others to move by handing them something.

Hearing

Don't generate sound from any source. Don't talk, or cause others to talk. Respect that silence, allow the rose petal to fall!

Touch

Don't touch the prospect, not even to put a pen in his hand.

Taste

Don't pass him the cookie plate, or a drink.

Smell

Don't push your chair too close to the heater, or light up a cigarette!

Now you might be thinking,

'Oh, that sounds simple enough, I can easily be quiet.'

But strangely it's not, and this is why. You will feel intense pressure, as your customer is under pressure to make a decision. Your instinct as a courteous and empathetic salesperson will be to alleviate that pressure, because you've been trained to make people feel comfortable and relaxed. But after a close, you must go against your instincts and be silent and still.

THE PERSON WHO ALLEVIATES THAT PRESSURE LOSES!

If either the salesperson or the prospect lifts the pressure of the decision from the environment, the likelihood of a buying decision either evaporates, or is postponed.

So make quite sure you don't!

When a sale is achieved, be quick with the mechanics of the order. I have seen a customer's enthusiasm wane while the salesperson fiddles about working out how he writes it up.

9.7.12 The Minimum Monthly Payment Close

The 'minimum or faster' terms payment close is another useful closing question. Use it when you are convinced that cash is not a consideration.

After explaining the price, suggest,

'We have an easy budget plan of only $--- a month which enables you to take delivery of our products now and hardly notice the involvement. Would \$--- a month suit you Mrs. Brown? Or would you rather take care of it a little faster?'

Mrs Brown has three choices;

1. \$--- a month;
2. a little faster than that, or
3. she will give you an excuse.

Any close involving payment should follow with a comprehensive explanation of the optional repayment plans as they affect the customer.

> A CLOSING QUESTION MUST OFFER THE PROSPECT TWO ALTER-NATIVES — BOTH NECESSITATE A POSITIVE SALES DECISION. THE THIRD ALTERNATIVE IS NOT STATED IN THE QUESTION, BUT IT IS THE UNDERSTOOD OPTION OF EVERY PROSPECT IN THE SALES ARENA — **THE EXCUSE!**

If a prospect constantly selects the excuse, keep on calmly piling up need, use, and value in his mind, and keep closing. At least it ensures that you know his thoughts. You will not 'sell' every customer, but you may plant a seed which germinates in time.

9.7.13   Memorize Closes Relating To Your Products

As you progress through the sales material, keep closing significantly. Give your prospect choices. Ask closing questions.

Examples:

'Would you prefer the black, Mrs. Barrett, or do you feel the red is more attractive?'

'How do you normally handle something like this Dr Smith?'

Would you like the first payment to fall due at the end of the month, or is the middle of the month more convenient for your budget?'

'Would you like a midweek delivery, Mrs. Hennings, or would you prefer the weekend?'

'Would you like me to arrange a service call in the morning, Mr. Harris, or would it slot more conveniently into the office routine if I came during the afternoon?'

'Would you prefer the superseded discounted model, Mr. Thomas, or does the latest design appeal to you more?'

9.7.14   The Assumptive Close

Originally I included this in the section on 'Attitude', because the so-called assumptive close isn't a close at all, it's an attitude. But because in sales circles it is well known as a close, and also because it is easier for you to come to grips with at a later stage of learning, I decided to include it in the Closing chapter.

BASICALLY, AN ASSUMPTION THAT THE PROSPECT WILL BUY IS AN ATTITUDE, AND YOU ASK YOUR CLOSING QUESTIONS WITH THIS ATTITUDE.

An assumptive attitude enables you to present the prospect with closing questions, which lead to both major and minor buying decisions. The prospect can agree readily to small decisions, and a successful salesperson, by achieving agreement on these minor decisions, assumes the major sale in the growing momentum of affirmative response. This assumptive attitude often succeeds when an immediate confronting decision on a perceived high price can result in the prospect's backing off.

If you are new to the profession of selling, it sometimes seems illogical to be tossing around minor optional decisions when the main product remains undecided, but it works!

The reason lies in feelings.

    'Mr. Carlisle, are you going to buy this product or are you not going to buy this product?'

That's the real issue, isn't it? And that is a closing question! But what kind of a response do you feel a salesperson would receive having phrased his close in so blunt a manner?

A salesperson's job is to lead. You will find the prospect arrives at the decision to buy more quickly and more comfortably after being led through minor, seemingly unimportant decisions. By going up the steps one at a time, he will arrive more safely at the point of sale and the journey will have been smoother than if you ask him to jump over a wall. Most prospects won't take off!

They are not high jumpers.

THE WEIGHT OF INBUILT CAUTION, FEAR OF MAKING WRONG DECISIONS, DOUBTS, LACK OF ESTABLISHED FAITH AND TRUST IN YOUR OPINION – **THESE THINGS BIND THEM TO THE GROUND.**

Regard your prospect as a partner, not an opponent, and the whole sales environment becomes more relaxed. Go with your customer, step by step helping him along, and you'll arrive at the point of sale together.

It's all exciting and so much fun.

9.7.15 **Practice Makes Perfect**

When you first attempt to ask a closing question, you may sit nervously on the edge of your chair, expecting your prospect to say,

'Aha, I can see what you're up to, how transparent can you be?'
and you'll fear having to handle such a situation. But if you follow professional closing techniques and they become a comfortable and natural extension of you and your demonstration, the situation doesn't occur because people genuinely need you to help them with a decision, and afterwards will value you, not just as a salesperson but often as a friend.

Take it in faith until experience can confirm it for you.

> CLOSING SHOULD BE SO PRACTICED, SO UNDERSTOOD,
> THAT IT BECOMES AUTOMATIC AND REFLEXIVE.

When you are doing a presentation and decide to close, strive to ensure that your tone of voice, the tempo of your speech, the movement of your body and your facial expressions do not change. Aim to achieve complete continuity as you move from the features and benefits of the product into the closing sequence. Be alert and conscious at all times of your customer's feelings and reactions.

Closing is a little like fishing. You cannot see the emotions and reasoning of your prospect, so you throw your line into dark water. You close by pulling up the line. As a result, either you have a catch, or the prospect scatters for a while. Throw in your line again. Nothing is final, and you will find that the fish will regather.

9.7.16 **A No-Close Story!**

Our daily environment constantly reminds us of the urgent need in the community for quality salespeople.

I would like to share with you a story from my experience in a large city department store, to emphasize in your mind the customer's need for the salesperson's help in making buying decisions.

I wanted to purchase a refrigerator and my opening words to the salesman were:

'Good morning, I'd like to buy a refrigerator.'
We don't always get it as easy as that, do we!

'This way, please ma'am,' he replied,
and took me to a row of refrigerators. He proceeded to give me twenty-five demonstrations for twenty-five refrigerators.

'This one has so much cubic space, and so many plastic containers. This one's pink and it has space for so many bottles. This one is square, it's automatic defrost. This one has a deep freeze compartment, which has so and so. This one's been reduced in price as it's a discontinued line. This one has two deep freeze compartments, and this one . . . and this one . . . and this one . . .'

Now, what happened to me? Twenty-five mini demonstrations! Yes, I became more confused by the minute and less and less capable of making a decision.

What should he have done?

Listen to your customer. He will tell you how to sell him.

He could have enquired about the space and color of my kitchen. He could have asked me about my family. I would have replied I had three boys. He might have gone on from there and suggested I would need a large fruit compartment and perhaps a large meat compartment.

He could have asked,

'Are you a busy person?'

I'd have said 'yes'. Almost everyone would say 'yes'. Then he could have suggested that an automatic defrost would save my time.

I'd have said 'Yes'.

He should have taken me with him up the steps towards a sale, shielding me from twenty-five confusing decisions, and made one major decision for me. It wouldn't have taken long, I was a confessed buyer!

Something like this, —

'Mrs. Moore (use your prospect's name accurately and often), from what you tell me your choice should be made from two of our models. Either would fill your needs exactly.'

Then he should have gone into a greater description of the two, and closed the sale.

'Which would you prefer, the one that suits your kitchen colors, or the one that has the double freezer compartment?'

Give two choices always. I would have made a choice and gone happily with his decision, *believing it to have been mine*. Instead I left empty-handed, too confused to make a decision, muttering the 'see husband' excuse!

I needed a salesperson to help me with my decision.

Unfortunately, I had a demonstrator.

9.7.17   In Summary

Why we close

1. We close because it's good manners. It shows consideration for the prospect not to belabor our demonstration beyond its effectiveness, and not to outstay our welcome.
2. We close because shorter, more professional demonstrations enable the salesperson to accomplish more demonstrations per day. This results in greater product radiation, more customers, and more dollars earned for the salesperson over the same period of time.
3. We close because our customers genuinely need our help in making decisions, and closing provides this help.

Kinds of closes

There are two kinds — the trial closes and the full closes.

Trial closes, or half closes

1. Trial closing questions, which do not offer the prospect choices, tend to build confidence in the salesperson, and an increased rapport with the prospect, who as a result feels involved and his opinion appreciated.
2. The response to a trial closing question can at least give you some inkling of his feelings.

Full closes

The other kind of close is the full close. This presents the prospect with a decision-making situation. He only has three choices of response (or variations of them). Two represent springboards into sales, and it is simply a matter of handling the mechanics from then on, and the other one is the excuse. Welcome even this, as this too is a benefit to the salesperson. The salesperson who knows the thinking of his prospect obviously has an advantage over one who is flying blind.

How to close

You close by asking questions and offering two choices, dropping them in strategically from the beginning of the demonstration.

When to close

You close during moments of heightened interest, or when you need to take a leading role. You should drop in closing questions during moments of awakening need awareness, through moments of feature understanding, and through moments of benefit realization.

You close as soon as possible, as often as is tasteful, and as constantly as the stars in the sky!

A close for you!

Last of all, let me leave you with a personal closing question.

Do you care enough to invest time in the theoretical study and the practical application necessary in order to become a successful salesperson?

Or would you prefer a lower commitment and a lesser result?

You must answer with either the first or the second, or give me an excuse . . . *and even then I might not believe you!*

9.8 OBJECTIONS AND EXCUSES

9.8.1 The Challenge of Selling

The business of selling is interesting, rewarding work, full of variety and challenge. This section is about the main challenge of the sales environment — excuses and objections.

The difference

Is there a difference? As a salesperson you need a clear definition of excuses and objections, the everyday words and realities of the language of selling.

There is a difference. It will help you to distinguish between them in this way, —

> EXCUSES ARE UNIMPORTANT AND OFFER NO THREAT TO A SALES RESULT, OBJECTIONS ARE IMPORTANT, AND CAN BE DANGEROUS, EVEN FATAL TO A SALES RESULT.

You will find it helpful to think of an excuse as inconsequential comment on which no great reliance need be placed.

An objection, on the other hand, usually reveals itself through repetition, and is deserving of careful attention. Excuses can flutter throughout a sales demonstration like confetti, but an objection, reinforced with reason, has greater substance.

As the demonstration progresses, the objections become distinguishable from the excuses, but at first both objections and excuses should be treated as excuses, and thought of as friends.

On average, more demonstrations arrive at an unsuccessful conclusion than come to a successful conclusion. Logically therefore, more often than not a salesperson receives objections, so they become constant companions.

9.8.2 You Are Experienced Before You Begin!

Excuses are not new to any of us. We start giving and receiving excuses from the time our mother first says 'No'. As children we become experts at handling excuses. We must learn to close, but we only need to adjust the handling of excuses to the sales environment.

Even babies instinctively know how to handle excuses. A baby who doesn't want to be put down to sleep uses his instinctive objection handler — a loud wail! Just like a salesperson, he makes an emotional appeal.

What parent hasn't had to handle objections of this kind:

'No Susan, you can't have a new tennis racquet until your birthday.'

'Do you want Milly to beat me in the tournament on Saturday Dad?'

'No, you can't go to the dance Jane, you're too young.'

'Well, Betty's mother doesn't think she's too young, but then she's not an old-fashioned mother.'

'Will you please switch off that television and go upstairs and do your homework John.'

'Oh, Mum, this is my favorite program and I've got all tomorrow to do my homework.'

Children handle their parent's objections masterfully. They know the value of persistence. They know by instinct not to expect an objection to change unless they supply more facts and benefits upon which a favorable and face-saving decision can be based. Experience has given them a successful record of influence from which confidence grows.

They believe in what they're saying and refuse to accept rejection. Each one of us develops from birth the necessary qualifications for a lifetime in the sales environment — which is the world!

You cannot escape childhood, so realise you're already qualified in this important aspect of selling, before you even start. The sales arena presents you with the same excuses over and over again. So you don't have to be innovative so much as adjustable. The repetition gives you no excuse for not being an expert. Practice brings mastery, as long as you are determined to succeed.

9.8.3 Common Excuses and Objections

Think of excuses and objections as friends and fellow travelers for, like friends, you're going to meet them often, and without them you probably would not have a sale, or even a job. If customers never made excuses companies could sell their products through the mail and save the commission costs they pay salespeople. Welcome excuses and objections!

Familiar friends

Here are some general excuses and objections which are common to most products, but every product attracts specific excuses.

Can't afford/Too expensive
Buy later
Won't use
Soon dates/Wears out
Satisfied with previous purchase
Consult another opinion

9.8.4 Format for Objection Handling

When you repeatedly receive excuses and objections take three consecutive steps in reaction:
1. The first time you hear an excuse inwardly congratulate yourself and ignore it.
2. The second time you receive an excuse ignore it again.
3. The third time you receive an excuse recognize it as an objection and handle it, unless the excuse given changes, and if so continue to apply the ignore rule.

INITIAL REACTION — **INWARDLY CONGRATULATE YOURSELF!**

Engrave indelibly on your conscious mind this statement:

WHEN YOU RECEIVE YOUR FIRST EXCUSE DURING A SALES PRESENTATION, INWARDLY CONGRATULATE YOURSELF!

That may sound strange but it's important, because it affects your mental attitude, and as a result a valuable boost of confidence is injected into the demonstration at a needed stage. You just achieved a salesperson's first objective . . .

You caused your prospect to want your product!

If a customer's response to your demonstration is indifference and you have not been able to establish a rapport or stimulate interest, he is more likely to extricate himself and vanish, or maintain a stony silence, than offer an objection. Then you have no reason to congratulate yourself. So, when you hear the first excuse, you can be justly pleased with your progress.

SECOND REACTION — **IGNORE IT**

Your second reaction, almost simultaneous with the first, should be to IGNORE it, just politely acknowledge that you heard it in an empathetic way,

'Well, I understand how you feel, Mrs. Brown, but while I'm here, let me show you . . .' and go on, or even simply reply,

'I understand Mr. Jackson . . .' and go on,

or simply an affirmative grunt!

New and unsuccessful salespeople often imagine that to handle excuses successfully you have to retaliate with some smart, influential response, and feeling unable to do this they retreat from the environment. But the best way to handle an excuse the first few times you are confronted with it, is to do the easiest thing — IGNORE IT!

No other reaction should be discernible to the customer.

THIRD REACTION — **IGNORE IT AGAIN!**

The same applies if the excuse is repeated or if it changes. Mr. Brown first said that he couldn't afford, then he changed it to buy later, then to the consult another person excuse.

> AS LONG AS HE CHANGES THE EXCUSE, STICK TO THE IGNORE RULE — JUST ACKNOWLEDGE IT AND GO ON WITH THE DEMON-STRATION WITHOUT GETTING OFF BALANCE.

Why does he change his excuse?

Why does he change from the can't afford to the buy later?

Consider this: there are always at least two people at a demonstration — the salesperson and the prospect. Therefore at least two pairs of ears are listening to those excuses. In other words, Mr. Brown is listening to his own excuse, and sometimes he simply doesn't manage even to convince himself, so he tries another one to see if that sounds more convincing! He's speaking as much to himself as to you, and that is why it is not worth handling.

Also, people build strong emotional reinforcements when they anticipate conflict. In the sales environment a prospect anticipating opposing opinion will summon fact, fiction, pride, and prejudice to support his objection, and thus fortified, it becomes less likely to disintegrate. Continue the demonstration, presenting the material as interestingly as possible, identifying with the prospect's needs. Don't spiel off learned passages which may not be appropriate or appealing to him. I liken that to an 'off the rack' suit. Rather tailor the demonstration to fit the needs and interests of the particular prospect, but at the same time build a reservoir of tested and tried sentences and phrases from which you can draw.

THE INFLUENCE OF A.E.I.O.U. ON A SALES DEMONSTRATION'S PROGRESS

DEMONSTRATION NO. 1

This sale's progress is left to 'chance'.
Undirected and uncontrolled, it will only reach a point of sale when the law of averages allows.

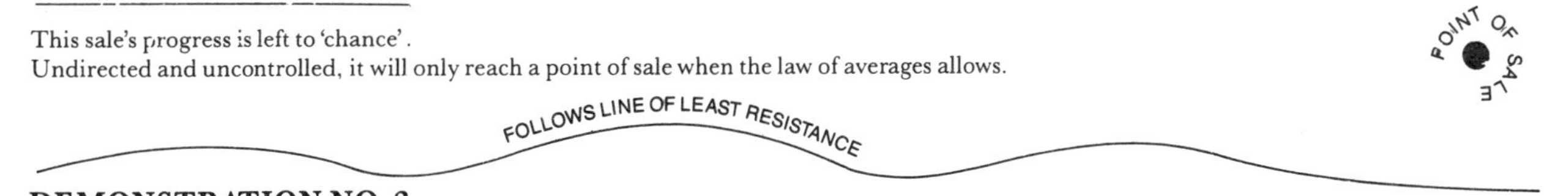

DEMONSTRATION NO. 2

Possibly because of poor product knowledge, confused features, unexplained benefits, inexpert closing or unconvincing handling of objections, this demonstration failed to reach the point of sale, even though closing was attempted. I.O.U. were less effective when not preceded by A & E.

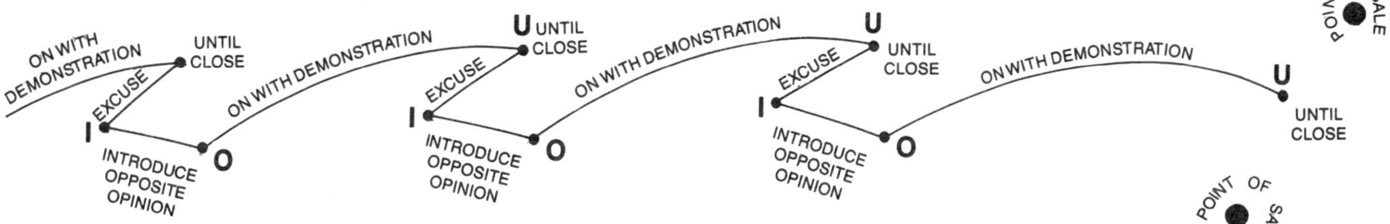

DEMONSTRATION NO. 3

Use of A.E.I.O.U. maximises likelihood of sales result.

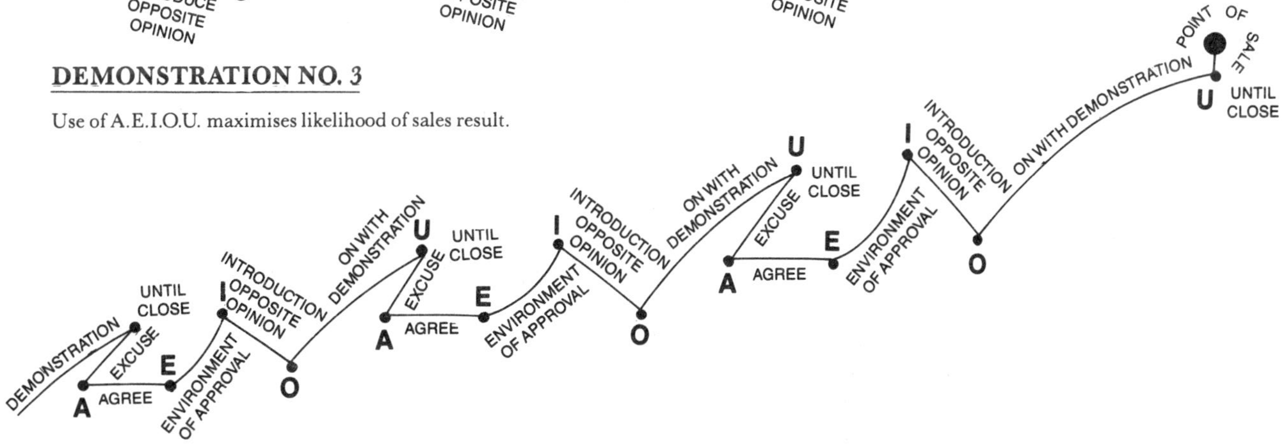

If the excuses change or weaken, acknowledge but ignore them, but if the same excuse comes through constantly and unwaveringly, an objection has emerged.

FOURTH REACTION — **IDENTIFY AND HANDLE THE OBJECTION**

A SALESPERSON MUST HANDLE AN OBJECTION TO THE PROSPECT'S SATISFACTION OR LOSE THE SALE.

AT EVERY DEMONSTRATION A SALE IS MADE,
EITHER THE CUSTOMER *BUYS* THE PRODUCT, OR YOU *BUY* THE OBJECTION.

Sales people tend to 'buy' excuses and objections too readily and pay highly for them. You lose the full commission, plus the chance of radiation and influence your product might have had in that environment, and the prospect loses the benefit of the product when a sale is needlessly lost. So be sure you haven't 'assumed' an excuse is an objection with insufficient reason.

The intensity and frequency of the prospect's excuses will be affected by the quality of your demonstration. Analyze an excuse; it is often a feeler, or simply a brake on the situation.

What the prospect means is,

'I'd like more information', or 'We're travelling too fast, I need a slower pace, time to think.'

So he puts on a brake that slows your performance. When you have ignored the objection at least twice and it just won't fade or vanish, then you must handle it to the prospect's satisfaction or lose the sale.

9.8.5   **The Vowel Progress Plan For Handling Objections**

I'm going to introduce you now to the formula on which I built my sales career. This system enabled me to write national and international records, and helped many hundreds of new sales people through training classes to handle excuses simply and successfully.

Stick to this sequence only as long as the action of writing up the order is premature or inappropriate.

BREAK IN WITH THE ORDER WRITING ACTION EITHER BETWEEN, OR IN THE MIDDLE OF ANY ONE OF THE VOWELS, WHEN THE RIGHT TIME SUGGESTS ITSELF TO YOU.

This precious moment, the appropriate moment to start writing the order with the prospect's permission, can present itself at any time. The skill comes in recognizing it; but mostly you need to wrest it from the sales environment by means of a closing question.

The Vowel Progress Plan for handling objections provides you with valuable planned activity, which you blend into the demonstration while waiting watchfully for the right moment.

Here's how it works:

The five vowels A.E.I.O.U. each represent a specific action when applied to an objection, and these vowels act as pegs upon which you hang your performance.

A STANDS FOR AGREEMENT
E STANDS FOR ENVIRONMENT
I STANDS FOR INTRODUCTION
O STANDS FOR 'ON' WITH THE DEMONSTRATION
U STANDS FOR 'UNTIL' THE NEXT CLOSE.

First you practice it, then it becomes natural, and finally instinctive.

'A' for agree

When an excuse emerges as an objection, and takes you out of the 'ignore' area, (in other words your prospect has said it at least three times), it's time to AGREE. React as you would to a fire alarm, move quickly and without panic into a state of agreement, thus taking the heat or discomfort out of the situation.

Words such as,

'I understand how you feel, Mrs. Brown and I'm sure you're right . . .' or

'I know exactly what you mean, Mr. Smith, and I agree with you' or 'That makes sense to me, Mr. Johnson,' are suggested opening replies.

'E' for environment

This places responsibility for the maintenance of a cordial atmosphere during a sales demonstration squarely on the shoulders of the salesperson. It warns against letting the negative influence of the objection sink deep, or spread wide, in a demonstration situation. React quickly, prevent the fire from spreading. Create an environment where the prospect feels approved of by you. To achieve this you need to communicate understanding and even approval of his objection. You will find a prospect is much more receptive to your influence if you show a respect for his opinion.

A suspicion that the salesperson considers his objection inaccurate or unadmirable, which is allowed to linger in the mind of the prospect, can build a barrier between you.

Confrontation makes losers of everyone.

The relationship you should aim to achieve with a prospect is one of 'I like you, you like me,' a comfortable balance in an environment of mutual respect.

> MOST SALESPEOPLE REALIZE THE NEED FOR THE PROSPECT TO APPROVE OF THE SALESPERSON, **BUT TOO FEW UNDERSTAND THE PROSPECT'S NEED TO FEEL APPROVAL FROM THE SALESPERSON**.

Many sales demonstrations take a wrong direction, because of failure to grasp the significance of this need. After giving an objection, the prospect needs reassurance that his differing opinion has not affected his approval rating with the salesperson.

'I' for introduction

The next vowel is 'I' . . . Now is the time, calmly and interestingly, to introduce the opposite point of view. Make allowance, at all times, for your prospect's intelligence, feelings, and priorities. If you have done the job all successful salespeople need to do of establishing a friendly relationship with your prospect, he will usually give your opinion a hearing. Prospects expect a salesperson to present an opposite view to an objection . . . don't disappoint him . . . when the time is right DO IT!

As persuasively as possible, weave your viewpoint and the reasons why you hold it with the benefits of your product's ownership. Do it with sincerity and conviction but not so as to denigrate your prospect or devalue his opposing opinion. When you introduce the opposite point of view, don't show either by change of tempo, tone or movement, that you are under pressure — as if you were frantically extinguishing a fire!

Just logically put forward the reasons why the prospect might reconsider. Don't expect him to change his mind there and then, but be alert to the possibility. Usually a salesperson must give his prospect new facts, added features, extra benefits, on which he can base a new decision, before he can expect a positive change. This is called face saving, or

> ALLOWING A CUSTOMER TO BUY FROM YOU,
> RATHER THAN TO BE SOLD BY YOU.

To argue with an objection is like trying to put out a fire with gasoline. It magnifies the objection, and strengthens it.

The fifteenth century Italian author Niccolo Machiavelli may not have been an admirable man, but he made a sensible statement when he wrote:

'NEVER FIGHT A BATTLE YOU CANNOT WIN.'

Battle with your prospect, and at worst a sales opportunity will die, or certainly be wounded, and at best you will be forced to retreat!

The truth about handling objections is that even if you expound righteous argument until the prospect runs out of responses . . . you would be better advised to harken to the perceptive words of the British statesman, Viscount Morley:

'YOU HAVE NOT CONVERTED A MAN BECAUSE YOU HAVE SILENCED HIM.'

'O' for 'on with the demonstration'

The fourth vowel 'O' stands for 'On with the Demonstration.'

This is the nucleus of the soft sale, which is representative of empathetic selling. After a close, you proceed without delay to your order pad if the prospect selected one of your offered choices but, if you must handle an objection, it is sensitive and timely to continue on with the demonstration before closing again. This minimizes your psychological victories as felt by the prospect and rescues him from a face saving response. It gives him time to rethink the points you made in handling his objection and feel the impact of your persuasion. Build your relationship with the prospect on firm foundations as you go up the steps towards your goal, and you will find in the long run your sale is more secure.

'U' for 'until the next close'

The fifth and final vowel is 'U', and it acts as a reminder always to be poised and ready to introduce a choice-offering closing question. Each time you close you test your influence with the customer. Closing ensures you capitalize on the work you have done. Always be watchful for a timely moment to slip in a new closing question.

The A.E.I.O.U. method is a thoroughly professional way of handling objections . . . *try it*, and double your effectivity.

The vowel progress plan works with every objection.

9.8.6   **Let's A.E.I.O.U. With the 'Won't Use' Objection**

'A'. First agree . . .
> 'I understand how you feel, Mr. Haig. If neither you nor Mrs. Haig ever benefited from this product, then I would agree with you — there is no point whatsoever in making the investment, and personally I would not like to feel that I had encouraged anyone to order a product that was not of benefit to them.'

'E'. Create an environment of approval . . .
> 'And I respect people who don't rush in and buy everything they see, unless they are convinced it will be of real value to the family.'

'I' introduce the opposite opinion . . .
> 'But I would just like to say that I believe it is difficult to assess the amount of use the family will have from it until they have access to it. You could be surprised by the benefits . . .'

Now present the facts, features and figures which refute the statements the prospect made as an objection, and go back over the advantages of immediate ownership, adding, where possible, third party endorsement in support of your refutation. Mention other benefits that may have clarified in your mind, or produce a special benefit you decided to keep as a powerful surprise for when interest was at a peak, such as a discount, or a premium. If appropriate, point out the possible consequences of non-purchase. Explain the function and purpose of the service call, and how it helps ensure full and beneficial use.

Then continue smoothly on,

'O' for 'On with your Demonstration' . . .

This can include emphasis on the prospect's need for the product, further description of the features, facts and figures, and/or additional explanation of the benefits of ownership.

'U' for 'Until' . . . you feel it's appropriate to close again.
> 'Mr. Haig, would you prefer your service call during the week or would the weekend suit you better when all the family can be present?'.

Always be physically and mentally prepared after a close for a smooth transition to the order pad, should your close result in a positive buying response.

9.8.7   Let's A.E.I.O.U. the 'Consult Other Opinion' Objection

This usually takes the form of 'see husband', 'see wife', or 'consult with so-and-so, he's the expert,' or a decision-responsible group.

Remember, the first two times your prospect gives an excuse, ignore it: just acknowledge but ignore it. But when it persists, and is clearly an objection, bring A.E.I.O.U to the rescue!

'A' — agree,

> 'I understand how you feel, Mrs. Burton, and I agree anyone who might use the product would benefit from seeing it, and I'm happy to come back at a time convenient for Mr. Burton.'

Now 'E' — build the environment . . .

> 'And may I just say it's really special to meet a husband and wife who make decisions as a team. So few married people think and act as partners today.'

Then 'I' — introduce the opposite opinion,

> 'But if you feel your husband will agree with your decision, and don't want to be bothered with my coming back, I can leave this cancellation form which guarantees your deposit will be returned should he insist that you change your mind.'

Don't suggest the order be written up to save you returning, but rather to save the prospect the inconvenience of having you back!

Then proceed with 'O' for 'On with the demonstration.'

Seeing and feeling more value will encourage the prospect to go ahead and order anyway. Have confidence in your product; many times it answers objections more effectively than the salesperson can . . . so don't forget to be quiet from time to time, and give the product every chance to do the persuading!

Lastly 'U', — 'Until you close again',

> 'Mrs. Burton, I was with a mother the other day who made a decision to go ahead and invest in this product. She told me that her husband on several occasions had ordered surprise gifts for the family, and how much the children appreciated them, so she felt justified in giving her children a special gift which they would remember their mother had given them. She used the government family allowance, which is sent to mothers to invest valuably for the children. Would you like to do the same, Mrs. Burton, and use

your family allowance in that way or would you prefer to handle it in another way?'

If she still prefers not to sign an order, don't hassle her. Good salesmanship is all about good judgement. You might be suggesting a course of action that would cause friction between husband and wife. Show yourself to be her friend by suggesting an appointment for the husband, and offer at least two choices of appointment time.

There's a wise old saying salespeople do well to remember,

'IF YOU CAN'T MAKE A SALE — MAKE A FRIEND!'

However, be aware that if you meekly leave without having established a definite time and date for your return visit, *you will be unlikely to ever achieve the sale.*

This Vowel Progress Plan simplifies your job by giving you a format to run on. It puts you in control.

9.8.8   Let's A.E.I.O.U. the 'Buy Later' Objection

When applied to the 'buy later' objection it can progress like this:

The prospect states:

> 'I see your product would be beneficial to me, it's just that at the moment I've got a lot of expenses. But if you come back at Christmas time. . . . I really think it would make a beautiful Christmas present.'

Now provided you have already ignored the excuse, and are convinced it is an objection, answer with,

'A' for Agree.

> 'I understand how you feel, Mrs Thomas. We can't all have everything we want the moment we see it, can we? It wouldn't be very good for us, if we could!'

Then 'E' — tend to the Environment.

> 'And you're quite right, everyone should plan ahead and budget for Christmas. It's such important family time and so many people leave Christmas presents until the last desperate moment and pay the highest prices. Every member of the family benefits when the mother plans Christmas well in advance.'

You have created an environment of approval.

Now continue with 'I' for 'Introduce the opposite opinion,' and say:
'But, Mrs. Thomas, I wouldn't be doing my job if I didn't point out that we have an annual price rise, so that if you genuinely wanted it for Christmas, you may pay more and yet receive the same value. It doesn't make sense to pay more in a few weeks, when for a small deposit you can have the same thing for less. Everything goes up all the time, doesn't it?'

If you know no price rise is imminent, mention other Christmas purchase benefits related to your product, and if your company launches special incentives or discounts at Christmas and you know no price rise is imminent mention them at this point. Alternatively you can point out the convenience of having Christmas decisions made in advance.

Then carry on naturally,

'O' for on with the demonstration, . . .

Elaborate on the features and add value to the benefits of the product, until. . . .

'U' for 'Until' you consider it timely to close again.

THE DEPTH OF A SALESPERSON'S PERSUASION IS REVEALED AT THE MOMENT FOLLOWING A CLOSE.

9.8.9 The Benjamin Franklin Method Of Handling An Objection

At times when your prospect presents you with a number of objections, you may find it helpful to take out a piece of paper and write them down. This method is well known to professional sales people as 'the Benjamin Franklin Close', but in my opinion it is a method of handling excuses rather than a close.

Benjamin Franklin was, of course, one of America's greatest statesmen, a man who prided himself on making well-considered decisions. When in doubt, it was his habit to take a piece of paper, draw a line down the center, head one column 'Reasons For' and the other 'Reasons Against'. After he had filled it in, he had the pros and cons clearly and analytically laid out before him. This enabled him to make a carefully assessed decision.

9.8.10   **Let's A.E.I.O.U. the 'Only Pay Cash' Objection, Using the Benjamin Franklin Method**

Mr. MacDonald is the Managing Director of a small company. He states,

> 'I only pay cash and I haven't got the cash now.'

'A', agree,

> 'I know how you feel Mr. MacDonald. I understand cash flow problems and that one needs to budget sometimes years in advance, and it is difficult to change.'

Then 'E', create an environment where he feels approved of by you, and say:

> 'And may I say I always like to meet experienced organizers, people who plan well — maybe because I'm not so good at this myself, and I like to learn. Too many people make impulsive decisions all the time. Would you agree?'

You are showing yourself to be sensitive to Mr. MacDonald's situation, and have created an environment of approval. He relaxes.

Then 'I', introduce the opposite opinion by saying AND doing!

> 'Would you mind if I write down the points you are making, Mr. MacDonald? It will help me assess how I can best help you. I believe this product holds the solutions your company seeks, and that very quickly it will prove a most profitable investment, but I would like to fully understand . . . first the reasons you might consider investing in this program, and then the reasons why not'.
>
> Or . . . 'If I could show you written proof of how this product would pay for itself in benefits, I believe you would be glad you took a closer look at the figures. Am I right?'

Then 'O' for 'On with the Demonstration', . . . listing the features and benefits as you go. Help him if he needs help with the reasons for purchasing it. Lead his thinking like this,

> 'Would you say that this program would have lasting benefit for your company, Mr. MacDonald?'

He's likely to say 'Yes.'

> 'Would you say that any one department would find it especially beneficial?'

He'll tell you — write it down. Ask lots of questions which you anticipate will receive a positive answer. Little yeses are steps towards a big

'YES'. When you have run out of reasons, facts and figures to support why he should proceed with the purchase, invite him to put forward reasons why his company should not be involved with the product, while you sit and write them down without contributing. This column usually can be reduced to the cost factor. Then point out that the result of this analysis indicates many more reasons for going ahead than for not going ahead, and, if relevant, sell the benefits of time payment plan at this point. 'Sell' your company's credit facility as the language of the twentieth century. Point out that the company with no established credit line can suffer inconvenience. Put forward every argument in favor of your plan and then go on smoothly, refining the features and benefits in the light of a better understanding of his needs.

'U' for until.

Until it's time for you to close again, when the influence of your arguments will be measured.

> POSITIVE RESULTS ARE MORE OFTEN ACHIEVED FROM A CLOSE MADE ***WHEN THE PROSPECT HAS BEEN CONSIDERING A BENEFIT***, THAN FROM A CLOSE MADE ***WHEN HE HAS BEEN DWELLING ON THE SALESPERSON'S OPINION OF HIS OBJECTION!***

'You've just given me many more good reasons for going ahead than against, Mr. MacDonald. They stand out from the page. It's a decision I'm sure you'll never regret, . . . may I arrange the delivery this week, or would you prefer it in month's time?'

Always be ready, after a close for order-writing action!

9.8.11 Let's A.E.I.O.U. The Price Objection

Most prospects object verbally to the price, even if they are happy with it. To others the price looms as a genuine hurdle in their minds. They say they 'can't afford' or 'it's too expensive,' or words to convey this. The salesperson's job is to help the prospect perceive the price as manageable, and the A.E.I.O.U. method nestles comfortably into the response.

First 'A' for 'Agree':

Just assure your prospect that you understand how he feels, and then cover

'E' for the 'Environment,' . . .

. . . by remarking that you would not expect an obviously sensible or intelligent person to invest in anything until he had time to understand and be convinced of its value.

Then 'I' for 'Introduce the opposite opinion' . . .

by taking the total cost figure and

BREAKING IT TO THE BELIEVABLY BUYABLE!

If your prospect is a time-payment customer, this step is absolutely vital, but even a cash customer benefits as he feels good about the interest you can show him he is saving by paying cash. You break the price down to the buyable by taking a piece of paper and doing two little sums.

1. Calculate the monthly payment figure by dividing the price by the period of time selected for payment.
   Example:
   $1000 over 2 years
   is $500 per year
   is approximately $10 per week
   is approximately $1.50 per day.
2. Then divide the daily figure among the number of people who will benefit from the product. This is 50 cents each for a family of three.

This is a demonstration of 'the product of the moment' — the price. Now you need to insert the choice-offering closing question:

'This is barely the price of an ice cream, or a can of Coke. I'm sure you could fit this into your budget, and give your family all the benefits this product has to offer, couldn't you Mrs. Green? Shall I go ahead and arrange for the parcel to be addressed to Bobby, or would you prefer the labels made out to the The Green Family?'

or —

'When you see the price in its true perspective, Mrs. Brown, that is dollar value per week, per person, I'm sure you can see how any family can have the benefits and hardly feel the investment at all. In fact, if you divide the cost between Stephen, Jane and Peter, it is little more than the price of an ice cream, or a can of Coke! Would you like to go ahead on this easy budget system, or would you rather take care of it a little faster?'

She must reply by selecting one of the offered choices, or by exercising her option of the excuse.

Often it is also valuable, simply as a benefit building exercise, to spread the cost over the life expectancy of the product. To compare period of benefits with cost is an accurate way of assessing value.

Example:
$1000 divided by 10 years equals $100 per year which equals approximately $2 per week.

Then ask the closing question:

'If you spread the cost over the ten years that this product will serve your family, Mrs. Smith, you're only looking at $100 per year. That's only $2 a week. Considering the important benefit you will receive, the figure is hardly noticeable, don't you agree? Which do you prefer, the brown or the multicolored model?'

When breaking the price to the believably buyable, point out that a product whose value is on-going is more justly compared with other commodities which are paid for on a regular basis, such as the weekly food bill, electricity, the telephone, than with a product like a vacation where the whole benefit is experienced in a short up-front period. People can seldom tell you what they pay per year for potatoes, or soft drinks, or electricity, and yet on an annual basis they add up surprisingly.

Then end the discussion with your closing question:

'Mrs. Jones, obviously these small amounts could not worry you, and my product's small payments won't worry you either. In fact, I am sure with a little intelligent rechanneling of existing resources, you will be able to have the product for the family without having to find anything extra. It's a decision I am sure you will never regret . . . and it's always better to be able to say, "I'm glad I did," rather than "I wish I had." Would you prefer to arrange the deposit with a credit card, or would cash be convenient as it's only a small amount?'

Point out too, if applicable, that the benefit will continue to be received long after the payments are finalized.

It can be seen from this reply that the length of time allocated to any one 'letter,' either A.E.I.O. or U. is flexible, but that 'I' usually deserves the longest period. This is followed by. . . .

'O' 'On with the Demonstration'

which may only be a single perfunctory addition of fact, . . .

then . . .

'U' for 'Until,'. . . .

you decide to introduce a closing question.

9.8.12   **Let's A.E.I.O.U. With Resilience**

A salesperson must always be versatile. From time to time your prospect will throw out an objection that will distract you from your planned path, and you will have to think quickly to apply the vowel progress plan. Go with the prospect's line of thought, and come back when the time is right.

Recently I was observing a trainee demonstrate Zondervan's *The Book of Life* to a Mr. & Mrs. Anderson. Mr. Anderson announced,

> 'Well, the books are great, the children would love them and I do have the money, but I couldn't order them because they just don't match the carpet.'

Both Rachel, the sales representative, and I were momentarily stunned. Fancy ordering our beautiful books for the covers! But see how the A.E.I.O.U. plan rescued us all.

> 'A' for 'Agree,'
> 'Why, Mr. Anderson, I hadn't even noticed. You're absolutely right — they don't match the carpet, not at all, not one color, do they?'

Rachel had agreed.

> 'E' for 'Environment'. . . .
> 'And may I say Mr. Anderson, how nice it is to meet a husband who considers color schemes in the living room. Why, you're a very rare person. I wish my husband would take more interest in the color schemes of the house. He leaves all that to me.'

Tackling the excuse in this manner allowed her to restore his self-esteem. Had she faced him with the shallowness of his excuse by saying, 'Surely Mr. Anderson, you don't buy books for the carpet?'   . . . she would have alienated her prospect.

Next I introduced the opposite opinion and simply explained that the books were designed for one purpose, to give people a knowledge and understanding of the Bible. Then she continued with,

> 'O' for 'On with the demonstration,' until. . . .

> 'U' for 'Until'. . . . a little later she was able to close.
> 'I've got an idea, Mr. Anderson. Perhaps we could put them in the hallway. It's darker there, and the colors would hardly be noticed. Would you like to include the bookrack? It would stand there neatly against the wall. Or would you prefer them on a table?'

Rachel was rewarded with an order from Mr. Anderson, and I rejoiced that her resilience, courtesy, and problem-solving attitude had given her the success she deserved.

9.8.13   Anticipating Excuses

Successful salespeople anticipate excuses. They make statements with which the prospect is likely to agree before he has thought of the excuse. Then, when he has thought of the excuse, he doesn't say it because by so doing he would be contradicting himself.

Examples

Let's look at some examples.

If he has agreed with you that your product would cut his costs, it's more difficult for him to tell you that he can't afford it.

If parents have agreed with you that reading is the key to a successful school career, it is more difficult for them to tell you that their children won't need books.

If a father agrees with you that the breadwinner should plan for his family's future, it's more difficult for him to tell you they won't need insurance.

If a mother has agreed that clean carpets can affect a family's health, it is more difficult for her to tell you that they don't need a quality vacuum cleaner.

ANTICIPATING EXCUSES CAN ALSO BE DONE BY A STRONG EMPHASIS ON NEED.

Intersperse product need throughout the demonstration. A strong need banishes argument!

9.8.14   Listening Can Handle Excuses and Objections

Sometimes just listening can handle excuses and objections, and in many instances it is the most effective way of all.

Aim to become a skilled listener. There is no faster way of communicating genuine interest. Objections can be like footballs, if not caught and passed on, they disappear over the line and out of the ball game!

9.8.15   Handling the Objections of a 'Know It All' Prospect

Sometimes you will be demonstrating to a person more qualified than you to assess the product. And sometimes you will come across a person who only thinks he is an expert. React in the same way to both. Still apply the vowel progress plan, but when you introduce the opposite opinion, sensitively seek out his opinion. Let silence play a major role. If you expect a prospect to buy because you fully answer his questions, you will be disappointed.

> PEOPLE DON'T LIKE TO HAVE YOU SELL THEM THINGS,
> THEY LIKE TO BUY THINGS FROM YOU.

You can produce a perfectly logical reason why the customer is wrong, and still not get the sale!

Too often frustrations are experienced by salespeople striving to handle objections because they have not realised the truth of these words:

> PREJUDICE IS RARELY OVERCOME BY ARGUMENT.
> NOT BEING FOUNDED IN REASON, IT CANNOT BE DESTROYED BY LOGIC.

If you feel that you have won an argument, minimize the impact of your victory. You'll remove the discomfort by diverting the prospect's attention and feelings back into your product. When handling objections always remember,

> YOU'RE NOT THERE TO WIN THE ARGUMENT, YOU'RE THERE TO ACHIEVE THE SALE.

9.8.16   Callback Objections

These vary with the nature of your product. Experience in the book industry taught me that, except when a price rise was imminent, time invested in call backs was less productive than a fresh demonstration to a new prospect; but let instinct direct you.

> A PROSPECT WHO HAS ALREADY MADE A DECISION AGAINST A PRODUCT IS HARDER TO PERSUADE THAN ONE WHO HAS MADE NO DECISION!

Hope sometimes sends salespeople back, where experience would have advised against it.

However, attempts should unfailingly be made to set up call backs when the prospects cannot be dissuaded from the 'consult other opinion' or 'buy later objection'. Never agree to a prospect ringing you after discussing it with the 'other opinion'. In the home market, the chances are the homemaker won't ring you, and the sale is lost. If the prospect won't agree to a call back appointment, simply explain that you are hard to catch as you are out a lot and that you'd hate to think that she was ringing and not getting through to you, as indeed you would! Suggest that the next time you're in the area you will call by, and she can give you her decision. Don't return for some weeks, and when you do, pick a time when her husband is likely to be home, and plan to do a complete demonstration. Go cheerfully to the door, knowing that the sale is not there, because what has happened is this, she has said to him, ...

> 'Oh, I saw something I really want today, something that I'd love to have for the family.'

And he says,

> 'What's that?'

She names the product, and he asks

> 'How much?'

She gives the price, and he says

> '*What*? Well you can forget that right away, I don't want to hear another word about it . . .!'

And your sale blows out the window.

When you return, approach the door with undisturbable cheerfulness. Mentally prepare yourself to be unaffected by rejection. When she tells you her husband is not interested, she will know she is disappointing you, and this discomfiture will increase her desire to end the interview quickly. Come through positively with friendliness and lack of disappointment, and she will be more likely to agree to your request to see her husband. It can go like this . . .

> 'Good afternoon, Mrs. Rankin, it's Jane Woods from Everyhome Productions.'
>
> 'Oh yes, I'm sorry, I meant to phone you but my husband's really not interested, thank you.'
>
> 'That's all right, Mrs. Rankin. (Remember to be bright and friendly.) You told me you'd need to discuss it, and you weren't sure. Did he think he might be interested at some time in future, perhaps in a couple of years?' (Suggest a time far from the present, it removes the pressure which accompanies a decision.)

'Oh yes, but at the moment we can't manage anything.'

'I understand how you feel. When you have a family there are always so many things you need. But I do have a little time . . . Is your husband home, may I ask? If I could just give him a quick look, then when the time does come to think about it, he'll know what it's all about.'

'I don't know, he's pretty busy at the moment.'

'Well, he might like an opportunity and I'm happy to give him a little time and a chance to see it. As I'm right here, could I see him for just a minute?'

Usually she calls to her husband, and when he comes forward, consider his feelings. He's probably thinking,

'Oh dear, I've got to talk to this salesperson about something I'd rather not be involved in.'

So take that unpleasant task from him, . . . do it for him. Tell *him*! Say, 'Good afternoon, Mr. Rankin, I did enjoy being with your family the other day. Sorry I missed you. Mrs. Rankin has just explained to me that at the moment you're not wanting to order anything, but as I'm right here, you might just like to have a quick look, so that if you considered something like this in the future, then you'd know what it's all about.'

'Well, I haven't got much time.'

'I can show you the basics in just a few minutes. May I come in?'

'All right. Come in then.'

And you will find that with the two together, and Mrs. Rankin already wanting it, that 90 percent of the time — within the hour — you will have that sale!

IT HAS BEEN MY EXPERIENCE THAT COURAGE, PERSISTENCE AND A DETERMINATION TO DEMONSTRATE ARE NOT JUST WORDS, AND APPLIED TO A SALESPERSON'S ROLE WILL CONSTANTLY BRING SUCCESSFUL RESULTS.

I have seen it proven many times, by hundreds of salespeople, and heard it confirmed by hundreds of grateful customers.

9.8.17   A Summary

1.   Sales are seldom made without excuses and objections, and a salesperson needs to learn to distinguish between the two. Both

excuses and objections should be handled as excuses until the objections become distinguishable.

2. The first time you hear an excuse congratulate yourself, you've earned it, and at the same time simply ignore it.
3. The second time you hear an excuse, simply ignore it again. Acknowledge it but ignore it.
4. The third consecutive time you hear an excuse, recognize it as an objection and handle it. Apply the vowel progress plan —

A for Agree, agree with whatever their statement is;
E for Environment, create an environment of approval;
I for Introduction, introduce the opposite opinion;
O for On with the Demonstration;
U for Until it's time to close again.

IN THIS WAY YOU WILL ACHIEVE ONE POSITIVE GOAL AT LEAST — EITHER YOUR MAIN OBJECTIVE, THE SALE, OR YOU MAY HAVE MADE A FRIEND, OR YOU WILL AT LEAST COME AWAY HAVING GAINED THEIR PROFESSIONAL RESPECT.

Selling is, and always will be, about people. Never forget to keep moving back into your product. Excuses dissolve there. And have unshakeable faith in your product, believe that *it won't let you down*; then work, study and practice to ensure that *you don't let down your product*.

You are partners.

Learning to handle excuses is a major step in your sales career.

Accept the challenge they represent with humor, compassion, and determination.

And expect to be challenged as . . .

A KITE ONLY RISES AGAINST, NOT WITH, THE WIND.

9.9 REJECTION AND FAILURE

9.9.1 The Difference

Rejection and failure touch the lives of every salesperson somewhere, sometime, and in some form. Reaction to either can depend on character, severity, circumstances, and even available advice. Some salespeople dwell too long on the pain of failure, paying it an undeserved compliment, perpetuating its influence. Others, sometimes unwisely, pay it insufficient due.

> WHEN IT IS YOUR TURN TO EXPERIENCE FAILURE OR REJECTION,
> FACE IT HONESTLY AND TOTALLY, ***BUT TEMPORARILY!***
>
> REJECTION AND FAILURE ARE NOT THE SAME THING.
> **THE CUSTOMER DOES ONE, AND YOU DO THE OTHER!**

The customer rejects you, and you choose to fail, or not to fail, by your reactions and subsequent actions.

Even the pain is different.

The pain of rejection is sharp, like a knife wound, and if it does not receive proper attention, it can become infected, and spread, and resentment can set in.

The pain of failure is a like a virus, which causes an aching sickness to move through your body affecting your ability to continue.

They have similar consequences; they both immobilize.

The salesperson who permits failure or rejection to play a dominant role in his life will feel restricted and tend to shrink from the market place to the protection of home or office environments.

9.9.2 The Trauma of Rejection

Did you ever eat a bad oyster?

If you ever did, you would know that it is literally a shocking experience, and what's more, your mind somehow compounds the situation, and subconsciously determines to dispense with that oyster immediately, whatever the cost, to protect you from ever being exposed to that experience again.

Rejection can have the same dramatic effect.

Both new and experienced sales people react to rejection, and subconsciously tend to maneuver themselves into a more comfortable environment. The easily discouraged simply stop going out, and experienced sales people, who handle isolated incidents with ease, may fall victim to a compounding reaction which eventually drives them to a lower risk area, and deprives them of success.

Rejection hurts, but many of the most inspiring human achievements were associated with the pain of rejection or failure, and invariably, if you run away from rejection, you escape to failure.

> A SALESPERSON CANNOT AVOID REJECTION,
> BUT HE CAN LESSEN THE LIKELIHOOD OF FAILURE.

The sales industry offers an unlimited growth environment, both for the development of human potential, and for professional and people skills. It also offers security to successful salespeople; they are among the highest paid in the community. The path over which you must make your way is full of potholes but it does not lead down a gully; it runs to the top of a mountain!

Kikuso Okokura, the Japanese artist, said,—
'The art of life lies in a constant readjustment to our surroundings.'

A salesperson must adjust, even on a daily basis, from rejection to acceptance, and from acceptance to rejection; and handle either imperturbably as it presents itself. He must have an attitude of expectation of rejection and failure, and a knowledge of combatant procedures. Literally thousands of failed salespeople can be found sheltering from rejection and apparent failure behind corporate desks in futureless jobs, as a result of a self-imposed lifetime sentence for the minor offence of ignorance!

> SELF-ANALYSIS SETS YOU FREE FROM THE TYRANNY OF FAILURE FEAR, AND REJECTIVE RESPONSE.
>
> KNOWLEDGE AND UNDERSTANDING BOTH LESSEN THEIR IMPACT AND HELP AVOID THEM.

9.9.3 **Your Reaction to Rejection is Your Choice**

What exactly is rejection?
The World Book dictionary defines it as:
To refuse to take, use, believe, consider or grant.

In the sales arena, any one of these choices of reactive behavior is instigated by the customer.

The salesperson has choices too. You can choose to respond to the customer's reaction to your approach or product in any way you please. You can choose to laugh; you can choose to shrug it off and forget it; you can choose to try another approach or technique, thereby learning from experience; or you can choose to allow the customer's attitude to immobilize your actions and even terminate your career!

THE DAY YOU REALIZE AND ACCEPT THE FACT THAT YOU HAVE A CHOICE OF REACTION TO A CUSTOMER, IS THE DAY YOU BECOME LESS VULNERABLE TO REJECTION.

Twelve ways you can beat rejection and failure

1. Summon up the strongest qualities of character within you, some of which may be lying dormant, or underdeveloped, because of lack of previous need for them. Courage, determination, self-control, pride of performance, resilience, humor, tenacity; how often have these qualities rescued people from failure?
2. Work hard: put in the hours success demands.
3. Break failure related habits.
4. Accumulate valuable experience. Work with successful people; result-related activity is a winner.
5. Seek out positive timely advice. A problem shared is a problem halved, and it is quicker, and less painful, to learn from the experience of others.
6. Develop the ability to recognize the approach of threatening failure, and learn to assess accurately the extent of its impending influence. Quick decisions are often necessary to prevent failure. Should you abandon the path you are traveling on, or read the signposts and take a new direction? Too many salespeople approach the signposts at the junction of failure and success, and pass through with closed eyes.
7. Consider prevailing alternatives honestly; rash judgement and unwise changes are prompted by reaction to rejection.
8. Expose yourself to learning, and analyze its influence. Read motivational books, memorize inspirational quotations; listen to tapes and stirring music. Music is motivational. (I knew a salesman who kept a cassette of 'Zorba the Greek' permanently in his car. He listened to it en route to every appointment, and declared

the music lifted him to the peak of performance!) Change your thinking. Mature in the marketplace of life.

9. Do not allow a disproportionate emotional response to control you. Say NO to yourself!
10. Commit yourself to a goal.
11. Believe. Get closer to your product through study and service. If it's a lovable product, love it and what it can do for your customers with all your heart! Expose yourself to customer satisfaction and appreciation; a customer's gratitude can provide powerful rejuvenation.
12. Pray. Seek God's strength and support, it is freely available at all times. The most positive definition of failure I have read is, 'Failure is God's way of preparing us, so He can enter in.'

9.9.4   The Importance of Self-Analysis

Of these twelve suggestions, self-analysis is the most difficult, but it offers permanent protection from the pain and immobilizing effect of rejection. Adopt the attitude of an interested bystander and observe yourself handling rejection and contemplating failure, and you open your mind to a wealth of exciting and valuable learning.

Self-analysis occurs when you deliberately reach deep within yourself without pride or prejudice.

The Scottish poet, Robert Burns, urged each of us to look closely within, with his words:

'O wad some power the giftie gi'e us, to see oursels, as ithers
see us!'

While you are still vulnerable (and experience will help you become less vulnerable), self-analysis and situation analysis will help you achieve a victory of your strengths over your weaknesses; you will become what you want to become! Think of each experience, however painful, as a learning experience, and you will never feel it to be final, but rather a step towards your goal's achievement.

Self analysis brings self understanding,
Self understanding brings inner strength;
Inner strength brings renewed conviction,
Renewed conviction brings control,
Control brings action,
Action brings results.

This kind of thinking is positive thinking. When you realize you are mentally running from the job in reaction to rejection or apparent failure, stop and think. Say to yourself: 'Let me understand what's happening here' . . . and you will realize you're not failing, only learning. You are reacting to a feeling of failure, not failure itself. Intelligent analysis will save you.

> THE WORLD HAS LOST MANY POTENTIALLY GREAT SALES-PEOPLE WHO DID NOT REALIZE, IN TIME, THAT HELP WAS AS CLOSE AS WITHIN THEMSELVES.

9.9.5   Customer Failure

It is important to diagnose rejection and failure correctly.

Sometimes a salesperson accepts failure personally, when in fact it is the customer who has failed.

Did you realize customers can fail?

When a prospect fails to become a customer, the responsibility for the failure does not necessarily lie on the shoulders of the salesperson.

Decide to suffer only when it's justified!

Prospects fail more than salespeople do.

They are often handicapped people. They can be slow to recognize value, blind to the benefits, deaf to reason, and dumb when you ask for the order! Now, if you find a prospect as handicapped as that, how can he ever graduate to becoming a customer?

You can't expect him to make a success even of being a prospect!

Humor turns situations right round, and acts like a bandaid on wounded aspirations.

9.9.6   Failure Attitudes

People who are unlikely to achieve, and people who haven't yet achieved are two groups of people who will help you fail. They heap their uninformed, inexperienced and fear-filled opinions in your lap, wrapped up in a package labeled 'indisputable fact'. Please untie the string, and you will find inside only gas and shadows.

Failures seldom say,

> 'I am a failure, I haven't got the ability to learn, or the courage to try.'

If they had the courage to express themselves in this way, they'd have the courage to do the job. Recognize them through statements such as,

'I'm too busy' or
'I'm not well actually' or
'This has happened to me . . .'
'I don't think I'm the salesman type . . .'
the inference usually being that the sales environment has failed. They don't arrive at an expected appointment, or phone to cancel it . . . they'd rather not explain, they just fade out.

Be aware they did not leave of their own volition.

Rejection and failure got 'em !

9.9.7   The Influence of a Spouse's Attitude on Failure

No research on the causes of failure in salespeople would be complete without mention of the deleterious affect of a negative spouse. An unsympathetic spouse is often the root cause of a failed sales career; other reasons may have been put forward at the time, but the real reason is a discontented spouse. Conversely, many a successful salesperson owes his success, in large measure, to his spouse's encouragement.

A husband whose self-esteem is dependent on his wife's constant and complimentary attention *will work to prevent any threat to this environment.*

A husband who disapproves of irregular hours *will work to control them.*

A husband whose character traits include resentment, even jealousy of the success and recognition his wife achieves, *will force her to decide between him and her sales career.*

A saleswoman needs a husband who is supportive and encouraging. Ultimately he will reap many benefits. I know well how much of my achievement in the sales arena should rightly be accredited to my husband, Michael.

A wife whose self-esteem is dependent on her perception of her husband's image, or on a salary or wage rather than commission, *will work to change his career if it is not filling her needs.*

A wife who is discontented with irregular hours *will work to regulate them.*

A wife whose character traits are destructive to her husband's success *will heap her insecurities on his head at every homecoming, and often send him scurrying into the apparent security of a futureless job.*

A salesman needs a wife who is supportive, understanding and encouraging. Ultimately she will reap many benefits.

Unquestionably, a spouse's attitude carries great influence, and rightly so.

The difference between success and failure is so very often dictated by a spouse.

Success is a very precious plant. It takes root and grows under certain conditions. John and Janis Smart of Brisbane are two people who created an environment where success could flourish. John achieved national sales records in Zondervan of Australasia, setting himself high goals which challenged all his components. John was the first to acknowledge the vital role Janis had played in his success by creating a home environment from which he could derive motivation, support and rejuvenation.

9.9.8 The Relationship Between Failure and Complacency

Complacency is often a reason for failure. This ubiquitous attitude permeates behavior so gradually that the victim is usually unaware of his affliction, and failure patterns creep in and control the activities upon which sales results depend.

Complacency hovers in the shadows of successful people, fed by disproportionate congratulation, erroneous assumptions, and self satisfaction.

Salespeople and sales managers who neglect to focus on the activities which made them successful suddenly can be flummoxed by a downturn in production.

The answer lies in *immediate realization and curative action*! Sift through old ideas and seek out new ones. Dig into old sales bulletins, files, books, records, newsletters, seminar brochures — the reasons for past success can be rediscovered and activated! Delve into the minds and hearts of motivated people, the answers often lie there. Spend a little time in thorough contemplation of the consequences of failure; tighten your belt! Excitement banishes complacency. Shake your potential awake, for it is when you think you are successful that you need to double your efforts and triple your care.

9.9.9 Rationalization

Rationalization is a major contributor to personal failure, and is a contributor to the failure of others. It is often highly visible in salespeople who seek to avoid the challenges of the sales arena, and indeed in people who have difficulty in facing the challenges of life.

The tendency to attribute one's actions to creditable motives is a defensive process aimed at cushioning the conscience, and rendering it more comfortable to reason. Rationalizers seek and find excuses, often unconsciously, to justify their actions, or refusal to act, their attitudes, opinions and behavior. This deprives the salesperson of valuable redirection which failure and mistakes very often suggest.

A rationalizer ignores the interests of others and puts his wants and hopes before even truth. Although he obtains a measure of gratification, it is achieved at the high price of reputation loss. The practice of rationalization puts restrictions on personal and professional growth which only the acknowledgement of truth can set free. Rationalization is fear-based and underlies eventual failure, which often approaches from an unexpected direction.

The first part of its cure is recognition, followed by a chunk of honesty and a decision to reject anything but the whole truth however unwelcome.

9.9.10 Attitudes Which Combat Rejection and Failure

Once you have made the decision that you will not allow a feeling of failure or rejection to deprive you of an opportunity, then you will graduate to welcoming failure. It is a stage of experience you reach, or sometimes pass unconsciously through. You will look back and may wonder how you survived or why you were so affected at the time. But pass through it you will.

You should welcome failure because you learn from it much more permanently and quickly than you do from success.

We would not expect to associate the early motion picture celebrity, Mary Pickford, with failure, yet she wrote:

> If you have made mistakes, even serious mistakes, there is always another chance for you. And supposing you have tried and failed, again and again, you may have a fresh start any time you choose, for this thing that we call failure, is not the falling down, but the staying down!

Sometimes we can only discover what will do, by finding out what will not do!

HE WHO NEVER MADE A MISTAKE, NEVER MADE A DISCOVERY

Imagine living without making a new discovery!

Dare to fail, and fail again and again and again. Work on the reasons for failure in each case, and know you are becoming more valuable in the marketplace.

9.9.11   Failure is a Teacher

The most rewarding teacher is the success which follows failure. That is the most satisfying success of all, but unachievable without failure.

My husband Michael and I are authorities, through experience rather than aptitude, on rearing boys, as we had three ourselves. Along with their friends, we noticed how success came readily to some and then later, the scene changed. Often the ones who had experienced immediate success without a great deal of effort and certainly little failure moved on into their work environment and perhaps marriage with the expectation that things would come just as easily.

The ones who hadn't run the fastest or jumped the highest, or been rewarded with academic recognition, the ones who battled to receive an improvement award, moved into their work place or marriage with the knowledge that they would be required to put forward their best effort to find a place in the sun. They learned some of life's most valuable lessons through apparent or temporary failure, while their contemporaries, anticipating accustomed acclaim, were ill-equipped and actually deprived of important lessons vital to their eventual success in the adult world.

It should be a matter of concern rather than satisfaction to see your son or daughter go through school, where attitudes are established, and if wrong, have to be unlearned, without experiencing a setback. Adversity arms you for life.

As long ago as the century before Christ was born, the Roman poet Horace wrote:

'Adversity has the effect of eliciting talents, which in
prosperous circumstances would have lain dormant.'

In the sales industry, failure gives us a yardstick by which success can be measured. Valuable experience results.

How many advertisements do we see from employers wanting experience? Employers often recognize that experience is more valuable than that piece of paper recording qualifications.

9.9.12   The Value of Example

Biographies and autobiographies of the lives of achievers provide us with multiple examples of the way to handle failure and rejection.

Let's look at the lives of two people.

First, the life of Jesus Christ. There can be no greater life from which a salesperson can draw inspiration. Jesus experienced rejection in so many areas.

1. Lazarus rejected Him as Savior; that must have disappointed Him.
2. Most Church leaders of His day rejected Him; that must have saddened Him.
3. The people rejected Him when they cried out for Barabas; that must have been hurtful.
4. Some of the disciples rejected Him; even Peter denied Him; that must have been a most painful rejection.
5. Last and perhaps the worst, right at the end, He must have felt rejection when He cried out from the cross:

'My God my God, why hast thou forsaken me?'

How pathetic the rejections we experience seem by comparison.

Abraham Lincoln's fight against failure and rejection is an inspirational one, from which every salesperson can draw fortitude!

1. 1831   He started in business, it failed and he went bankrupt.
2. 1832   He stood for legislature, and was defeated.
3. 1833   He started another business, and that failed too.
4. 1836   It was all too much, and he had a nervous breakdown.
5. 1838   He got back on his feet and was defeated again in parliament when he stood for Speaker.
6. 1840   He was defeated again.
7. 1848   He was defeated in Congress.
8. 1855   He was defeated for the Senate.
9. 1856   He was defeated for Vice President.
10. 1858   He was defeated again for the Senate.
11. 1860   He was elected President of the United States of America.

He must have been just plain stubborn!

But the world needs more leaders like Abraham Lincoln, people who totally and perpetually reject failure. Look what he did with the rest of his life.

A more recent example is the Prime Minister of England, Margaret Thatcher. This courageous leader was rejected by nine constituencies before being accepted by Finchley, and subsequently, she showed the world that she didn't believe in giving up!

9.9.13   **Work Spurns Rejection and Failure**

It was Lincoln who said:

> 'Things may come to those who wait, but only the things left by those who hustle.'

Most failure and rejection can be cured by work. If you stayed home because you had a day of rejection, it compounds in your mind. If you ventured out and found some work experience, very likely you would have gotten over it.

> IT IS NOT ENOUGH TO HAVE THE WILL TO WIN,
> YOU NEED TO HAVE THE WILL TO WORK TO WIN.

Many salespeople announce a will to win, but not so many actively demonstrate it!

9.9.14   **Turning a Negative Into a Positive**

If you feel yourself developing a negative attitude as a result of rejection or failure, take control, and turn it around. Count your blessings, focus on the job's advantages. This will sound easier to advise than to do, but a salesperson who can rely on a positive attitude soon bounces back. Never block out the memory of rejection, or forget your failures, just mark them up as learning experiences. Forget them, and it's likely you'll forget the lessons too!

Every salesperson has negative thoughts from time to time; you can't avoid them, and I believe you are not meant to avoid them! Your intellectual component is simply looking after your interests by saying:

> 'Check the status quo of your environment; is it as bright as you believe or as futureless as you fear?'

Varying moods of optimism and pessimism provide you with different 'views' of your life's situation, and this balance can help you decide on corrective action or redirection, or strengthen your appreciation of the life you have been given to lead! Recognize negative thoughts as contributors, but never allow them to take control; deliberately give positive thoughts air time too. Make your mistakes strengths, and your strengths, stronger.

Once, I took two managers to a sales seminar. They had done well and I wanted to reward them. I bought the tickets thinking,

> We'll have a day out.

The seminar was a disaster. The food was bad, the speakers were worse, the planning was non-existent. The hall was uncomfortable and cold; it surely was an unproductive day!

I apologized to my guests because I felt responsible for wasting their time.

The first said,

> 'Yes, it really is too bad that people have the temerity to hold such a poorly planned function. I can't help thinking of the many things I could have been doing.'

I agreed, and apologized again.

The other one said,

> 'Just a moment, . . . *not at all* . . . I have been to many seminars, and learned a great deal, but never before have I been to one that was a failure.'

He was just becoming a district manager, about to run his own seminars, and he said,

> 'I learned more today about running seminars than I ever did when I went to a successful one, because I didn't realize until now what made a seminar valuable. I have learned today what an organizer needs to provide.'

I suddenly realized I was listening to a winning attitude turning a negative into a positive. I wasn't surprised when this same manager, one year later, won an international award.

Failure teaches you what's unsuccessful, and assists you to assess more accurately what's likely to be successful. It gives your experience a broader base.

9.9.15 How Criticism Contributes to Failure

Another reason for failure is criticism. To combat it you need to have a knowledge of its cause and effects. Like fear, it can inhibit and even devastate achievement.

Think of a new sales agent as a little snail, slowly approaching his task, gathering confidence as he reaches out with trust to experience his environment. Then someone takes scissors and snips off one of his protruding feelers. The result is dramatic devastation of his whole career. This may be a cruel analogy, but criticism is cruel and the best shield against it is diagnosis.

Criticism is seldom recognized for what it is. It is seldom presented directly, and you need to decide, after sleeping on it, whether to ignore it or whether direct action is justified.

Criticism can be written or spoken, true or false, intentional or unintentional.

It usually becomes distorted as it travels, and therefore becomes more hurtful, as an untruth tends to hurt more than a truth, and your reaction is accompanied by a sense of injustice, and its companions, outrage and anger. Make no decision on a course of action until you are sure you have it in proper perspective.

The first cure is to look with understanding at the motives of your critic. Deliberately carry forgiveness in your heart if only because anger and resentment are more damaging to you than to anyone else. An intelligent assessment of your accuser's motives will lift you above your critic and the problem, and helps ensure that your judgement will not be simply emotional reaction.

Don't exaggerate the criticism in your heart.

> WORDS OF CRITICISM ARE LIKE PIECES OF AN INCOMPLETE JIGSAW; TOO OFTEN WE CUT THE MISSING PIECES FROM OUR IMAGINATION TO FORM THE PICTURE WE FEAR MOST!

Understand that half of our language is communicated by expression, emphasis, body movement, pauses and tones. In general, words are the only repeatable part, and often the emphasis is changed to suit the intentions of the repeater.

Take a single sentence:

'Betty's aunt took the green bowl.'

A simple statement of an event.

The emphasis placed on *Betty* changes the whole impression.

'*Betty*'s aunt took the green bowl.'

We are made to wonder if someone else's aunt was expected to remove the bowl.

'Betty's *aunt* took the green bowl.'

This could convey that, contrary to expectations, neither Betty's Uncle, nor anybody else, had a part in it.

If a strong emphasis is placed on the word *took*,

'Betty's Aunt *took* the green bowl.'

Betty's poor old aunt suddenly becomes a thief!

Emphasis on *the* . . .

'Betty's aunt took *the* green bowl,'

. . . implies that the bowl taken had some special significance.

Emphasis on *green*, might suggest that the other colored bowls weren't taken.

Emphasis on the word *bowl* might communicate to us that the bowl was taken, but other dishes were left behind.

Without changing the words, we have completely altered the sense.

And consider the manager who, describing a representative, stated, 'Susie *really* tries to make a contribution', and the secretary overheard the remark repeated — 'Susie *rarely* tries to make a contribution.'

A reputation belittled on a vowel sound!

Tone of voice conveys to the listener the speaker's feelings about the events — his irritation, approval, or whatever emotional reaction he has had to the news. Therefore repetition of comment or criticism must at least be unreliable. The original sense must alter when the emphasis is changed, and the criticism falls within the hearing of people who have their own reasons for changing its sense. By implication, or innuendo, or the repetition of only a portion of what was originally stated, meanings can be altered and intentions misinterpreted. Mischief can be caused between the critic and the criticized. Truth is dishonored.

Three centuries ago the English poet John Dryden, wrote:
'As long as words a different sense will bear,
And each may be his own interpreter,
Our airy faith will no fountain find,
The word's a weathercock for every wind.'

Criticism may be made to you and of you by a loved one. Assess his reasons and let your reaction to his criticism take into account his motives. In my experience, criticism presented as 'in the interest' of the person criticized usually has the interests of the critic at its source. Learn to understand human nature, and let a sense of humor direct your response. It is a great rebuilder.

I have found too much listening to critics stultifies achievement, and too many critics are non-achievers who cloak their failure in attack because their defences are built on insecure foundations.

Listen, and learn, and temper your judgement with kindness.

Every day is a new day — as the sun gets up to start afresh, so will you.

SUCCESSFUL PEOPLE MINIMIZE CRITICISM

Friendships have been initiated through criticism. Critics often have needs that are not being filled, and criticism is an attention grabber!

React always with a generous spirit. Give everyone the benefit of a doubt and, as you become successful, expect to be criticized.

Simply regard it as confirmation of your success.

The British Prime Minister Winston Churchill once said,
'If you don't want to be criticized,
do nothing, say nothing, and be nothing!'

IS CRITICISM EVER JUSTIFIABLE?

When, if ever, are you justified in criticizing?

At any time, if justice demands, and wrongs can be righted!

Most of us have the privilege of living in countries where freedom of speech and expression are upheld, but we must respect this privilege, and only launch criticism which is improvement oriented, and has a worthy cause.

9.9.16   Constructive and Destructive Criticism

Basically there are two kinds of criticism, destructive, and constructive.

Don't be in the business of destructive criticism, the kind of criticism that leaves the victim nowhere to go. The deadly criticism that puts a stop to his dreams, his growing confidence, and his developing skills. The criticism that takes away a reputation without justification, offers no second chance, and makes it hard to carry on.

Do be in the business of constructive criticism. This can be a form of sincere friendship, or can be motivated by a sincere desire to solve problems, and right wrongs! You have a right to your opinion, but take it where it will do most good, usually to the group, person, institution, family or company concerned.

IT SOMETIMES TAKES COURAGE, AND CAN BE A DUTY, TO STAND UP FOR WHAT YOU BELIEVE IN; AND SOMETIMES EVEN MORE COURAGE TO STAND AGAINST WHAT YOU DON'T BELIEVE IN. If you must criticize, couple it with kindness and ask yourself,
'Do I genuinely have the betterment of the company or person or institution or whatever at heart, or just a concealed self-interest that I have not even recognized myself?'

Be careful with humor; it is easily misinterpreted. I know I have been guilty of saying things in jest, which repeated seriously have a different meaning.

9.9.17   Direct Action, or No Action, Not Lateral Action

Too often we react with righteous anger when we are criticized. Form the habit of searching for lessons of value in any criticism made of you, without jumping too quickly into retaliation. This way you will be able to turn criticism into a benefit.

Unless you have an exceptional reason, translate criticism from someone whose opinion you respect into direct action. Give an honest and open explanation of what you heard, and how it affected you, not a sideways retaliation through a third or fourth person. Give the critic a chance to explain; this demonstrates openly the fact that you do not indulge in gossip. It pays him a compliment and shows courage, and you might get some good advice!

Statements such as,

'It is because I value your opinion that I was saddened to hear . . '
or
'I wanted to contact you directly to know how you really felt, and if it was true . . .'

. . . indicate a sincere desire to remedy the situation, which is usually transferred to the critic. Without realizing it, the critic may have anticipated no greater benefit from his criticism than at best, an improved situation, at worst, a sense of superiority! The chances are that by paying him the compliment of your time, and showing respect for his opinion, you will clarify a miscommunication and end by making a new friendship, or strengthening an established one. Respect will have replaced criticism, and courage will have converted a potentially harmful situation into a benefit.

If the criticism stems from someone whose opinion you do not respect, ignore the criticism. The chances are that others won't value his opinion either.

Write this jingle in your diary . . .

Ignore the guys
Who criticize
The other guys
Whose enterprise
Helps them rise
Above the guys
Who criticize
Their enterprise.

. . . Throw the memory of the criticism out the window, grab your sales kit, *and take yourself out the door!*

It has been my experience, working over many years with thousands of salespeople, prospects and customers, that people are basically good, and any detraction from goodness has a reason behind it.

A salesperson can often find himself in a position to help with that reason.

9.9.18   The Influence of Fear on Failure

The most common cause of failure, in my opinion, is fear. Because it is so often the root cause of failure, I want to encourage you to analyze the degree to which you are allowing fear to influence your destiny.

Fear is one of the most influential forces in the world; only love is stronger. For purposes of survival you are born with a seed of fear. It grows and gathers strength only if it can draw the nourishment it needs from the environment. It cripples like creeping paralysis, and inhibits and confines the quality of life. Think of it as you might a prescribed drug — a little taken at the right time is good, but too much is addictive and deadly.

The Bible directs us to fear God.

A schoolchild needs an attitude of respect to those in authority, and if it is laced with a little fear, it can be beneficial; but in general fear-motivation retards progress and meaningful learning.

As long as fear's influence is limited and acts only as an advisor in your life, and not the decision-maker, it is fulfilling a valuable role. But if its paralyzing hand takes the helm and steers the course of your life, you need to work to diminish its influence. You need to be aware of fear's affect on your achievement level. Fear can narrow your vision, immobilize your actions, shake your convictions, weaken your resolutions, and reduce your potential.

> FEAR IS AN INCUBATOR FOR ALL THE INGREDIENTS OF FAILURE, AMONG THEM — SELF-DOUBT, DISTRUST, GUILT, FALSEHOOD, AND STRESS.

It was the American President Franklin D. Roosevelt who said:
'The only thing we have to fear is fear itself.'

Fear is like fire — harnessed, fire serves man, and plays a valuable role in assuring survival and raising our living standards; but like fire, unleashed and undisciplined, fear will destroy.

The finger that presses the button that will turn the world into a nuclear holocaust will not be motivated by greed, but by fear.

There are two fire extinguishers for fear.

The first is understanding, the second is direct action.

WHEN YOU ACKNOWLEDGE THE FACT THAT IN THIS LIFE,
YOU ARE RESPONSIBLE FOR YOUR OWN MENTAL ATTITUDE,
THEN YOU HAVE ALREADY TAKEN A HUGE STEP TOWARDS
ACHIEVING A BALANCE BETWEEN FEAR AND FOOLHARDINESS!

The rejection of fear's influence puts you in a position to decide on the direction of your life. Make sure the direction is upward, and the goal is worthy of your life's dedication.

9.9.19   How to Overcome Fear

Let's look at how we can overcome fear.

It was Marie Curie, the Polish physicist, who said,
'Nothing in life is to be feared, it is only to be understood.'

Take a look at some of the things you fear. Fear taints so much of our thinking; from big fears such as possible job loss, exam failure, loss of a loved one, catching a disease, age, to little fears like getting fat, being late, or being left off an invitation list. If you nurture these fears they grow, but if you meet their cause with understanding, you can contain fear into its rightful place in your life.

FACE YOUR FEAR, AND TURN ITS SUBSTANCE INTO SHADOW.

Change your thinking, and fear abates. Understand the cause and effect of fear and worry, and it fades. Worry is only a form of fear. Draw from past fears and realize that you are no happier today because you worried yesterday, and will be no happier tomorrow because you worried today.

In this way you can find yourself doubting the value of worry, and overcome your fears.

Allow fear to change your course of action only if you have thought through the value of its influence.

Is it a wise warning, or an unworthy negative?

Knowledge of fear as it affects you brings understanding, and understanding acts as a shield against fear.

Direct action acts as a sword.

Fear is wretched enough on its own, but unfortunately, it usually comes with accomplices. It attracts cowardice, falsehood, cruelty, fatigue, and guilt. The easily fear-filled person has usually a shortfall of courage, and the fear he serves and constantly feels can drive him to uncharacteristic and irrational acts and words of cruelty and even crime. Guilt follows. Fatigue is a constant experience as the pressure of this imbalance of fear in his life demands a heavy emotional toll.

Understanding what is happening weakens the fear. When fear leaves the scene, cowardice goes with it. There is room now for courage to emerge. Courage and action move in partnership towards success.

Direct action puts a sword through fear.

I remember once a woman who feared not being invited to a party which her sister was giving for her daughter's birthday. The invitations went out and her fears were confirmed. The fear, like fire, got away and she launched into cruel and damaging gossip against her sister's daughter. Cowardice accompanied the fear, so she did not go to explain her feelings to her sister.

The day after the party an apologetic neighbor arrived with a bunch of unopened envelopes, which she found her three-year-old son had removed from the woman's letter box and hidden in his room. Among them was the invitation. Guilt, fear's accomplice, swamped her. Her neighbor listened to her story and urged her to visit her sister, but fear weighed too heavily on her heart and she could not bring herself to go. So her neighbor, feeling her son was to blame, offered to accompany her. Her sister, who had been hurt by her non-attendance, on hearing her story forgave her. Not only was fear restored to its proper place, but their friendship grew deeper and love was rekindled between them.

Courage was rewarded as it so often is.

If fear has forced you into a failure situation — squarely face what you fear and regain control of your life. Failure is the child of fear and, like parent and child, they have a very close relationship.

Life is full of adventure, *and how exciting it is!*

9.9.20   **Your First Birthday Gift Was Life**

The birthday gift of life, which you receive on the day you are born, is so seldom opened fully. You should regard the gift of your life with the responsible attitude with which you regard the gift of your children's lives, as something to nurture, discipline, expose to experiences, and develop to its fullest potential.

> THE TRAGIC WASTAGE OF LIFE LIES
> IN THE TIME WE HAVE NOT SHARED,
> THE MISTAKES WE NEVER MADE,
> THE LOVE WE HAVE NOT GIVEN,
> AND THE HAPPINESS WE NEVER FELT.

Never allow failure or rejection to sap your potential to enjoy life in all its abundance.

A salesperson who has properly assessed his product and his customer does not fail because it is hard to sell, as many salespeople will tell you.

A needed product seldom fails.

> A SALESPERSON ONLY FAILS WHEN HE ALLOWS HIMSELF TO BE INFLUENCED BY THE NEGATIVE PERSUASION OF OTHERS, AND WHEN HE IS UNABLE TO CONVINCE HIMSELF THAT HE CAN BE SUCCESSFUL.

Wouldn't it be wonderful if in our world, we could be free of the fear of failure? If we could all go out and welcome it as the blessing failure inevitably proves to be. If we could go out and face it, challenge it, turn it around through familiarity, through humor, through work, into success, again and again and again.

Winston Churchill exemplified this thinking. When invited as guest speaker to his old school, he stood before the boys at Harrow, and delivered five words only, and sat down. The words he chose were:

'NEVER, NEVER, NEVER GIVE UP!'

If you choose (and you always have a choice), if you choose to remember only one message from this chapter.

I would choose it to be this:

> SO MUCH OF FAILURE,
> THE REAL AND PERMANENT FAILURE OF OUR WORLD,
> CAN JUSTLY BE LAID AT THE FEET OF SINS OF ***OMISSION***,
> NOT ***COMMISSION***.
>
> APATHY ABOUNDS:
> THERE ARE SO MANY PEOPLE WHO SAY NOTHING,
> ***WHEN SO MUCH NEEDS TO BE SAID;***
> THERE ARE SO MANY PEOPLE WHO DO NOTHING,
> ***WHEN SO MUCH NEEDS TO BE DONE***.

That's the crux — people do nothing instead of going out and caring enough to be active.

We have a choice always whether to succeed or to accept the dominance of rejection and failure. The marvelous, stimulating, thrilling fact of life is that we have a choice every moment of the day; and it is on the result of this choice that our failure or success depends.

I would like to end this chapter with a poem which emphasizes the choices every salesperson has:

The salesperson's choice

You can walk in valleys, but I'm not coming too,
Cause I'll be climbing mountains, where I can see the view.

You can look through windows, and see the world from far,
But I'll be out there reaching to catch a rising star.

You can lie there watching the best of life go by,
But I'll be out there dancing, on the hill where the eagles fly.

You can sit in shadows, wishing you could see,
But I'll be out there selling, wherever I'm called to be!

And if you want the secret of how to win or lose,
Then listen and I'll tell you — *all you do is choose!*

9.10   TIME MANAGEMENT

9.10.1   Take Time to Evaluate Time!

Salespeople constantly talk about time, but seldom think about it.

'I haven't got time,' we wail.

'Next time, I'll . . .' we promise.

'Time flies, . . .' we complain.

'If only time permitted!' we lament.

Poor old time . . . it is always blamed!

The truth is, it moves at a constant measurable pace, and permits anything!

The objective of time planning is simply to fit effectively as much result-oriented activity as possible into the available time period. Time is the stuff of which life is made, and the dividend you receive from life can depend on the quality of your investment.

The start-button of successful time management is planning. Develop the capacity to interweave profitable activities, and you will maximize your time's potential.

9.10.2   Step By Step to Time Management

1. First, focus on a simple, easily grasped, and highly visible goal.
    It may be a set number of sales, demonstrations, or committed hours, or perhaps a promotion, or a dollar target. Carve this indelibly on your intellect, and summon all your other components to the support of its attainment. Demand a commitment from your mind, heart, body and soul. The forces within you, which make you what you are, must be in agreement from the beginning. They must be united in their commitment, and not fragmented along the way. Failure occurs when the heart would love to achieve the goal, but the mind commits its attention in another direction; or the body braces to exert the physical effort, but the soul is convinced that there is something unworthy about the goal.

    THE FIRST STEP TOWARDS SUCCESSFUL TIME MANAGEMENT IS TO SET A GOAL, **FOCUS ON IT**, AND DEMAND A COMMITMENT FROM **YOUR TOTAL SELF**.

2. Set annual, quarterly, weekly and daily goals, as steps to the achievement of your main goal. Keep your eyes fixed on the horizon of your main goal: never allow minor goals to take on disproportionate importance. Goals set in support of an overall objective should be flexible, and valued only in perspective to their contribution. Now, plan your time around the goals!

3. The single most important realization for a success-committed salesperson is this:

   YOU ARE NOT PAID UNTIL THE PEN IS IN THE CUSTOMER'S HAND, AND HE SIGNS THE ORDER!

   When a salesperson fully grasps the close relationship between this fact and success, he will act to bring the two together more often! His time, therefore, should be planned with this result-oriented activity maximized, and side issues minimized. Too many salespeople delude themselves that they are working effectively when they prepare the sales material, sort through prospect lists, plan, make charts, do bulletins, attend meetings, motivate their team, or drive around visiting team members. These activities are only valuable when they directly support the main goal, but too often they are allowed to become main goals in themselves.

   The truth is everything can be a waste of time, *unless you are sitting in front of a prospect*, or contributing towards increasing the likelihood of sitting in front of a prospect; or, if you are a manager, contributing towards the likelihood of a team member *sitting in front of a prospect!*

   A HIGH SALES GOAL CAN ONLY BE REALIZED WHEN THE SALESPERSON CIRCUMNAVIGATES THE PERIPHERALS, AND CONCENTRATES HIS TIME ON ACTIVITY WHICH DIRECTLY CONTRIBUTES TO BRINGING THE CUSTOMER'S PEN AND THE COMPANY ORDER FORM TOGETHER.

9.10.3   Think About Activating Time Planning

Tom Johnson had to drive thirty miles to an evening appointment. He turned on his car radio, drove to his destination, made a sale, and returned.

Bill Rosen had to drive thirty miles to an evening appointment. He planned to maximize his time en route. He left earlier, and took time to deliver a pamphlet on 'closing the sale' to a team member; he called, with flowers, on another team member who had been hospitalized; he listened to a sales tape on his car cassette as he drove. Next, he called on two unlikely sales leads, and succeeded in making an appointment with one for the following evening. He continued to his destination, made a sale, and on the way home, called to give a recruiting talk to a nominee.

Bill's evening represented time planning in action! It all started with thinking about time planning and an awareness of its relationship with success.

Which are you, a Tom or a Bill?

Possibly you stand somewhere between the two, and rationalize . . .

'If I have time I'll call and see . . .'

The successful salesperson doesn't acknowledge the possibility of 'ifs'. He plans his time, and effects his plan in the time.

9.10.4   Twelve Time Saving Suggestions

1. The sales demonstration itself can consume time needlessly. To gain maximum results from your selling time you need to achieve a qualified, cogent sales presentation. This will secure more orders, and increase productivity. You're less likely to waste time with non-prospects, if you learn to qualify.

2. Don't procrastinate: to comply with a task takes the same time now as later. Approach it at the beginning, not at the end of the time available. Form the habit of asking yourself,

    'Is there anything I can do without disadvantaging today, that will make tomorrow's goals more attainable?'

    Never put off till tomorrow what you can do today.

3. Fill in a daily report form which has been designed to reveal the productivity of time invested activity. Analyze the association recorded between results and activity. Draw conclusions. If the daily, weekly, or quarterly goals *are not proving supportive to the main goal*, change them. Allow time to teach you. A salesperson who declares reports are time wasters is either not taking corrective redirection from their analysis, or filling in an unhelpful report form. Unless he has nothing to learn, which is unlikely, eventually his results will reflect decreasing productivity.

4. Keep competitive. If you feel your commitment to even your main goal is weakening, enlist personal pride of performance and loyalty to strengthen it. Give listening 'air time' to worthy priorities, rather than to justifications. They'll jostle for position!

5. Discipline yourself, become a watch watcher. Discipline is a tough environment, . . . but failure is tougher! Failure can be a relentless taskmaster, extracting devastating dues. Learn to distinguish between the things you want to do and the things you need to do. Discipline is the price you pay for success; it is always regretted at the time, but seldom in retrospect!

6. Delegate everything that *profitably* and *fairly* can be delegated. Often, efficient people are convinced that because of speed and accuracy, time is saved if they do everything themselves. This can be justified for the short-term, but in the long-term ensures time loss.

7. Modernize. Become familiar with equipment, gadgetry, and office and field systems which technology has made available to lighten the load and conserve a salesperson's time. Videos, computers, dictaphones, tape recorders, time saving domestic devices, sales oriented diaries and planners can all contribute to time conservation. Be open to change, and rethink basic assumptions in relationship to change. Nothing is as constant as change and yet we allow it to constantly surprise us! Adopt an attitude of:
    'If there's a better way of doing it, I want to know about it!'

8. Learn to make quick, accurate, on-the-spot decisions; indecision is a notorious time waster. The skill, of course, comes in recognizing the right decision, because wrong decisions are time wasters too. Experience helps, so practise making immediate decisions, unless procrastination offers advantages. Too often, people who delay decisions only regurgitate the same facts and considerations, in the same environment, but at a later date. The result — slow progress, and wasted time!

9. Prospect efficiently. Of all a salesperson's activities, the work of prospecting is most prone to time wastage. Time filters away through unnecessary phone conversation, house calls, lunch and tea breaks. Abruptness, of course, can be interpreted as discourtesy, so the skill comes in matching brevity with courtesy. Sorting, searching and unearthing leads *should be done in hours when demonstrations cannot be made.* Implementing an efficient prospecting record system is closely associated with time saving.

10. Become a paper work shrinker, not a magnifier; a simplifier, not a complicator. The less paper work you, your office staff, your customers and team members generate, the fewer obstacles stand between you and result laden activity. Follow through right away when the envelope is opened. Resist the temptation to become immersed in paper work and then abandon it without good reason; you will have to repeat the process with no gain at a later time.

11. Realize that the work expectancy of achievers invariably extends beyond the work expectancy of non-achievers. Each day has twenty-four hours; allocate six for sleep, two for eating, and eight for normal work time, nine to five. This still leaves eight floating hours. *Therein lies the secret of success.* The difference between achievers and non-achievers is spelled out in the application of those precious extra eight hours!

12. Use the phone instead of the mail, it's more personal, more motivational, and quicker. When you need to impart information uniformly, book multiple number hook ups instead of individual calls.

9.10.5 Time is Money

Most salespeople don't have to invest money in an office or equipment to get started, but the one capital asset he does have to invest is time. A salesperson should think of his time as his money! The more money you invest in a business the greater is your expected return. So it is with time. The more time you invest, the higher return you can legitimately expect.

Every salesperson should calculate his worth per demonstration. For example, in a fifty week year:

Earnings per year	Demos. per week	Earnings per demos.
$80,000	24	$64
$60,000	24	$48
$40,000	24	$33
$20,000	10	$40
$15,000	5	$60
$15,000	10	$30
$10,000	5	$40
$10,000	10	$20
$ 3,000	3	$20

By spreading your earnings across your demonstrations, you learn, your actual worth per hour in the market place. Calculations based on sales give you an incomplete picture. Five factors will cause variations in worth per hour, but one of the challenges of salesmanship is to strive to increase your personal earning capacity, within the time you allocate for selling.

These five major factors are:
1. Talent — *Are you extending your potential?*
2. Knowledge — *Are you reading, listening, learning?*
3. Technique — *Are you experimenting constructively?*
4. Attitude — *Are you thinking positively?*
5. Experience — *Are you practising regularly?*

Careful record keeping also enables you to calculate your worth per call, per approach, or per close. It makes you aware of the high price you pay for a casual cup of coffee, and rewards you with the reassurance that all result-associated action is earning time, even if it would appear that only sales are income producing.

Time is the father of equality: each of us receives the gift of the same amount per day.

Winners put it to effective use, *losers don't know where they put it!*

9.11 GOALS

9.11.1 A Person Without a Goal is Going Nowhere

Imagine for a moment that you were given a brochure of a luxurious holiday resort, and although you desired to be in such a beautiful place, you made no plans to be there. Imagine, further, that you did not know where it was, or how you would get there, or whether it had a vacancy, or what the cost might be! If you just kept hoping to be there, without finding the answers to these questions, do you think you would ever find yourself at that holiday resort?

When a salesperson approaches the sales environment without goals, mediocre success is the best he can hope for. An achiever recognizes that goals are crucial, and that a salesperson without goals waits for things to happen, but a salesperson with a goal can't wait, he has to make things happen! You will never know the thrill of arriving if you never aim to go anywhere.

9.11.2 Goal Priorities

Both your personal goals and your business goals, whatever they may be, should be interwoven with a commitment to be a credit to everything to which you owe allegiance.

Personal goals can be defined or immeasurable, private or publicised, and can include family goals which focus on a particular member or the whole family team. Business goals should be attainable, challenging, measurable and motivational.

It is important to identify and strike the rightful balance to ensure the stability and happiness of life, and then to give those goals top priority in your life's thrust.

9.11.3 Samples of Balanced Goals

For example, this might be typical of a **part time** homemaker's goals:

I will get out of bed at 7 am every day.

I will spend half an hour every day reading sales books, or listening to motivational tapes.

Part of my earnings will be put towards a holiday for my husband and myself.

Your *family goals* can include your contribution, or be specifically individual. For example, written in your diary:

I will take Betty swimming twice weekly to enable her to achieve her swimming badge this summer.

I will take Harry to the library once weekly.

I will make a list of the household chores to ensure that all family members share the responsibility equally, and will inspect what I expect!

We will volunteer as a family to contribute three hours a week to a local charity. (Seek family confirmation before writing family goals down!)

Part time business goals can include personal team, or company goals. For example:

I will be top district in my division in the first quarter.

I will spend more time developing John Brown and Sally Meakins.

I will achieve my quota of the company's annual goal.

I will earn $15,000 minimum.

The goals of a **full time** career salesperson might read as follows:

Personal goals:

I will reduce my golf handicap.

I will introduce time management into both my business and private life this year.

I will build a new barbecue this spring.

Family goals:

I will spend more time with the family.

(Specific goals with named family members are more compelling.)

Full time business goals:

I will qualify for promotion.

I will recruit forty new representatives.

I will make three sales a week before attending to team development.

I will have a 15 percent increase in business.

Be careful not to set too many goals, or your perception of them can become blurred, and they nullify each other. Set just a few clearly defined goals and let nothing deter you from their realization.

9.11.4   Effective Goal Setting

When contemplating goal setting, consideration should be given to the character and life's circumstances of the person for whom the goal is set.

CODE LETTERS

REPRESENTING THE FINAL
OBJECTION RECEIVED

CA   Can't afford
TE   Too expensive
CO   Consult other opinion
NI   Not interested
AS   Already satisfied
WU   Won't use
PF   Product failed to meet needs
BL   Buy later
O   Other

Appropriate letters to be inserted
in 4th box from left

Evaluation and Recapitulation

For the period of . . . .

The object of this analysis is to accurately
assess your effectiveness.

Total hours worked . . . .

Number of demonstrations . . . .

Total sales . . . .

Total commissions on sales . . . .

Earnings per hour . . . .

Earnings per demonstration . . . .

Was goal achieved   Yes ☐   No ☐

DAILY PROGRESS RECORD

Date	No. of demon- strations	No. of hours worked	Most frequent objection	No. of closes	No. of sales	Amount earned

Goals should motivate, but they can demotivate. They should challenge but be attainable; they should stretch and strain but never crack a salesperson's potential. When it is set too high a goal breaks a salesperson's mainline thrust, which will splinter and fragment in an urgent search for a happier environment. Both the goal and the salesperson can be lost. A salesperson and his goal are in partnership. *When they achieve their objective, the salesperson has made the goal a success, and the goal has made the salesperson a success.*

Just as a tailor's experience and his customer's preference are taken into consideration before the cloth is cut, so must the the company's experience and the salesperson's preference be co-ordinated before the goal is set. Ideally a manager should sit and co-author, motivational and realistic goals with the salesperson, sharing his hopes, building his aspirations. People are more committed to decisions they contributed to, rather than to decisions made by others for them. When they have no blame escape valve, they tend to stay on track!

9.11.5 Setting the Right Goal

The planners of both individual and collective goals should be mindful of the fact that for maximum motivation, company goals need to contribute to the salesperson's success, and not purely manipulate him to contribute to the company's success. Likewise, every salesperson's business goal should contribute to his company's success, and not be achieved to the detriment of the company. Conflicting interests are damaging to both.

Goals can be contentious issues when a salesperson takes them as seriously as he should and perceives them as inequitable. He must feel his goal has been 'cut to fit with caring hands.'

Temporary, even spectacular success, can be achieved in the sales arena without goals, but continuous success and a sales career cannot. Whether a salesperson is setting a personal goal, or a salesmanager is planning a team goal, his long term success depends on finding the right goal to maximise the opportunity's potential. The most satisfying goal *is the progressive realization of a challenging objective.*

If in doubt set two goals, a 'must get,' and a 'hope to get.' In this way the goal is perceived as helping to make the salesperson a success, and not threatening him with failure even before he has started.

COMMITTED DEMONSTRATION GOAL

I . . . . of . . . . Tel. No. . . . .

commit myself to the achievement of ☐   demonstrations over ☐ weeks

Signature . . . .

CODE LETTERS

REPRESENTING THE FINAL OBJECTION RECEIVED

CA	Can't afford
TE	Too expensive
CO	Consult other opinion
NI	Not interested
AS	Already satisfied
WU	Won't use
PF	Product failed to meet needs
BL	Buy later
O	Other

Each box represents one complete demonstration. Each square within the box enables you to record the result of the demonstration.

1. First Square; insert a circle when a sale is achieved or a cross when no sale is achieved.

2. Second Square; insert the dollar value of the sale or the letters representing the final objection given.

3. Third Square; insert the number of closes you used during the demonstration.

4. Fourth Square; insert the number of excuses/objections you received.

5. Fifth Square; insert the date of the demonstration

PROGRESS RECORD CHART

EXAMPLE

Demo result	Dollars or objection
Nos. of closes	Nos. of excuses
Date	

SALE

0	$512
3	4
4 August	

NO SALE

X	B.L.
5	5
5 August	

Relate to them in this manner:

1. First level — Survival Goals
2. Second level — Growth Goals

These challenge in steps; the survival goal eliminates the demotivational effect which can accompany a failed goal, and the growth goal avoids the danger of an undeserved sense of achievement!

GOAL STEPS TO ACHIEVEMENT LEVELS REASSURE THE TREPID, AND CHALLENGE THE INTREPID!

9.11.6   Commitment to Goals

It is important to realize the difference between having a goal and being committed to a goal. Some salespeople have written down their goal at their meeting, but have lost it. Others know their goal but are not propelled to action by it. Successful salespeople are committed to the achievement of their goals. A goal can run parallel with a salesperson's thinking, or be dangled out in front like the donkey's carrot, *but a winner's goal is part of him!* It runs like blood through his veins, affecting every move he makes.

Commitment to a goal depends on:

1. Attainability —
2. Desirability —
3. Immediacy —
4. Co-authored setting —
5. Established loyalties to beneficiaries.

9.11.7   Percentages and Averages

Goal setters should be aware of Lakein's 80/20 rule.

This brings into focus the fact that . . .

'80 percent of value comes from 20 percent of the items.'

In other words, 80 percent of your time, brings in only 20 percent of your results, and conversely, 20 percent of your time brings in 80 percent of your results. The validity of this observation of 'the average,' against which the superiority or inferiority of anything can be measured, will make the highest goal attainable, as you concentrate more attention on the 20 percent of activity which brings in 80 percent of your results.

9.11.8   The 'Musts' For Goal Conscious Salespeople

1. Decide to be a goal directed salesperson.
2. Set and accept a limited number of challenging goals.
3. Write them down, under Personal, Family, and Business headings.
4. Make a sincere commitment to their achievement.
5. Focus on **deadlines**.
6. Break them into manageable packages of place, calendar time, and specific action.
7. Think **countdown**.
8. Chase them with dedication, and with your complete self — *your total being.*

> SUCCESS IS DIRECTLY RELATED TO GOALS, AND THE GOAL SETTER SOMETIMES IS SURPRISED TO FIND THAT THE WORLD WILL STEP ASIDE FOR ANY PERSON WHO KNOWS WHERE HE IS GOING!

9.12   HANDLING GRIEVANCES AND CONTROVERSY

9.12.1   The Destructiveness of a Neglected Grievance

As surely as the sun rises, a salesperson will one day feel aggrieved about something! It's a part of life, and everything that happens in life is accelerated in the sales arena.

Salespeople are emotional people, and they feel things more deeply than unemotional people. This statement seems to hold no surprises, but what is not commonly realized is the devastating impact of a deep grievance on a salesperson's performance. An aggrieved feeling can be likened to a snowball allowed to run down hill. It grows, and becomes more damaging as it gathers momentum. What started as a comparatively minor irritation can lie at the base of disillusionment, distrust and terminated careers.

> A SALESPERSON HAS EMOTIONAL, INTELLECTUAL, PHYSICAL, SPIRITUAL, AND FINANCIAL NEEDS. UNLESS HIS ENVIRONMENT MEETS HIS NEEDS, HE WILL CHALLENGE, AND PROBABLY CHANGE HIS ENVIRONMENT.

Hope will prompt him to make moves which sometimes offer little guarantee of improvement. Sales managers should be conscious at all times of their people's needs, and seek to create an environment which fills those needs. A sales manager who neglects the grievance of a valued salesperson risks losing him, but the salesperson acting to extract retribution for a grievance puts his job at risk, and may find he is not as valued as he supposed!

When a sales manager becomes aware that a salesperson feels aggrieved immediate contact should be made, preferably in the form of a personal visit. A phone call or a letter is never more than second best. Messages to return calls or conversations with a spouse are inadequate, and usually fuel the flames!

A wise salesmanager gets into his car and drives or flies to the problem of a valued salesperson; an unwise salesmanager leaves half a message with a spouse, and pops the other half under the proverbial carpet, and deludes himself he has coped!

PAY PAIN THE COMPLIMENT OF TIME AND ATTENTION, AND IN-VARIABLY YOU WILL SOLVE THE PROBLEM, AND GAIN RESPECT.

ANGER NEARLY ALWAYS HAS PAIN AT ITS BASE.

Care and concern, both for the aggrieved and the importance of the problem, need to be clearly demonstrated, an explanation and remedy supplied and justice administered.

9.12.2 How to Handle Personal Grievance

When you feel aggrieved, translate it into intelligent action!

Mentally step out of your shoes, and look at yourself objectively. Imagine placing time and distance between the problem and yourself, and visualize it as someone else's situation. Don't wallow in a grievance. It has been my observation that grievances accumulate in direct proportion to the time available for their contemplation. Some salespeople take a pair of bellows to grievances and exert enormous energy blowing them out of all proportion: others put them through a shrink process so they can no longer see or feel them. The tendency to rationalize is usually irresistible, but consciously examine your grievance from every possible point of view, deliberately extracting emotional reaction. Apply humor to every grievance; there was never a load that wasn't at least lightened by a sense of humor.

There is a wealth of profound wisdom in these words from Ella Wheeler Wilcox:

> Laugh, and the world laughs with you,
> Weep, and you weep alone,
> For the sad old earth
> Has to borrow its mirth,
> It has troubles enough of its own!

ALWAYS SLEEP ON A GRIEVANCE AFTER YOU REACT, ***AND BEFORE YOU ACT!***

Then take action, and action is usually the right course.

Consciously and deliberately put courtesy and understanding like a cloak over your hurt, and go with a desire to solve the problem to the source of your hurt, or to the person in a position to alleviate it.

There is a wealth of wisdom in the words:

COMPLAIN UP, NOT DOWN THE MANAGERIAL LADDER, AND NEVER SIDEWAYS!

In other words, minimize a grievance by confining it to the problem solver. Give an open and honest explanation of the facts and your feelings, and ask to understand the reasons for the hurtful decision, action, or comment. If it was your manager to whom you have taken the grievance, consider his position unselfishly, but point out the effect of your feelings on your performance. Create a problem solving atmosphere and ask for help in finding a satisfactory solution.

We do not live in a just world. Would so many of the world's people live without hope even for adequate food if we did? Justice, if not always expected, should be sought and honored; but it has been my constant observation of life that time administers justice, where people and circumstances fail. Frequently advantages emerge from new situations which were not anticipated at first. Courage is more reliably rewarded than indignation, so bring courage to the judgement table, but make sure you do not simply bring it to the defence of pride, jealousy, envy, self-interest or greed. Seeds of all these qualities lie within each of us.

9.12.3   The Sandwich Method of Handling Grievances

John Lembo's suggestions for handling grievances have long been my favorites. Many managers instinctively employ his recommendations, but John Lembo analyzed them. His 'sandwich' method handles people with sensitivity. This method simply recommends the insertion of two honest compliments on either side of the complaint. This provides refuge for the accused and gives him opportunity to present his case without the handicap of condemnation. It stands in marked contrast to the 'jam him in the corner, and face him with the facts' attitude. The first lesson for a salesperson when handling a grievance is to make allowance and build latitude for human dignity.

9.12.4   Unsolvable Grievances

If facing a grievance factually, and attempting to solve it face to face does not eliminate, or lessen the problem, you must decide whether to tolerate, or terminate!

Some of history's greatest achievements sprang from an intolerable grievance which turned the achiever down a new path.

Remember that . . .

THE MIGHTY OAK ONCE WAS BUT A LITTLE NUT THAT HELD ITS GROUND!

There are times in life when we are called on to make irreversible decisions. If possible, give your decision time; ask advice only from people of judicious judgement, not necessarily from those who would be expected to support you. If you become convinced that the position is intolerable, and you can justify a change, and have faith in your ability to make a success of a new environment, don't compromise your happiness. Pick up your dreams, take them with you, remember only the good things, and don't look back.

9.12.5 Old Fashioned Good Manners Can Avoid Grievances

The sales industry is a people industry. Often grievances are avoided in the first place when good manners between office staff and the salespeople, the salespeople and their clients and colleagues, are anticipated and received!

What are good manners? How can they help a salesperson?

In her book, *Australian Guide to Etiquette*, Barbara Murray-Smith defines 'a lady,' as,

> 'A woman who remains poised, calm and collected, in even the most difficult situation, and who is kind and sensitive to the feelings of others.'

She defines 'a gentleman,' as,

> 'A man who is courteous, kind and considerate to all with whom he comes in contact, whether they be his subordinates, his contemporaries, or the Lord High Executioner!'

THESE DEFINITIONS ARE EQUALLY APT, APPLIED TO SUCCESSFUL SALESPEOPLE.

My favourite definition of 'a lady' is a woman to whom a man feels obliged to react as a gentleman. To be able to bring out the best in others is a huge asset for a salesperson.

Basically, manners are concerned with the physical, mental, and emotional comfort of others. You open a door or pull out a chair prompted by concern for the comfort of another; you write a note of thanks, or pass a kind comment to give gladness to someone else. You stand when someone enters to acknowledge respect. You carry thought for the situation of others into the simplest of functions, and in so doing communicate quality of character, and care for your fellow man.

Salespeople who make a habit of good manners lay successful foundations. When your full concentration is on the presentation, or on handling an objection, inbuilt and natural good manners infiltrate your performance. Unnatural, contrived manners vanish under pressure. Truth exposes insincerity whenever it can.

9.12.6 Controversy

Controversy involves at least two people; a grievance is usually felt by one! Handle controversy with the same attitude as you would handle a grievance, only spread it wider.

Controversy should be perceived as productive, as it brings much of worth to a sales environment.

1.   It promotes enquiry.
2.   It sharpens analysis.
3.   It encourages objectivity.
4.   It fosters opinion.
5.   It attracts involvement.
6.   It generates solutions.
7.   It banishes complacency.
8.   It challenges potential.

When a salesperson perceives controversy positively he is unlikely to ignore, suppress, or withdraw from it. This places him in a position to benefit from it. So often short-term evasion of controversy spells long-term calamity.

You may have heard . . .
'Necessity is the mother of invention.'

Controversy provides necessity: necessity invents the solutions.

Salespeople and salesmanagers learn, and ultimately benefit from the experience of contributing to problem solving. Unexpected and helpful alternatives are unearthed, creative solutions formulated, relationships deepened, and mistakes anticipated. Controversy judiciously handled can result in synergy, through team interaction.

9.12.7 It's Attitude to Controversy Which Determines its Value

It all comes back to attitude. Perceive controversy as constructive and invariably something valuable will be wrought from it. 'I win you win' solutions can replace the 'I win you lose' imbalance so often found at the root cause of controversy and grievance.

Insurmountable controversy seldom occurs when sensitive and unselfish principles are adhered to; but when all else fails, the literal interpretation of prevailing rules, and the company's long term interests should be the overriding consideration.

All salespeople, indeed all human beings, should remember that the problems of tomorrow have their origins in today.

9.13   DECISIONS

9.13.1   The Decision Maker

Salespeople and sales managers need to be decision makers. They need to be able to make quick, timely, result-oriented decisions, then activate the circumstances which will prove them right! New salespeople may find it helpful to think of the journey to success as a road through a strange city. A decision as to which direction to take needs to be made at each street corner, and sometimes you must turn and retrace your steps.

Harry Newton, Australian entrepreneur domiciled in New York, alerts us to the close association with success of constant decision-making. He said:

> 'Gambling is going to Las Vegas. Business is not a gamble. All you're trying to do is figure out the number of ways a venture can go wrong and anticipate them. If too many things go wrong, kill the plan.'

I once had the valuable experience of attending one of Gerry Harlos's sales seminars. Among the subjects discussed were the three major approaches to decision making, and Gerry's analysis redirected our thinking.

9.13.2   Authoritarian Decisions

Usually these are made by a designated leader. This is the quickest method of decision making, and many successful organizations, churches, groups, and families are run this way. However it weakens commitment, and can leave festering emotions and issues which would be better aired and shared.

Authoritarian decisions encourage participants, through necessity, to suppress 'concealed agendas' and to lobby politically. The ambitious maneuver to manipulate the decision maker. Resentments are 'locked in', with no outlet, and in an atmosphere of mounting emotional pressure, the logical voice of wisdom can be suppressed.

9.13.3   Majority Decisions

These usually alienate a valuable minority. Your problem solving entrepreneur is often in the minority group. Those who passively follow the leader can swell a majority decision on a personal basis, thus rendering ineffective a knowledgeable and more qualified opinion. If all things were equal this would be a recommended method of decision making, but as everyone knows, all things are never equal!

9.13.4   Consensus

This method results in high quality decisions. It provides the environment where creativity and innovation can find expression. It enables each participant to contribute, and every opinion to be valued. Consensus ensures a commitment to decisions made and goals established from each contributor.

Consensus does require advanced levels of people skills, especially at large meetings, as the feelings, convictions, and ideas of each member, on every issue, can reveal the unexpected! The aim of consensus is 100 percent agreement. Time pressure must be minimal, or it inevitably lapses into majority decision, which, requiring only 51 percent agreement, can be finalized more quickly.

At high sales management levels, no other decision making method should be contemplated, as it ensures the group's resources are fully tapped. This method builds esteem and optimism, elicits commitment and loyalty, and fosters a developmental environment.

In the beginning the leader needs to explain that the objectives of consensus are not unlike those of a jury, and that it is the group's duty to strive together for a rightful decision. He should discourage dominance from one, or reticence from another, and give consideration to all ideas and opinions.

9.13.5   Factors Which Influence Decisions

1. The perceived importance of the decision and its consequences.
2. Ignorance, in one, or even all involved areas.
3. Fear, of the responsibility, and of the possibility of influencing a later regretted decision, or of critical reaction to an idea or opinion.
4. Conflict of interests — Participants who harbor conflicts of interest have differing perceptions of the considerations, and opposing desires for the decision's outcome.
5. Misunderstanding or mystifications.

6.　Existing structured methods of decision making which have resulted in entrenched habits of behavior not conducive to effective decision making.
7.　Insufficient time allocation.
8.　Characteristics such as jealousy, resentment, or ambition, which result in prejudiced contribution, and endanger rightful decision making.
9.　Low self-esteem deprives the decision making group of valuable input.
10.　Prevailing distractions.

The leader needs to decide which, if any, of these ten factors are in the process of influencing the team's ability to make effective decisions, and where necessary, counter-balance their influence with facts, figures, and an unbiased opinion which is perceivably sincere, confidence-building, and motivational.

9.14 DIFFERENCES IN SEX CAN INFLUENCE SALES RESULTS

9.14.1 Sex Plays a Part

Salespeople are sometimes surprised to learn that sex differences can influence the outcome of a sales demonstration, but they can contribute to or detract from the likelihood of a sale.

In our office a higher percentage of sales cancellations are received from demonstrations where a saleswoman has sold a husband on his own (his wife initiates the cancellation), or a salesman has sold a wife on her own, (her husband initiates the cancellation), than from demonstrations made to prospects of the same sex as the salesperson. It is valuable, therefore, for salespeople to have a knowledge and understanding of the causes, in order to minimize the possibility of cancellations.

Selling is closely associated with feelings, and the feelings of both the salesperson and the customer can be deeply involved during a sales demonstration. Successful salesmanship is based on consideration for the prospect's feelings, and an understanding of how feelings are affected.

A prospect responds with varying degrees of feeling to,
1. What you say.
2. How you say it.
3. What you do.
4. How you do it.
5. What you show.
6. How you show it.

If the first impression a *salesperson* makes on his *customer* is a pleasing one, he is likely to be more receptive to the salesperson's message.

If the first impression the *customer* makes on the *salesperson* is a pleasing one, he is likely to give a higher quality demonstration. So start by making yourself as personable as possible, in a professional sense.

9.14.2 Dos And Don'ts for Each Sex

1. Dress neatly, and wear freshly laundered clothes, which in themselves will not attract the prospect's attention. Low cut, tight, or

inadequate clothing can provoke a reaction from a member of the opposite sex, which is much more likely to be unfavorable than favorable, and distract from your product or its message.

2. A saleswoman demonstrating to a man on his own should sit at least three feet away from him. Men feel threatened and vaguely resentful if women invade what they feel is their territory! Quite contrary to what might be supposed, men do not like women to come close, they prefer to assess them at a respectful distance. Usually a man likes to dictate the terms of the sales demonstration — its length, its tone, and its depth of involvement. Any perceivable attempt by a saleswoman to take charge, or to neglect to invite and appreciate his opinion, however contrary, is inadvisable. During a sales demonstration the average man likes to feel challenged, and is irritated by ignorance and nervousness. He likes to be impressed professionally, and rewards genuine endeavor with warmth and encouragement. He likes facts and figures. A man sometimes likes to put either a salesman or a saleswoman 'through the hoop'! You should not be intimidated if you meet such a prospect; it is as much a compliment as a discourtesy. My advice is simply go through the hoop willingly and professionally. Smile cheerfully, answer good humoredly, and stay on track.

A man likes to feel he has *bought from*, and not been *sold by* a saleswoman.

A MAN BUYS AN OBJECT, A WOMAN BUYS WHAT AN OBJECT WILL DO.

Visit a department store or a car lot and watch couples making buying decisions. Invariably it is the man who touches, handles and feels the object; whereas the woman listens, looks, and has a need to be convinced that it will do the job required. The differences are pronounced and fascinating, and a salesperson can learn a great deal from observing people under the pressure of buying decisions.

A salesman demonstrating to a woman should sit a considerable distance from her, but only until trust has been established. It then becomes appropriate and usually advisable to move nearer.

MOST WOMEN HAVE A NEED FOR APPROVAL;
MOST MEN HAVE A NEED TO APPROVE.

A woman has a stronger need to feel personal approval, even from a salesperson, and she will interpret a move closer to her as a sign of friendship, as long as the move coincides with the onset of trust and doesn't precede it! He needs to allow sufficient time for care to be communicated, and credibility to grow. Insincerity, if sensed by a woman prospect, will immediately put an end to the possibility of a sale; to her it is a betrayal of trust. A man is more tolerant on the whole and will give the salesperson a second chance.

There is no third chance to establish trust and no sale will result without it.

A saleswoman, demonstrating to a woman, may ignore 'respectful distance' rules, and sit next to her prospect in offered friendship, sharing ideas and information from the start. She still needs to establish trust, and can achieve this by communicating genuine care and interest in the prospect and her life's situation.

Demonstrations made to a husband and wife together have danger zones for both saleswomen and salesmen. Position yourself in front of them, enabling both to view your sales material with equal ease. If a salesman concentrates on the wife, even if it is a domestic product, and she is the likely decision maker, he still enters a high risk area. If a saleswoman concentrates on the husband, and can be perceived to value his reactions and opinion more highly that those of his wife's, then she can wave her sale goodbye! Never enter into an argument between them, except to a make a conciliatory comment. When a wife overrules her husband's opinion usually you may assume she is the decision maker, but when a husband abruptly overrules his wife, he's not necessarily the decision maker, he may have a self-esteem problem. I have found a man will make an emotional snap decision faster than a woman. If the product represents a benefit he personally has not the time or expertise to bestow, he tends to buy the solution. A woman on the other hand will ponder the pros and cons more logically. A man approaching a positive decision to buy often tosses it to his wife, as if to say,

'I'm about to buy, rescue me if you want!'

She will toss it back to him in a tone which he can readily interpret as approval . . .

'It's up to you dear, you must share this decision.'

She knows that if it ever becomes a regretted purchase, he won't be able to blame her!

Communication between a husband and wife is a most interesting challenge for the salesperson; understanding each other so well, their surface movements are minimal and often highly individualistic.

SELLING IS SO MUCH FUN,
AND AS THE FRENCH SAY, **'VIVA LA DIFFERENCE!'**

An understanding of psychology helps both saleswomen and salesmen at all times!

Any kind of flirtatious overture made by the prospect to the salesperson during a demonstration should be shrugged off as a friendly compliment.

Any kind of flirtation instigated by the salesperson of either sex to the prospect, or customer, is a denigration of your company's reputation and to the profession of salesmanship.

9.15   BODY LANGUAGE

9.15.1   How an Understanding of Movement Can Help

Body language is a method of interpreting the movements and stances of a prospect in order to have a better understanding of his thinking. An understanding of his thinking enables the salesperson to present the product, service, idea or cause in the manner most likely to influence a positive buying decision. Some salespeople have found a knowledge of body movement to be a great encouragement to them, particularly after a close, and salespeople who wish to delve deeper into this area of communication should purchase two excellent Australian books, one by Joe Braysich, and the other by Allan Pease on the subject of body language. In the beginning, however, new salespeople are best advised to concentrate on the quality of their demonstration, and to allow their instincts to evaluate the customer's thinking while actively listening and reacting to what the customer is saying, rather than becoming distracted in an effort to interpret body language.

Generally, the body language of a man is more easily interpreted than the body language of a woman. His feelings usually are the more readily discernible of the two sexes. A woman is more complex and critical. She tends to make quicker decisions, but she is less likely to project her thoughts or reactions to sales material. She listens more and moves less.

A successful salesperson aims at total awareness in all aspects of the business.

9.16   PRESSURE SELLING

9.16.1   What, When — and Who Judges Pressure Selling?

Have you ever heard it said,

'A salesman called to see us and pressured us into buying.'

This occurs when a salesperson ardently pursues a sale without regard for the prospect's feelings or interests. It has been my experience that customers exaggerate and even invent the pressure they have experienced from a salesperson, either to justify their decision not to buy, or to defend their decision to buy a later regretted purchase.

Every salesperson needs to have a knowledge of situations in which he conceivably might find himself in order to maintain his reputation above reproach.

In the sales arena, however, the sole measuring stick of pressured selling must be the customer, as the attitude of every salesperson should be that the customer is always right! If the prospect sees, hears, or feels pressure, then it is pressure, even if the salesperson is guilty of nothing more than misassessing the prospect's reaction.

A critical and reluctant prospect can interpret a professional approach, a suspected spiel, a discernible technique, or even enthusiasm as pressure, and the result is immediate credibility loss.

9.16.2   How to Avoid the Accusation of 'Pressure Salesperson'

1. Do your homework! Learn and practise your presentation until it becomes a natural extension of your personality.
2. Make it a principle never to be inaccurate, or to enthuse without sincerity.
3. Be aware of the value of giving the customer adequate time to make a buying decision; don't bulldoze!
4. Show respect for his opinion and convictions, even if contrary to yours.
5. Never show irritation or impatience.
6. Make your closes tasteful and timely, and handle objections with tact.
7. Listen attentively when the customer speaks.

8. Follow through and do the things you have promised to do.
9. Send a thank you note, whether or not your demonstration was successful.
10. Express happily your willingness to return at a later date if the customer insists on a delayed decision. .Conceal your disappointment; it can spark a feeling of guilt or discomfort in the prospect, who will counteract by rationalizing at the expense of your reputation!

The salesperson who maintains an attitude of service, and nurtures a genuine concern for his customer's best interests, is seldom described as a pressure salesperson, or thought of in this way in retrospect.

9.17   EQUILIBRIUM IN WINNING AND LOSING

9.17.1   The Value of Winning

Winning is too often presented as coming first.

Recently it saddened me to read a sales magazine exhorting its readers to, *'Win, Win, Win, — there is no try!'* This attitude reminded me of the newly successful man who grows ashamed of his origins, and does not want to acknowledge his parents, *for winning is the child of trying.*

The winning every salesperson must pursue should be conditional on the continuance of the things which constitute your success and total well-being. At the level of achievement of your choice you must *stay competitive*, and challenge both your own potential and that of your colleagues.

Have you ever noticed how often a *new* salesperson becomes the company's contest winner, and then next year he has left?

What happened?

Winning can be a misguiding business! Often, he finds himself in a congratulatory environment which convinces him *he is a winner*, then when for some unfathomable reason his winning performance does not repeat itself, suddenly *he is a loser*. This misconception of winning is responsible for the loss of many salespeople of potential. What happens to the new salesperson who perceived himself as a natural winner when the acclamations fade? The approval environment has focused on someone else. Puzzled, he flounders, and if he has been led to believe that 'only coming first' matters, he can be lost to the company and even the sales industry. The fact is no one is a born winner or loser; he simply performs functions which ensure winning or losing results. Logically therefore, as circumstances vary, a salesperson is likely to qualify for either title from time to time! A first-time winner quite often has not identified which of the functions he performed were the ones which brought about his success, and inadvertently he does not repeat them!

> THERE IS NO SUCH THING AS A NATURAL WINNER OR A BORN LOSER, THERE IS ONLY WINNING ACTION, LOSING ACTION, OR LACK OF ACTION.

Winning is something you do, not something you are!

A winner performs winning work, but if you:

1.   Forget what it was you were doing when you were the winner, and stop doing the things that once made you successful, or
2.   Fail to identify correctly what areas of work ensure results, or
3.   Engage in unproductive or insufficient activity . . .

you are unlikely to achieve winning results.

Constant endeavor, with preparation, planning and long term goals, keeps producing perpetual winners.

If only one salesperson can win, does the race make losers of the rest?

Decidedly not. I have always believed that everyone who tries is a winner in some way. Being involved and trying invariably produces surprising benefits. A trier may not take home the trophy, but he receives lateral benefits of many kinds.

IT'S NOT FAILURE, BUT LOW AIM THAT'S A CRIME!

One summer holiday, as a schoolgirl, I learned the value of endeavor. Being competitive, I wanted to win the tennis tournament, but looking at the list of entries, I noticed several players whose age and standard of performance was higher than mine.

Turning to the coach I said:

'I don't think I'll enter, I'll never win.'

Her reply has remained with me all my life,

'Possibly not, but by entering you may give someone else the experience and pleasure of being a winner!'

Wow! I certainly hadn't considered that angle. I entered, I played several enjoyable matches, I lost — but the stranger who beat me became a lifetime friend.

What a win I had!

I remembered my coach's words, twenty years later, when my son was the favorite for the school 1,500 meters. He had trained hard and had a successful record. The day came and I went to watch the race, but it never took place. He was declared the winner by default, as there were no other entries.

'Why didn't you enter?' I asked a group of his friends.

'It's no good running against Moore,' one replied, 'he always wins.'

There will never be winners of worth, without triers!

Life doesn't give you a 'no show' card. You compete from dawn to dusk, starting the day with your conscience when you don't want to get out of bed. Your first victory may be 'mind over mattress!'

Winners find the winning things in every situation, but only after every effort has been made to cross the line first.

> AN ATTITUDE OF SEEKING THE BENEFITS IN EVERY SITUATION, EVEN UNAVOIDABLE FAILURE, IS NOT A LICENSE TO LOWER YOUR ACHIEVEMENT LEVEL, BUT AN ENCOURAGEMENT TO CONTINUE.

There are winning aspects in coming second if you search to find them. You will have learned and gained experience, and you will have contributed to your team or company's success.

> REAL WINNING OF WORTH IS NOT SPASMODIC,
> IT IS A CONSTANT COMMITMENT TO WINNING ACTIVITY.

The world loves a winner; and I believe we all carry the responsibility of trying and trying to become one, or be guilty of neglecting our potential.

And then when *you* succeed in becoming a winner, remember to thank the triers, because without them, there would have been no race for you to win.

9.17.2   The Value Of Losing

Take pride in doing everything well.

'Anything worth doing is worth doing well.'

This includes losing. Losing is part of life's experience: those who claim they have never lost are either fanciful or specialists!

> DO EVERYTHING HUMANLY POSSIBLE NOT TO LOSE,
> BUT WHEN IT IS INEVITABLE, DO IT WELL, AND FIND THE BENEFITS.

They include:

1. Lessons of value. Learn from losing, realign your direction and dedication. You have an opportunity to correct losing causes.
2. Appreciation. Losing can result in greater appreciation and less taking for granted of people, possessions and the environment which contribute to your happiness.
3. Wisdom. You're likely to be wiser next time.
4. You will have earned more money by trying hard and coming second or third, than by not trying and coming twenty-second or twenty-third!
5. Your team will have benefited, even if your contribution was small. Rejoice in knowing you helped.

Finally, you still have an active and challenging job to do — *lose well!* Be a 'winning loser', not a 'losing loser'!

Forget yourself, this moment of victory belongs to the winner. Honor him! Add to the quality of the occasion by giving a winning performance of 'how to lose'. Take immediate steps to congratulate the winner. This is hardest if you expected to win, and you really cared.

Realize you have been given a friend-making opportunity; demonstrate a character of worth.

Look the winner in the eye! Shake his hand. Say something kind, encouraging and sincere, even if your heart is broken. If they are far away, send a card, make a phone call, send a gift.

I remember once, as a new representative, beating a much respected champion in a sales contest. Indulging in a little self-satisfaction, I was spending a day at home catching up after the contest.

What did she do?

A special courier arrived with a bunch of violets, and a copy of Ziglar's book, *See You At the Top*. Inside was written,

'You'll always be a winner, but this book might help you know why!'

In one small act, she showed me the hallmark of a winner of worth, and my new-found superiority vanished in a rush of humility and gratitude.

A WINNER FINDS A WINNING OPPORTUNITY EVEN IN LOSING!

9.17.3   Winners versus Losers

A little book, *Winners and Losers* by Sydney J. Harris, cleverly differentiates between winning and losing attitudes.

A few of these, and others, are repeated here:

A WINNER paces himself;
A LOSER has only two speeds, hysterical and lethargic.

A WINNER learns from his mistakes;
A LOSER learns not to make mistakes by not trying anything different.

A WINNER leans on himself, and does not feel imposed upon when he is leaned on.
A LOSER leans on those stronger than himself, and takes out his frustrations on those weaker than himself;

A WINNER is not afraid to contradict himself when faced with a contradictory situation;
A LOSER is more concerned with being consistent than with being right.

A WINNER rebukes and forgives;
A LOSER is too timid to rebuke and too petty to forgive.

A WINNER acts the same toward those who can be helpful, and those who can be of no help;
A LOSER fawns on the powerful and snubs the weak.

A WINNER wants the respect of others, but does nothing with that end in mind;
A LOSER does everything with that end in mind, and therefore defeats his purpose.

A WINNER knows how much he still has to learn, even when he is considered an expert by others;
A LOSER wants to be considered an expert by others before he has even learned enough to know how little he knows.

A WINNER isn't afraid to leave the road when he doesn't agree with the direction it's taking;
A LOSER follows the 'middle of the road' no matter where the road is going.

A WINNER makes commitments;
A LOSER makes promises.

A WINNER focuses;
A LOSER sprays.

A WINNER looks first to blame himself;
A LOSER looks first and fastest to blame others.

A WINNER seeks for the goodness in a bad man;
A LOSER seeks for the badness in a good man.

A WINNER tries to judge his own acts by their consequences, and other people's acts by their intentions;
A LOSER gives himself all the best of it by judging his own acts by his intentions, and the acts of others by their consequences.

A WINNER faces the truth;
A LOSER rationalizes.

A LOSER keeps his eyes on the pavement to pick up dropped coins.
A WINNER never sees the dropped coins because his eyes are on the stars.

Chapter Ten

MANAGERIALLY

10.1 Why a salesperson should become a manager

Every successful salesperson should consider the benefits of sales management. It offers challenge, and brings privilege and responsibility — the privilege of money and prestige, the responsibility for people, and for company goals.

> THE SALES MANAGER WHO IS COMMITTED TO HIGH GOALS AND STRIVES FOR THEIR ATTAINMENT, INSPIRES OTHERS TO FOLLOW HIS LEAD.

> *This is the epitome of successful sales management.*

> THE CHIEF PREOCCUPATION OF A SALES MANAGER SHOULD BE TO CREATE AN ENVIRONMENT WHERE HIS PEOPLE CAN BE SUCCESSFUL.

> *His own success will follow.*

> THE CHIEF NEED OF EVERY SALES AGENT IS TO HAVE A SALES-MANAGER WHO WILL MOTIVATE HIM TO DO THE BEST HE CAN, AND YOU MUST WANT TO BE THAT MANAGER.

> THE SECRET IS TO TREAT PEOPLE AS IF THEY WERE ALREADY WHAT THEY OUGHT TO BE, AND YOU WILL HELP THEM BECOME WHAT THEY ARE CAPABLE OF BEING.

In the beginning . . .

When you first contemplate taking a step in management you may wonder if the commitment is what you want, or if you have, or can develop the necessary skills. My advice is always accept a new challenge. If your company has faith in you, have faith in yourself!

The first step is to ask to have the privileges and responsibilities given to you in writing. Look closely at the company's goals, and the expectation it will have of your contribution, then estimate how you can plan time around your inflexible commitments to help achieve those goals. In other words, before accepting the position have a clear understanding of what the promotion will do for you, and ask of you.

Some companies don't ask sales managers to concern themselves with company profitability. They expect you to promote sales and let accountants worry about the figures. But I have always believed that a sales manager who has a knowledge of the relationship between sales and profitability is of greater value to his company. An increase of sales regardless of cost can result in a decrease in profitability, and an understanding of the factors that influence profit margins and cash flows helps the sales manager to put his thrust in areas where sales and profits go hand in hand. Every company must eventually make a profit or it won't be there in the morning!

Start with the attitude of wanting to learn, and wanting to teach, and let this attitude direct your action. The greatest sin against your team members is to be a poor performer.

As an old Chinese quotation says:
'Man, in order to succeed, must first help others.'

How can you do this? What does sales management involve?
Someone once answered in this way . . .
A laborer uses his hands.
A craftsman uses his hands and brains.
An artist uses his hands, brains and heart.
A salesperson uses his hands, brains, heart and feet.
A salesmanager uses them all at the same time!

10.2   The four major differences

Where do the functions of a successful sales manager differ from those of a salesperson?
Firstly, a sales manager:
1. Needs to maintain the level of sales expected of his position, without detriment to his managerial responsibilities.

2. Needs to communicate the skills of salesmanship to his people, and to share a responsibility for their success.
3. Needs to be able to attract and train recruits to his team.
4. Needs to communicate the skills of recruiting to his people and share a responsibility for their success.

These are the four major important areas of difference.

10.3   What does sales management involve?

It involves developing an ability and willingness to perform the following:

Hire/Recruit
Set Goals
Class Training
Field Training
Make Decisions
Handle Grievances and Controversy
Care
Manage Time
Run Meetings
Motivate
Develop Managers

In all management, time management takes central place, whether it is managing self or organizing to help your team members manage themselves.

10.4   How to recruit successfully

The opportunity and responsibility of inviting others to join the company, and of benefiting from the results, are available in most sales companies. Success in hiring/recruiting is important to sales managers, and the communications skills required are similar to those of selling. Recruiting is a sales job, so approach a prospective recruit as you would a prospect. You have something important to offer, and you need to communicate the features and benefits of the job, close the sale and handle the objections.

Parallels in selling and hiring

Selling	Hiring
1. Discuss the 'need' for the product.	1. Discuss the 'need' for the job.
2. Explain the features of the product.	2. Explain the features of the job.
3. Communicate the benefits of the product.	3. Communicate the benefits of the job.
4. Close the sale. Example: (a) Would you like to include the optional extras, or do you feel the basic product covers your needs at this time? (b) Would you prefer to pay by check, or would one of our easy budget plans suit you better at this time?	4. Close the sale. Example: (a) Would you prefer a weekend training class, or would a weekday suit you better at this time? (b) Would you prefer to come to our head office for training, or would a local class be more convenient?
5. Handle the excuse. (a) Can't afford. (b) Buy later.	5. Handle the excuse. (a) I'm too busy. (b) I'm really not a salesperson.

Selling and hiring activity involve a similar process and persuasive skills.

Successful recruitment is dependent upon seven major factors:

1. Your attitude should be one of enthusiastic conviction of the benefits for the prospective recruit.

2. Your approach should be sincere, informative and exciting.

3. Your qualifying should be minimal; on the whole, direct selling companies offer opportunity to most people. If in doubt, ask yourself,

   'Do I feel I can trust him? Would I be happy to invite him to my home?' If so, he qualifies.

   Nevertheless, seek out people who need to work and who are adaptable, resourceful, honest, and sincere. Look for people who have a habit and expectancy of success; experience is valuable, *but not if it is only of prolonged failure and mediocrity of performance!*

4. Your ability to communicate the need for the job to be done — the satisfaction of the mission.

5. Your ability to 'sell' the product's value in the market place.

6. Your application of choice-offering closes such as:

   'Would a Saturday class be convenient, or would Monday evening of next week suit you better?' or

   'Would you care to be picked up, or would you prefer to come on your own?' or

'Would you care to bring a friend, or just come along yourself?'
There are dozens of closes — the customer either chooses one of
the alternatives or he makes an excuse!

7. Influential handling of objections. Anticipate a response of:
    'I'm not the salesman type,' or,
    'I'm so busy,' or,
    'My husband/wife wouldn't approve,' . . . or some such.
    You need to overcome the excuse, or lose the sale. Sounds familiar
    to selling? That's because you are selling!
    'Sell' the benefits of the job, add more value, and close again.

10.5   Hiring or recruitment sources

There are eight main sources of new recruits.

1. Walk-in, write-in, or phone-in advertisements in newspapers and
    magazines provide reliable results.
2. At the close of a sales demonstration a job opportunity can be
    offered.
3. Products or services which involve service call back-up offer
    recruitment opportunities.
4. Friends and acquaintances may welcome a new opportunity.
5. Cold calling can bring surprising results.
6. Product radiation opportunities. Most products expose you to
    specific recruitment opportunities related to the product's
    characteristics.
7. Radio or television advertisements can be used to interest new
    people.
8. Government employment agencies provide a 'quantity' of appli-
    cants, but usually the 'quality' you require is already employed —
    but there are exceptions and a sales manager of worth aims al-
    ways to help others develop skills and gain confidence.

10.6   Advertisements

The wording of an advertisement is important.

The advertisement is *selling* for you. The *'sale of the moment'* is the selection and presentation of words attractive to promising applicants. The
next step — the interview or training class is in itself a mini 'product of
the moment'. Word your advertisement to stimulate response from the

type of person you want to attract, not purely to inform. Too many words, too few words, words which invite wrong judgements, can discourage enquiry. On the whole only the ambitious and qualified answer large display advertisements. Housewives and young people tend to identify more comfortably with small advertisements, as their perceptions of their qualifications are often small. Natural sales talent often lies dormant in people who do not realize their potential. It has been proven that the skills of coordination of family activities, leadership, arbitration, and decision-making are equivalent to those required by many executive positions.

You may be instrumental in introducing an environment where these skills can find recognition and fulfilment.

Experiment with different advertisements and record the cost versus response in a book kept for the purpose. *Never lose it!*

10.7 Group recruitment

A hiring talk is a sales talk, only the product has changed — you are now selling the opportunity. First, select a venue which builds company confidence, arrive early and prepare the room, the facilities, and set up the materials. Have job application forms which absorb the interest of the applicants while they wait for you to start, to avoid starting and stopping as new people arrive. Answer all job-related questions with an assurance that all aspects of the opportunity will be covered fully during the session, or individually afterwards.

Serve, or have your assistant serve, each waiting applicant with coffee and refreshments. It relaxes the applicant, and demonstrates thought for his comfort.

A group or walk-in
These embrace five consecutive subjects, and each one needs to be treated as 'the product of the moment,' — *a sale in itself!*

1. **Yourself** — Introduce yourself with a short autobiography; tell the group your story and how you came to join the company, and the benefits you and your family have received as a result. Keep it short. Request questions be kept until after you have finished.

2. **The Product** — Excitedly but briefly 'sell' the benefits of ownership, explaining that details will be described at a later session.

3. **The Opportunity of the Job** — Describe the benefits of the work environment, the company ethics. Mention the remuneration positively, and explain that details will be given in writing at the training class.

4. **The Training Class** — Explain its impact, value and necessity.

5. **The Class Trainer** — Enhance the character and life's experience of the trainer, to stimulate a desire to meet him.

10.8   How to encourage your team to recruit

1. Take team members field training to watch you give hiring talks and interviews. Implement a *do as I do*, rather than a *do as I say*, style of management.
2. Plan incentives, and reward results. Give visible support, through contact, enthusiasm and back-up.
3. Take pride and invest time in keeping your team fully informed of facts, advantages, and opportunities related to recruitment from which a team member may stand to benefit.
4. Emphasize the mission, or community service aspects of the work. People like to feel good about what they do!

10.9   Class training

Basically the class trainer's job is to instil in the new sales agent a knowledge and enthusiasm for the products he will represent. He should communicate an understanding of the company and its ethics. The training program should also include a thorough grounding in the use of the sales material, the basic skills of salesmanship, and a knowledge of the sales and recruiting opportunities.

Take pride in providing first-class training: any compromise is paid for later. Build getting-started incentives into the class, and ensure the trainee leaves with a respect for your expertise and integrity, and the confidence and desire to go out and make immediate sales.

I had the privilege of being trained by Margaret Christensen, who became the National Director of Sales for World Book in Australasia. She always made the members of her class feel we were about to launch on a great and adventurous voyage of discovery, which indeed we were. Excitement gathered momentum as the class came to a close and we felt ready to burst out the door and find our first prospect! Much of the success I was eventually able to achieve I owe to the foundation and continuous training I received from this great sales manager.

10.10   Field training

This shared activity time is where skills are nurtured, knowledge imparted, and loyalties built.

THE BASIC OBJECTIVE OF FIELD TRAINING IS TO INCREASE THE TRAINEE'S SUCCESS POTENTIAL. PROFESSIONALLY, *THAT IS THE ONLY CRITERION UPON WHICH THE DAY'S SUCCESS SHOULD BE MEASURED.*

The trainee must be left at the day's end with faith in the job opportunity, and belief in his ability to achieve his goals.

He should be taught that each call represents four opportunities.

1. A possible sale.
2. A possible lead to a sale.
3. A possible recruit.
4. A possible lead to a recruit.

1. Can we sell?
2. Can they suggest a potential prospect?
   A friend? An acquaintance?
   A business associate?
   or . . .
   Someone in a position to recommend a potential customer?

3. Can we hire
3. Can they suggest a prospective hiree?
   A community worker?
   A friendly personality?
   Someone unemployed?
   Someone dissatisfied with their present job?

Someone in need of a new challenge
Someone who would welcome extra income?
or . . .
Someone who could recommend a possible recruit?

He needs to be taught which sales tool to synchronize with each of the four opportunities. Communication skills depend so often on a knowledge of what brochures, pamphlets, sales and recruiting material to show in conjunction with the explanation. He should be shown how both the eyes and ears of the customer can be brought to the support of the cause! In this way he learns that every call can be made a winning post.

If possible set up a field training day in class, but anytime can be beneficial — *or even a life-saver!*

Time is the highest compliment and the most precious gift a manager can give his people; possibly because often it is the hardest thing to give. But it is not only a gift; it is an investment. The greatest resource of any nation is its people, and if you invest time in helping your people, you build shared success on secure foundations, and the most lasting dividend you receive is loyalty.

If you plan to work with a full-timer, or potential full-timer, share a full eight hours. Maximize available time during the lunch break by including a positive analysis of the morning's experience, and if advantageous, plan redirection. Also simply take time to reach out in friendship. You may enrich his life by a word or by an example you set.

A normal day should include all the ingredients of the job in the market place — some successful and some unsuccessful results, some favorable and some unfavorable circumstances, some exciting experiences and some dull stretches.

If you agree to only half a day's training you risk exposing the trainee to an imbalance of experiences, which may have a deleterious effect on his attitude to the job. If he witnesses only success, and then goes out alone and experiences only discouragement, he may conclude he isn't suited to the job. If he witnesses only failure, he may decide that the job has no future!

Ideally a day's field training should be comprehensive of the average experience, but this never can be guaranteed. Some days success seems to compound; explain that this is exceptional! Some days everything seems to be in conspiracy against success.

What, then, of value can the trainee take away?

What will he remember?

If you can not even show the trainee a demonstration of the product, at least give him a demonstration of courage in the face of difficulty, persistence in the face of discouragement, stamina in the face of fatigue, all

FIELD TRAINING ANALYSIS

Training Manager __________ Trainee __________ Date __________

Manager's Travelling time	Trainee's Travelling time	Lunch/ Shopping break	Field Training time	Total Hours	Manager's Signature	Trainee's Signature

Demonstrations	Demonstrator	Demo. time	Venue	Product sold	Reason for not buying	Hiring talk result	Call back date
NAME							
ADDRESS							
N.							
A.							
N.							
A.							
N.							
A.							
N.							
A.							
N.							
A.							
N.							
A.							
N.							
A.							

Service or hiring calls	Done by	Venue	Product added	No. of leads obtained	Hiring talk result	Class

Guidelines by trainer

Signature

Observations by Trainee

Signature

blanketed with constant cheerfulness! These lessons he will never forget, and they become his self-expectancy.

Ground rules should be clarified at the beginning of the day, so the circumstances under which the trainee is entitled to claim sales and thus receive the commission, cannot be misunderstood. If a sale is achieved by a trainee, it is clearly his sale; but if a sale results from a demonstration to which both have contributed, or for which the manager has been entirely responsible, the manager is faced with choices:

1.   He must assess whether it would be of greatest lasting benefit to the trainee to be given it in kindness. Loyalty can result from unexpected kindness.

2.   He must consider the value of a lesson learned. Sales 'given in kindness' can convey the wrong impression; namely, that it's a manager's job to find sales for agents. Might he not derive greater long-term benefit from learning from the beginning that sales have to be earned?

3.   He must evaluate the solution of offering the sale as an incentive for a future number of sales, or committed demonstration activity achieved within a specified time period.

Each is right in certain circumstances. The decision is the manager's, and his success can be measured by the results his decisions generate!

Remember:
'Catch a man a fish, and you feed him for a day,
Teach a man to fish and you feed him for life!'

Successful managers demonstrate leadership

Another of the manager's decisions is to assess whether there is greater benefit for the trainee by his performing every approach and demonstration, or whether they should be alternated.

Sometimes, trainees prefer to learn by observing.

They say . . . 'I want to watch everything you do all day!'
and others who realize that best-remembered lessons include involvement. They suggest . . .

'Let's take turns, I want to watch you and to have you evaluate my demonstration and approach.'
The answer is,
'I'd appreciate your evaluation of my demonstration, too.'

This gives the trainee a listening goal. — Care for the trainee — assess what's best for him.

Practical field training for new sales managers
1. Check your kit the night before, and try to include a new brochure, clipping, magazine — something to communicate a new sales technique, idea or product information.
2. Be punctual: punctuality compliments both the trainee and the occasion.
3. Check the trainee's sales material; refuse to work with shabby material. Carry a file of replacement material in your car.
4. Ask for a guarantee, both at the time of planning the day, and before you start, that your trainee will follow up leads and implement suggested activity. *Plan to teach, not entertain!*
5. Co-author the field training report after discussion of the lessons of the day. Give it the importance it deserves — that's a God-given day of your life — plan to maximize its potential!
6. Follow through in a few days to check if the leads proved successful or how the new techniques worked out. Write a little note of appreciation and encouragement, asking to be informed of the follow up results.
7. Sincerely praise accomplishment, and approach weakness constructively. Catherine the Great, of Russia, wisely commented:
    'I blame softly, I praise loudly.'
    This protects self-esteem, and builds the confidence on which success can grow.

INSPECT WHAT YOU EXPECT!

If no follow-up has taken place when you phone a few days later, you are justified in expressing disappointment. Set another call-back time and ask yourself, 'Was he teachable?'
Did the day increase his success potential?
Was there anything you could have done, or said, to have improved it? You will find that he won't be the only one learning!
Every sales manager should memorize these words:

YOU CAN NOT TEACH WHAT YOU DO NOT KNOW,
AND YOU CAN NOT LEAD, WHERE YOU WILL NOT GO!

8. If it is applicable, before the day's end, remind the trainee of the current contests, and show him how to maximize his chance of being a winner. *Give him wings!*

9. Remind him of the next meeting, and unless it's inappropriate, suggest he aim to bring an order from the follow-ups of the day's work.

10. Thank him for his time, and if it can be sincere, tell him something you personally derived of value from sharing time with him. I always found this easy because I learned something new every day in field training, and people are precious!

10.11   Meetings

Successful sales managers soon learn the value of meetings.

The basic aims of sales meetings are to:
1. Motivate.
2. Develop skills.
3. Recognize achievement.
4. Teach and inform.
5. Provide fun and fellowship.

People will want to come back if these objectives are achieved!

AN UNSUCCESSFUL MEETING CAN DO MORE HARM THAN GOOD, SO A SALES MANAGER MUST PLAN TO MAKE IT A SUCCESS.

A good meeting is highly motivational: a poor meeting is worse than no meeting at all!

Here are some points to consider. Each one may not apply to every meeting, but ask yourself if it could be modified for the meeting you plan.

The twenty-two points for successful meetings
1. Select an accessible venue, with a friendly atmosphere and ample parking, and a date and time convenient for the majority.

2. Create an imaginative and comprehensive invitation bulletin. Make sure it *sells* the benefits and features of the meeting, and excites a desire to attend. Nearer the time, follow up with an encouraging phone call.

3. Plan an agenda; prepare a copy for attendees.

MEETING HANDOUT QUESTIONNAIRE   (Make up questions helpful in your situation)

What in your opinion were the major strengths and weaknesses of your experience with our company during the last 12 months?	What motivates you?	What kind of promotions activate you and your agents? How do these differ?	Is there any sales material which you feel would help you and which is not available to you?	Describe the morale of your agents — if necessary on a personal basis and the reasons for any problems that might exist.	Do you have a favorite quote or inspirational message?
How do you feel senior managers can help your personally?	What support can the company expect from you?	Do you consider your talents and contributions lie in the sales field, management field or a balance of both?	In which area do you feel you need the most help?	How valuable is contact to you, and how often do you like to be contacted? How often do your team members like to be contacted?	How important, in your opinion, is field training?

Create questions which will provide answers valuable to your management style and company's success.

4. Prior to the meeting gather together:
   The door prize (suitable for all attendees).
   Tickets for door prize, and appropriate receptacle.
   Awards and prizes for presentation.
   Attendance book.
   Current bulletins and incentive brochures.
   Replenishment of sales material.
   Gift for guest speaker.
   Name tags.
   Supper/refreshments.

5. Delegate subordinate managers specific tasks, such as writing out name tags, getting coffee etc., welcoming the people, introducing people to each other. If it is a small meeting latecomers should be introduced individually on arrival.

6. Be early yourself, and ask subordinate managers to be punctual. Rehearse the meeting while you wait; this ensures a more poised, confident performance, and a smoother flow of events.

7. Deliberately brush up your mental attitude. You need to be enthusiastic. An unenthusiastic manager will turn a good meeting into a mediocre meeting, or a mediocre meeting into a poor one! Your mental attitude is contagious — work on it.

8. Anticipate pitfalls. Ask yourself,
   'With what may I be confronted?'
   An antagonistic agent? A disillusioned new person? Two people in conflict? An interruption from family or phone call can suddenly and seriously spoil the atmosphere. A contentious item in the agenda allowed to take control may detract from the success of the meeting. Anticipate. Plan to minimize their impact.

9. Refrain from apologizing. Apologies weaken meetings; they are an admission that the meeting could have been better!
   Avoid sentences such as: —
   'I am sorry we are starting a little late . . .'
   'I apologise for the weather . . .'
   'It's too bad that Jim Jones could not be with us . . .'
   'Had I known about it, I could have . . .'

10.   Welcome everyone, starting with new agents and their spouses, the guest speaker, then the team.

11.   Introduce each speaker with a few sincere morale building sentences; give credit and thanks where due. This achieves these objectives:

>   The speaker performs better, because you have given him a higher expectation of himself.
>
>   The audience listens better, because you have given it the feeling the speaker might be worth hearing!

Your introduction should cover: Who, What, Why.

>   Who is this? What are his qualifications?
>
>   What the subject is about.
>
>   Why the audience should listen.

Nominate someone in advance, other than the original introducer, to thank the guest speaker. If you select one of the team to talk about an experience, a success, or a known skill, pay him the compliment of asking him to address the meeting *in advance of the occasion.* This ensures the talk is of better quality, and that he receives maximum impact of recognition, to which he is entitled. Casual consideration can be demeaning.

PUBLIC APPRECIATION RESULTS IN PRIVATE GRATITUDE

Leave your motivator, or guest speaker, until last on the agenda, so your people leave on a high note.

12.   Listen attentively throughout the meeting, and pay all your speakers the compliment of taking notes during their addresses. From time to time the audience, or gathering, will be conscious of you, and if you are appreciative and obviously interested in the addresses, they will take their lead from you and listen more attentively. Concentration is a compliment to the speaker, and your enthusiasm for learning is communicated to the group.

13.   Invite guest speakers or their spouses to present awards and prizes, and perhaps the newest agent to draw the door prize or raffle ticket.

14.   Use humor! When participants are amusing your contribution may not be necessary, but often a lighter note needs to be introduced by the manager. When humor is related to the subject

matter, the subject matter becomes more memorable. Unrelated humour is purely entertaining.

15. Make everyone feel important and valued as a team member. Recognize promotions, results and endeavors!

16. Plan participation. Who is more interested in the football game, the players, or the spectators? The players are; they never take their eyes off the ball! Make everyone a player, and deeper interest and involvement results. Invite the agent with his first sale to share it. Ask the person with no results to tell the meeting where he found his determination to continue. After you've called for 'orders in the house' invite your top scorer to share his expertise with the group. Recognize achievers in proportion to endeavor and results.

17. Keep control. Either you are in charge or the audience is! Be courteous, but never abdicate the leadership role.

18. Keep it moving. A meeting can become 'bogged' down on an issue. Take over, tie the ends together; give a reason for continuing, then continue.
    Interruptions of this kind may be made like this:
    > 'I wish we had time for a comment from everyone, and if anyone feels strongly about it, I'd ask him to come and talk to me after we have adjourned, but right now . . .' or
    > 'Tom, I can see you have given this matter a lot of thought, and I'd like to know your ideas. I value your opinion. Would you talk with me afterwards, or when you are free next week sometime?'

19. ·Give credit where it is due. Congratulate everyone present for investing in themselves and attending the meeting. Don't thank them for attending. If you have conducted a sparkling meeting, *they should thank you!*

20. Bring your sales meetings to a climax. Plan a peak of interest and excitement at the end of the agenda. Only one highlight should be introduced — usually this is a new promotion, product, or piece of sales material. Sell the benefits; relate the ability of each person present to the goal's achievement, and elicit a commitment to demonstration activity.

21. Finally it is important to remember, if only one turns up, be positive, and treat that one as if ten were present. And if ten turn

up, treat those ten as if twenty were present, and your meetings will grow in numbers and effectiveness.

22. The next day phone, or write hand-written notes to all active participants, expressing gratitude for the specific contribution made to the meeting's success.

The supper which follows the meeting represents care and expresses a compliment. Make it delicious and plentiful. Think creatively about its presentation: ice a sales target on a cake, the name of the current winner, welcome newcomers or acknowledge a birthday. If all else fails the expectation of a good supper may be the reason for coming next time!

10.12 Motivation

Motivation influences our lives as soon as we step out of our cradles! Literally, to motivate means 'provide with a motive, induce to act.'

'Pick up your toys Toby, or you'll have a good smack.'

First class motivation!

'Get good results in your exams, Ann, and I'll give you a new pen.'

A provided motive and a reason to act!

A basic responsibility of a sales manager is the motivation of:

1. Himself.
2. His team.

Every salesperson needs to learn to motivate himself, though in most companies he can rely on support motivation from senior management. Merle and Alan Anderson of World Book Encyclopedia in Queensland provide the best support motivation I've ever observed. Year after year they stand behind their people, providing them with reliable backup motivation, which is both a launching pad for high aspirations, and a landing ground for the battle weary. But the higher you climb the ladder of a sales organization, the deeper you must delve within yourself for the answers.

Motivation is a force which can be propelled from within a salesperson, or it can have an external source, but either way to be effective all motivation must be internally felt. It then induces action: results depend on action!

Successful sales management must include a working knowledge of how to identify, activate, and sustain motivation. This should run parallel with an understanding of demotivation, its effects, and remedies.

Motivation is not just incentives, nor is it something you do to people; *it is something you create inside a person which activates him.*

An understanding of motivation demands a study of human psychology. A successful sales manager appreciates that what motivates one salesperson may demotivate another, and is able to initiate an environment which challenges the potential of each team member.

Salespeople vary as much as customers do!

The motivation of belief

Belief is a powerful motivator!

A sales manager who gives his people a belief in the product, service or mission which they serve by selling, places his sales people in a winning position.

Enthusiasm is the offspring of belief; it is born of conviction. The motivation radiated by a strong belief carries the salesperson over obstacles, and through difficulties which might otherwise have checked his progress. In the sales environment, the purpose of motivation is to generate committed demonstration activity.

An unshakable belief in the value of a product sells the product. I have a cupboard of inferior cosmetics which stand in silent testimony to this truth! The saleslady's enthusiasm and faith in her product's powers caused me to buy the lotions without even examining them. I never regretted the purchase; just being with her was so much fun!

I do not suggest that the best in salesmanship is represented by belief and enthusiasm alone, but sales managers should recognize that there is no better starting point to a sales career than belief — communicated with enthusiasm!

Job definition

> THE MANAGER'S ROLE IS TO ANTICIPATE AND PROVIDE THE STIMULUS TO FILL THE NEED OF THE SALESPERSON.
> THIS IN RETURN RELEASES ENERGY WHICH ACHIEVES RESULTS.

Influence over the activity of others is a great responsibility. When motivation is used as a device to manipulate for selfish advantage or unethical ambitions, evil is unleashed. Hitler provided an unforgettable example of this; and the nine hundred suicides in Guyana, in South America, stand as a permanent witness to the power of corrupt motivation. History is riddled with motivation-based action.

How to plan motivation

A sales manager needs to insure:

1. That the results of his planned motivation are of benefit to the agent, the company, and to the sales manager himself, and not a disproportionate benefit to one.
2. He should consider how to motivate the team as a whole and team members individually. He must not only be just in all his dealings, but his credibility perceived to be unquestionable.

Lord Justice Hewitt gave all those in authority good advice when he said:

'Justice must not only be done, but be seen to be done.'

3. He should consider the timing of the motivation, and its duration.
4. He should plan the type, variety and management levels of the motivation.

He needs to learn to distinguish between the material and emotional needs of his people, and to create an organization which meets those needs. The material needs are usually money, merchandise, trips. The emotional needs are for promotions, recognition, mission responsibility and satisfaction. A manager needs to create a healthy climate which will induce the team to work willingly and well.

A manager gives support before asking for support.

A manager teaches the way to perform before asking for performance.

A manager recognizes the individual goals before pushing for organizational goals.

A MANAGER OF THIS CALIBER BECOMES THE CATALYST THAT CHANGES A COMMONPLACE CONDITION INTO AN UNCOMMON OUTCOME.

The ultimate of this kind of motivation is that the motivator becomes a manufacturer of motivators. He develops a team of salespeople who are self-disciplined creative decision makers, and they, by example, develop teams of people who are like themselves. The process is continuous, and this progressive manager is the generator of sustained company vitality and expansion.

The motivation of example

A successful sales manager leads his team by example. He is not like the general in the French Revolution who immortalized himself by shouting,

> 'Oh, there go my men, I must find out where they are going, to lead them!'

But motivation *can* be push or pull!

Pep-talks, a financial necessity, competition, a flagging goal, fear of failure, can all push a salesperson out to work, but a leadership example pulls him out. The top manager for Zondervan of Australasia Pty. Ltd., Jill Behne, led her Queensland team by example. Her people could always rely on Jill to fulfil the management demands her position required of her and yet challenge the field leaders by keeping her personal sales targets high. To the challenges of each day she brought a love and understanding of every team member. What inspirational leadership!

No motivational speech in the world will ever compare with the lasting motivation of successful example.

10.13   Contact

So much of worth in sales management is lost through lack of contact that it is valuable to consider where lines can be drawn between effective contacting, acceptable contacting, and inadequate contacting.

The nature of your product and your company's marketing methods have a bearing on the necessity for contact, but direct sales organizations who replace haphazard and unreliable communication with planned and regular contacting will experience an increase in productivity. When sales management puts total emphasis on hiring and training, lack of contact can become the drain hole where all your good work flows away to nothing. Conversely, excessive and prolonged phone conversations can drain your valuable time. Successful sales managers give thought and application to the balance.

What is contacting in the sales arena?

It is keeping salespeople informed of current opportunities, changes and incentives; it is alerting them to possible failure or danger zones; and it acts as a constant reminder of your interest and care in every aspect of your salespeople's lives, and the lives of their family members.

Five is the recommended number of direct reportees a manager can handle to maximum effectivity, but many more can be contacted on an irregular basis.

When should you contact?

You should contact at the first possible opportunity. Never procrastinate; at best procrastination lessens your impact, at worst it proves fatal to your cause!

Ask your team members the time when your regular call would be most welcome, and if you need to disregard the agreed time, apologize and explain. It is advisable to consider low cost charge times when establishing a contact time for long distance calls.

Why should you contact?

You contact to motivate, congratulate and commiserate.

You call or write regularly, not just to encourage the achiever and prompt the non-achiever, but to foster a team spirit of fellowship and involvement.

Beware of the question, 'Have you sold anything?'

It can demotivate the non-achiever; it can irritate the achiever, but it also can be just the question a successful salesperson is hoping for! An empathetic sales manager tries to sense the appropriateness of the occasion.

The objective of contacting is to serve people for mutual benefit, and to anticipate and fulfil their needs.

10.14   Care

CARE IS THE INTANGIBLE INGREDIENT OF SALES MANAGEMENT WHICH ENHANCES ALL ASPECTS OF YOUR DAILY LIFE.

You need to care genuinely about the members of a team, above and beyond their sales potential. Care about their success in the company, but also about their success as human beings. Care manifests itself in all sorts of ways in sales management.

Here, from my observation, are some of them.

Grow-know and *Shrink-think* are titles which represent the two most distinctive styles. You can learn the basics of selling with either, but only one will stretch your potential.

Ten signposts of care
1.   You can always recognize a *grow-know* caring manager when he reads the agenda at a manager's conference or meeting. He assesses it with the eyes and ears of his people, and raises issues

pertinent to their interests. A *shrink-thinker* majors in the subjects which affect him personally, and asks self-oriented questions.

2.   Another perceivable trait is the absence of *grow-knowers* at the end of conference sessions — they are on the phone to alert their people to the new changes and opportunities. Constant contact is a highly visible indication of caring managers.

SHOW ME A MANAGER WHO CONSTANTLY CONTACTS HIS PEOPLE AND I WILL SHOW YOU A CARING MANAGER.

The *shrink-thinker* is mingling and relaxing, he has calculated that the cost doesn't justify too much phoning. If asked he says: 'I tried and tried but couldn't find them home.'

HE WHO IS WILLING TO DO SOMETHING WILL FIND THE MEANS, HE WHO IS UNWILLING WILL FIND THE EXCUSE!

3.   The *grow-knower* keeps a watchful eye on the state of sales kits of his people, and makes sure they receive new material. The *shrink-think* manager isn't concerned.

4.   The *grow-knower* invests his own money, above and beyond the company allowance. When it is necessary he pays out quickly and willingly. The *shrink-thinker* has short fingers and long pockets! He is a slow payer of money owed, and tends to borrow.

5.   A *grow-knower* takes pleasure in seeing awards and prizes are presented promptly, and remembers timely phone calls. The awards and prizes of a *shrink thinker*'s people seldom reach their destination till long after the event.

6.   A *grow-knower* consistently paints the 'big' picture, and holds promotional opportunities in front of his achievers. He learns not to be more ambitious for a salesperson than the salesperson is for himself, but he extends encouragement at all times.
He recognizes the truth of the statement that:

YOU CANNOT HELP PEOPLE PERMANENTLY BY DOING FOR THEM WHAT THEY COULD DO FOR THEMSELVES.

He knows he must be good *for* his people rather than just good *to* his people.
A *shrink-thinker* shrinks his people's perception of their own potential, either deliberately or unwittingly. His reliable,

'You can't do that . . .' or

'It's not company policy to allow . . .'

crushes initiative, and squanders aspiration. If there is a genuine reason why something cannot be done, instead of an open explanation, he prefers simply to withhold permission in order that his authority appears omnipotent. A *shrink-think* sales manager constantly reminds his salesperson that he is the boss, and in so doing makes an open admission of incompetence, and demonstrates a lack of self-confidence.

7. A *grow-knower* supports company functions like conferences and meetings punctually, and performs activities like class and field training conscientiously. A *shrink-thinker* avoids functions unlikely to be well-attended, and delegates class and field training responsibilities too readily.

8. A *grow-knower* learns the tools of management. He is aware that his 'attention to detail' may contribute to the success of his people and to the realization of his own goals. He regards a knowledge of office systems and the mechanics of paperwork as fundamental. He accepts the job of reading books and magazines, listening to tapes on sales management and attending sales seminars, as his responsibility to his people.

HE KNOWS BY INSTINCT, RATHER THAN DESIGN, THAT PEOPLE MAY DOUBT WHAT YOU SAY — ***BUT THEY BELIEVE WHAT YOU DO!***

The *shrink-thinker* cannot work the machine, and regards cash flows and paperwork as time wasters. If he reads sales literature at all, it is purely for his own benefit and advancement.

9. The *grow-knower* welcomes the opportunities which birthdays, family achievements, anniversaries and even illnesses provide for him to express the gratitude or the friendship he feels for his people. The *shrink-thinker* places little value on such things, or forgets, and is usually forgiven more times than he deserves.

10. The *grow-knower* is preoccupied with the achievement of his company's objectives and has faith that the company, in its turn, will work to benefit the interests of all its members. The *shrink-thinker*'s own interests eclipse those of the company and his people and his faith is conditional.

The most memorable *grow-know* manager I had the pleasure of working with was Jean Marshall of Bathurst, New South Wales. For many years Jean ran a large team of part-timers in country territory. The last person she ever thought of was herself. She assessed the incentive prizes through the eyes of her people, and would travel miles to meet their needs. She not only remembered the names of her team members, but the names of all their relations too, — even their dogs and cats!

What made her outstanding? *She genuinely cared.*

It all starts and ends with attitude.

These words of Richard Wolf's could have been written of Jean Marshall, or any caring sales manager:

'It is not what the world gives me, in honour, praise or gold,
It is, what I do give the world so others do unfold . . .
One tiny thought, one tiny word, may give a great one birth,
And if that thought was caused by me, I lived a life of worth.'

10.15   Talent spotting

One of the most important skills of a sales manager, is the ability to spot, and nurture talent. This is not necessarily found in the person you feel the friendliest towards. On the contrary, it is often the most difficult and demanding person whose talent has not found the outlet it needs. He feels confined and unappreciated, and perceives authority as a restriction. Meet his behavior with understanding, approach it with a problem-solving attitude and seek to create for him an environment where he can find fulfilment. A salesperson in this group has the power drive to go far: plan unselfishly to extend his horizon and unleash his potential.

The Irish author George Bernard Shaw recognized the potential of the non conformist when he wrote:

'The reasonable man adapts himself to the world. The unreasonable man persists in trying to adapt the world to himself. Therefore all progress depends on the unreasonable man.'

Every person in a sales team has potential for a contribution of some kind. The successful manager spots, develops, and as much as possible, publicly recognizes it.

One much beloved sales manager I have observed for years heads a team of talented salespeople, all of whom are better at most things than he is. He is *best* at only one thing, spotting and developing talent. With this skill he runs a large, successful sales organization through delegation.

Shaw's writings often displayed an empathetic understanding of the contribution made to mankind by entrepreneurial thinking. In his play *Back to Methuselah*, he clarified the creative individualist with these words:

'SOME MEN SEE THINGS AS THEY ARE, AND SAY WHY?
I DREAM THINGS THAT NEVER WERE, AND SAY WHY NOT?'

A sales manager should look for that attitude. There is usually a high flyer behind it . . . and when he finds it, he strives to create an environment where it can grow. Then in time, *swing with it to the stars!*

This doesn't mean you look for someone to do your work for you, it simply means that you spot the talent and unleash it.

10.16   Good managerial advice — two thousand years old!

The advice given to men in authority by Cicero, one of ancient Rome's greatest orators, can be pondered with advantage today. Thousands of years ago he noted six drastic mistakes:

1. Believing that individual advancement is made by crushing others.
2. Worrying about things that cannot be changed or corrected.
3. Insisting a thing is impossible because we cannot do it ourselves.
4. Refusing to set aside trivial preferences.
5. Neglecting development and refinement of the mind and not acquiring the habit of reading and study.
6. Attempting to compel others to believe and live as we do.

So what's new? *We're new* — new to our time and place.

But we may not have much time, and we may not hold our place, unless we recognize our opportunity, and move with our whole being to make it a reality.

GREAT MANAGERS THINK IN TERMS OF SOLUTIONS, NOT PROBLEMS.

They know that like so many things in life,

THE MORE YOU PUT INTO SALES MANAGEMENT, THE MORE YOU GET OUT OF IT.

Chapter Eleven

SPECIFICALLY

11.1   The customer and the prospect

11.1.1   The difference

Up to this point we have concentrated on the salesperson. Now we focus on other 'special' person — the *customer*!

Customers are people; as a salesperson you will spend your time with the world's greatest resource, its people. As your experience of people situations multiplies, you will grow in stature as life itself reaches out and arms you for the environment.

The basic difference between a prospect and a customer is —

A prospect is a person who might buy.

A customer is a person who has bought.

Mostly the salesperson is responsible for the transition!

A prospect is usually under pressure to make a decision, and a person under pressure is on unnatural ground. Expect him to show characteristics which he is unaccustomed to handling. He may present you with some tough resistance, yet in reality be a gentle, affable person.

A customer is not under pressure. Once you have discovered what he wants and helped him achieve it, his perception of the salesperson is invariably friendly, and he relaxes and enjoys sharing time with you.

11.1.2   An important similarity

The point to remember is that every prospect is reactive, some visibly, some invisibly. He reacts to the product, the sales material, to other opinion, to interruption, to time and above all to you — the salesperson! Your job is to elicit a favorable reaction to your product, therefore you should principally be concerned with the causes of the prospect's reaction.

11.2 Kinds of customers and prospects

11.2.1 The two basic categories of customers

There are two basic kinds of customers.

1. Satisfied.
2. Dissatisfied.

The salesperson, as well as the product or its service can influence the difference.

Sadly, some salespeople demonstrate with little interest in the aftermath of the order. Their objective is the sale and not the customer's long term satisfaction. Carelessly they make statements, claims, and promises which cannot be substantiated. The customer, signing in faith, ends up with a regretted purchase. These salespeople hurt and anger their customers, and bring discredit to the sales industry.

Some customers also approach a purchase carelessly. They have not done their homework, explained their requirements fully and accurately, nor asked the right questions and listened receptively to the salesperson's answers. If the product does not come up to expectations, they blame the product, the salesperson or the company, when in fact their expectations were at fault, or based on assumptions.

A salesperson and his prospect need each other; they should be partners moving in unison at a high level of communication towards the sale, not opponents pulling and pushing alternately towards the sale. A prospect doesn't instinctively feel himself to be a salesperson's partner, but this relationship should be a salesperson's objective. Both are rewarded when they come together mindful of those ageless words:

'Do unto others as you would have done unto you.'

11.2.2 Prospects are multifarious

What makes a prospect the customer he becomes? People have different characteristics; some are unchangeable, and others vary with mood or circumstance. A salesperson meets the mean and the generous, the suspicious and the trusting, the nervous and the courageous, the interested and the bored, the knowledgeable and the ignorant, the truthful and the liar, the rude and the courteous, the critic and the enthusiast. Armed with his own variable characteristics he goes forth to face this conglomerate of prospects and customers.

When you became a salesperson you wanted a challenge, didn't you?

11.3 The influence of character tendencies

11.3.1 Prepare to meet all kinds

The qualities of character which may lie dormant within the prospect, or which he may openly project, can affect the outcome of a sales demonstration. If it was possible for a salesperson to give two identical demonstrations, the outcome could be vastly different owing to the individual reaction of each customer.

11.3.2 The antagonistic prospect

Don't retaliate. Two wrongs never made a right. *Be humble but never humbled* and react with unfailing courtesy. Project impenetrable dignity and discernible pleasure in your work. Apologize for troubling him, and thank him for his time. Sarcasm, innuendo or invective — any kind of uncomplimentary response terminates opportunity and reduces the salesperson's stature. Realize the prospect has the problem, not you, and that sensitive handling can dissolve antagonism. Don't abandon hope too readily — if your product can meet his need you may yet walk together towards the sale. Give him every opportunity, but only a little time . . . and never dwell on his memory.

11.3.3 The distractive prospect

I call these prospects butterflies and grasshoppers! They are usually beautifully agreeable, but just when you think you have a sale, they rebound, fluttering off elsewhere on another line of thought. They prefer to change the subject rather than give an excuse. This response usually cloaks a deep-rooted fear or objection, which, unless discovered and reversed, will prevent a sale. Empathy is a real need here. Aim to weave trust-generating actions and statements throughout the demonstration, on which their confidence can build. Ask questions: you cannot handle what you don't know about!

Product information is still important but closing will prove inappropriate until the root of the problem has been reached and unrestricted communication achieved.

11.3.4 The excited prospect

What a joy they are! Keep the excitement running, match it with your own sincere enthusiasm for your product. With an itemized description of the features and their benefits, build to a peak of interest and use an assumptive close. Travel at their pace, pick up the momentum and sweep together down the path to the sale.

11.3.5 The nervous prospect

Convincing leadership and confident kindness receive the best response. If you appear representative of the qualities the customer would like to possess he takes a psychological step towards you. If you stampede over his feelings he retreats totally from a sales decision.

Use trial closes early and often, and listen encouragingly. Communicative empathy is often rewarded with growing trust, and only when this is established can a salesperson move to negotiate a sale.

11.3.6 The open-minded prospect

This customer's attitude ensures the demonstration is enjoyable whatever its outcome. He extends to the salesperson every opportunity to make the sale. Never allow his attitude to lull you into over confidence. He still needs knowledge and is entitled to the most comprehensive demonstration you can muster. Realize also that his attitude may stem from a lifetime habit of 'giving the other fellow a go,' and it may cloak a fair but tough interior.

Only use full closes; to use a trial close would be like asking for something you already have.

11.3.7 The pretentious prospect

This prospect would like to do, be, and have, a hundred things he doesn't, isn't, and hasn't! He craves the respect he believes others automatically receive. He is usually some way along a path of disillusionment, the pursuit of unworthy priorities, before the salesperson arrives. Even so he will bluff or lie himself out of every situation which doesn't reflect his self image in a creditable light. He rejects reality and demands constant reassurance from his environment.

Somehow he is unable to tell you he can't afford your product, because he wants to believe he can, and sometimes he buys when he shouldn't, as usually he's already over committed.

This prospect is an unlikely buyer, or, if he is a buyer, an unlikely payer. The demonstration is interrupted by ego building references to what he owns, where he's been, and who he knows. His excuses are of a lofty breed — he's giving hundreds of dollars to charity, planning a supermarket or going abroad. . . . Recognize his needs, and try to fill them. Listen with compassion, help if you can. Never judge; life is a continuous learning process for each of us. Close early to test your assessment, he'll usually slip out to a false excuse. Give him every benefit of the doubt, but where there is no doubt, thank him for his time, and leave.

11.3.8   The reluctant prospect

Start with your company demonstration, keep on track. Lead with strong need, follow with benefits interwoven with product knowledge. Place greater emphasis on logical reasons for ownership, apply emotion only lightly. Invite his input whenever you can, but continue nonchalantly if it is not forthcoming.

Enthusiasm can irritate because he doesn't share it; repetition bores him because it failed to convince him the first time. Give a full comprehensive demonstration and allow instinct to direct you if any response emerges. In this way you can unearth a personal interest, and find a starting point upon which you can build need, use and value. Thereafter, it may be a long walk but you can go down the path towards the sale together with growing confidence.

Meaningful not haphazard closing is a must.

11.3.9   The seemingly uninterested prospect

He's an assessor. You may have the feeling that you're not communicating but persevere; it may be that he needs statements confirmed and suspicions allayed before he takes a step in trust and indicates interest. He may be battling doubts that you cannot know about.

Delay closing until you have established a rapport.

11.3.10   The smart aleck prospect

His aim is to unbalance the salesperson, believing that as a result you will be thrown off your known track, and the truth will be more perceivable. His belief that people have a scant regard for accuracy and need to be hassled into the truth usually springs from the fact that he manipulates truth himself. Smart aleck prospects come in two kinds; either they have a low self-esteem and try to build it at your expense, or they like a fun challenge; they're competitors, and they like to keep even. They figure that they're suffering the demonstration so you can do a little suffering too!

The symptoms are the same, but the disease is drastically dissimilar.

The cure, or at least aid, for low self-esteem in a prospect is sincere compliment and genuine interest. This is best expressed by consulting his opinion, and listening attentively to everything the prospect has to say: gentle leadership and courtesy on your part every step of the way.

The cure, or at least aid, for customer challenge is humorous self depreciation, and an impressive professional demonstration.

11.4   The influence of heredity and environment

11.4.1   Why a study of both helps the salesperson

Any study of prospects and customers must include an analysis of what preconditions their thinking, and the following pages are not put forward as confirmed fact, but rather as conclusions drawn from experience of prospect reaction observed over many years.

Heredity and environment both can justly lay claim to influence thinking and reaction, but environment proves of greater significance time and time again. Indeed I have wondered if the reactional tendencies, which appear to be a result of heredity, have an environmental explanation at their base, as in many cases the different races of the world are exposed to different environments. However the reality of the sales environment confirms that certain reactional tendencies, apparently attributable to heredity, can be anticipated, although exceptions are common.

A salesperson is in a position to appreciate and enjoy the variety of reaction different people and different races tend to introduce to a sales demonstration. Every living thing has a right to an appreciated place on earth, and just as the delphinium, the rose and the pansy all contribute to the beauty and interest of the garden, so the different races of the world contribute to the beauty and interest of the human race.

The question a salesperson valuably asks himself as he approaches an intended customer is:

> 'What attitude, prejudice or priority might I anticipate, which I may have to counter, or upon which I may reasonably rely, to support my quest for a sale?'

11.5 Environment

11.5.1 Reactional tendencies as prompted by a work environment

The strongest environmental influence on attitude will always be the home and school environment. However, the prospect's workplace asserts an increasing influence on buying attitudes, and a consideration of these is of value to any salesperson.

The following occupations are some with whom I have had memorable experiences: and although there will always be exceptions, generally these tendencies can be anticipated.

11.5.2 Actuaries, Accountants, Scientists

Not surprisingly, these are figure people!

They are inclined to doubt the salesperson's accuracy, and I have always found it best to pass them any interest rate charts, discount calculations or price cards and ask their opinion. Detailed product information or endorsement should be handed over for examination, rather than read, and a period of silence allowed for assessment to take place. Never work in opposition to the impact and influence your sales material is able to achieve. Explain the product's features, and ask if the benefits are relevant. These people are usually academics and a product which appeals to their intellect or benefits their children is given a favorable hearing. Take an interest in the family's priorities and achievements; it fosters cordiality. Ignore their excuses as long as possible and allow the product every opportunity to do the persuading. They are not easily influenced by a salesperson's opinion however accurate.

Closing must be timely or it can be misinterpreted.

11.5.3 **Administrators, Managers, Supervisors**

Usually these people need to be led through the features and benefits of a product. They tend to like orderly demonstrations. Their environment develops in them an organized attitude which is uncomfortable with impulsive decision making. They respond best to a strong positive demonstration conducive to important decision making. Appointments are imperative as this group easily 'returns to track' when interrupted in their workplace, and the impact of the demonstration can be lost. Conscientious lookers and reliable buyers, they approach a sales demonstration with a sense of responsibility.

11.5.4 **Architects**

These are a disciplined people. Their environment seldom allows them a totally free rein. Their creativity is harnessed to the confines of specific requirements — price, size, shape etc. Their daily work requires careful consideration and precision. It is hardly surprising then that these are the qualities with which they view a sales demonstration. They will listen and look with the integrity the world has come to associate with their profession. Bargaining is out; they look for value and quality, particularly quality, with close scrutiny.

Give a comprehensive demonstration, and close evenly. Handle objections importantly through A.E.I.O.U.

11.5.5 **Armed Services: Airforce, Army, Navy, Marines**

1. **Officers**

They are accustomed to authority, and in their environment make constant and quick decisions. They are straight, likeable, fact dealing people, who expect honesty and give a salesperson a courteous hearing and a chance to make a sale. Give a comprehensive company demonstration, punctuated with trial and full closes. Their reactions are open and can be anticipated, and their objections are genuine and need to be handled to their satisfaction. They make no attempt to trick or trap a salesperson. Show a balance of need, use and value, and close confidently.

2.   Enlisted personnel

Perhaps because they have only spasmodic buying opportunities owing to frequent relocation, these groups are positive buyers. Willing to listen and learn, interested in everything, relaxed and trusting in the sales environment, it is a pleasure to work with them. Their instincts are sharpened in a survival environment. They jump at discounts and premiums, and the price or minimum monthly payment is your first choice of close. Trusting and trustworthy, fun to be with, I always feel privileged to share time and my product with soldiers, sailors, airmen and marines.

11.5.6   Artists: Painters, Musicians, Writers, Poets

Creative prospects tend to fragment easily. They usually consider salespeople as unlikely to have anything to say of originality, and therefore of interest, to them. They consider their requirements are different from most people's, and need to be convinced about the 'need' for the product. Achieve this and they often lose interest in the peripheral, and sign the order while talking about something of greater interest. It is advisable to pay them a sincere compliment and show interest in their work before attempting to demonstrate.

I have found artists, people who earn their living by expressing themselves artistically, to be happy people whose environment allows them to travel at their own pace, and in a direction of their choice. They are not accustomed to listening but rather to responding to creative impulse to the exclusion of outside influence. Only an inept salesperson, therefore, would try to establish control. Instead he should follow their train of thought and return at a time of their choosing. They do need a strong explanation of figures as they're basically disinterested in number work and need to grasp the cost scene. Don't bother handling objections; they probably won't listen. But close lightly and often, sooner or later a sale is likely to result. Demonstrations to artists are quite enchanting, and although they tell you they have no time, . . . invariably you end up staying longer than you ever intended — *and you are glad of it!*

11.5.7   Bankers

I've always imagined a banker's life as being spent listening to people asking for something he'd really rather not give . . .! I picture him sitting skeptically as his clients put forward their propositions. This is invariably the attitude he brings to a sales demonstration.

The salesperson needs to give a confident demonstration, lifting the communication level high to attract his interest. Bankers are listeners, but they are also ready to make a quick negative judgement; they protect their environments this way. Avoid statements which may be interpreted as exaggerations or unprovable; he is trained to identify misleading facts and concentrates on this. Sincerely present your product to his needs. Handle objections with the A.E.I.O.U. system, and close positively.

If the sale is not achievable, leave promptly. Nothing is gained by dalliance, but ask for referrals; bankers are accustomed to referring clients to people and do so most helpfully.

11.5.8 Barristers, Attorneys

Lawyers are less vulnerable to persuasion that most, even logical persuasion. Pressure is the daily expectation of their work environment, so the pressure normally experienced following a closing question barely registers! However they are specialists and if your product is outside their expertise, they are excellent listeners. You seldom find an uninterested lawyer — they're either interested or won't agree to the demonstration. Their training is in both concentrated analytical listening, and quick aggressive response. They are accustomed to sifting fact from opinion and differentiating between the significant and the insignificant through a mound of trivia, and will probably approach your demonstration with the same finely tuned instinct. Lightly introduce the opinion of people likely to impress them without expectation of a response and place emphasis on the features of the product clearly and with minimum repetition. Minimise the likelihood of non involvement with trial closes, and seek their agreement as you move through the material.

A.E.I.O.U. their objections.

11.5.9 Brokers: Wool, Stock, Insurance, Commodity, Futures

They are open minded people. Their environment dictates that they accumulate experience both in selling and buying, and they approach a sales demonstration much as they would like to be approached themselves.

They have highly developed people skills from coping with clients under pressure of decision on a regular basis, so courtesy and consideration for others become a natural extension of their posture. They don't give many excuses, but their objections once voiced are genuine, so move to the A.E.I.O.U. method of handling objections after you have ignored but acknowledged the first excuse.

11.5.10 Builders

They are very fair people, always ready to give value for value. Builders are usually experienced 'people' assessors. Their environment demands they deal constantly with challenging and changing people situations. They come to rely on their own judgement of people. I have always been conscious of being assessed by a builder during the first part of a demonstration, and I have needed to be aware that the features explained during this period would need to be repeated. Once they trust the salesperson and become convinced of the advantages of product ownership, the sale is normally forthcoming; reach for the order pad and assume the sale.

11.5.11 Commentators, Television and Radio Announcers

Talkers certainly, but good listeners just the same!

This group places strong reliance on the spoken word, and will tend to assess your demonstration this way, giving the sales material cursory glances. Words are their world, so take care to be communicative and comprehensive. Usually they ask lots of questions and need to be convinced of the advantages of ownership. Show interest in their work, and compliment their genuine achievements.

They think quickly and accurately under pressure, and will buy on impulse. Excuses are inconsequential and frequent, but objections need to be treated respectfully.

11.5.12 Dentists

Open-minded, interested, appreciative of value and quality. The vast difference between doctors and dentists as prospects always amazed me, as I had assumed they would be somewhat similar, until I considerd the contrasts in their environments.

A dentist has a captive listener who has very little opportunity even to edge a word out! Also, the consequences of a wrong decision are less severe — after all he simply pulls a tooth out and throws it away!

A dentist brings lack of pressure to a buying decision. He looks closely, assesses the advantage of ownership versus the understood need. When he gives an objection, handle it professionally and close the sale.

11.5.13 Doctors

In complete contrast to a dentist's routine, a doctor functions in an environment of listening to people continually, and it is unlikely that much of it is pleasing conversation. On the contrary it is more likely to be sad or worrying. He must listen with patience, courtesy and understanding, while the subject matter, length of discussion, and the tone of the interview is largely dictated by the patient.

When a salesperson visits the position is reversed. For these reasons, and the fact that his academic environment has convinced him of his intellectual superiority, and his waiting room is full of people with an attitude of deference, he extends little encouragement to a nervous salesperson. Sadly, I would advise any salesperson to approach physicians and surgeons with an expectation of patronage. However, they are buyers. The qualities you need are a professional dignity, a sound product knowledge, resilience, and an understanding heart. Demonstrate with an emphasis on the facts and features. Suggest the benefits, don't dictate them.

Intelligent prospects prefer to be directed towards, but identify their own benefits.

Answer objections with A.E.I.O.U., and close conventionally.

If there is any waiting to be done *expect to do it!*

11.5.14 Draftsmen, Data Processors, Computer Analysts, Technicians, Photographers

These people are concerned daily with careful checking. Mighty projects can be dependent upon their attention to detail. They are meticulous and have a highly developed ability to seek out and find influential fact. They bring these tendencies developed by their environment to a sales demonstration. The salesperson should give a comprehensive presentation communicating the features and benefits in combination, and move with an assumptive attitude to the closing question.

They're 'cause' and 'effect' people, concerned with supply and demand. This group responds to an understanding with an undertaking.

11.5.15   Drivers: Bus, Train, Truck

Perhaps they readily appreciate other people because they are alone for such long stretches, but without exception drivers are friendly, welcoming and humorous; the demonstration is always fun.

A driver is an experienced and accurate decision maker; his environment demands he make life and death decisions on a split second basis. He carries considerable responsibility, so a salesperson may sincerely acknowledge this. Show the features and benefits of your product and close purposefully with a mixture of trial and full closes. Take time to socialize.

11.5.16   Electricians, Mechanics, Fitters, Turners, Plumbers, Welders

These people work with their minds but express themselves with their hands. Their environment requires that they use their hands and brains in co-ordination. Therefore their tendency is to think 'follow through'; they like to grasp a complete concept. A sales demonstration should cover every interlocking consideration of the purchase, the need, the features, the benefits, the use and the value. Excuses and questions ricochet one off another and the salesperson is required constantly to divert into smaller 'products of the moment' sales demonstrations, traveling conscientiously through the standard sales process each time. A sale usually results in response to a close after a patient, informative demonstration.

11.5.17   Engineers

I have always been fascinated by the reaction to a sales demonstration by engineers. They simply don't enjoy buying. To them it is an unfortunate necessity, to be avoided if possible. Their environment demands they be problem solvers, and their training alerts them to the fact that good decision-making stems from a total awareness of the problem, and every influencing factor. When suddenly they are faced with making a decision on a previously unknown product, their entrenched tendency to check and confirm takes charge, and they search and enquire diligently for reasons not to buy, rather than for reasons to buy.

This seemingly negative response is best met with a logical approach to the facts and figures, the language of their workplace. Emotion can be an embarrassment and is regarded with suspicion. They recoil from an excess of enthusiasm. Cheerfulness and logic are appreciated, especially in retrospect, and even if a decision is postponed, a sale often results when time and thought have been applied to the product.

Engineers are among my favorite people (the fact I married one proves this!) — but they are out of their element when confronted with a sudden buying decision.

11.5.18   Entertainers

These people live in a congratulatory environment; it is home for them, so the salesperson needs to acknowledge their achievement to cross the threshold. Entertainers of all kinds are warm, responsive people once communication is established. Many people want their attention so you need to prove quickly that time invested in listening to you is in their interests. Their environment demands that they please their public, and they easily lapse into this frame of mind if you impress them. They thrive on enthusiasm, excitement and appreciation, and so make this the language of the demonstration. Like artists and other creative people they have a short concentration span, so get on with your job, — *you* have a performance to give! If you spend the time providing a willing audience you may find a proverbial curtain call has whisked away your sale.

11.5.19   Entrepreneurs, Chief Executive Officers, Chairmen, Managing Directors

These people bring to a sales demonstration an expectancy of positive, quick decision-making. You sense their strength, but salespeople who approach these business leaders are sometimes surprised to find a complete lack of superiority. They are invariably encouraging and helpful. Their experience of life has usually exposed them to such a variety of people and situations that they know, far better than most, the real values of worth in the marketplace of life.

They perceive the approach of a salesperson as it really is — a person contributing as best he can with the possibility of a new product which may prove beneficial. Remember, entrepreneurs and achievers have very often wrested their lifestyle from an environment which demanded much of them, and they came through winners. They know that courage, persistence, and work are admirable qualities, so demonstrate them.

Do your job professionally, use the AEIOU method of handling objections and close decisively — they appreciate it. In the same situation that's what they would have done!

11.5.20   Executives

Their environment provides the executive with many decision-making opportunities, but there is usually someone in authority looking over his shoulder. The result of a sales demonstration tends to be that he acquiesces verbally, but procrastinates the action of buying, just as he would if he was asked to make a decision he felt would be safer left to the Chairman or Company President.

An executive sifts carefully through all the facts, features and figures, without giving much indication of his feelings. Comfortable trial closes help to bring you closer to the prospect's thinking. Don't decide he isn't a customer because he doesn't buy on the first few full closes. He invariably presents an array of excuses which are best ignored, but perseverance and the influence of authoritarian recommendation are often rewarded.

11.5.21   Factory Workers

The first task of the salesperson demonstrating to a factory worker is to 'sell' himself. Trust must be established, and genuine care communicated right at the beginning for, until convinced of your motives, he tends to assume a salesperson is motivated only by self-interest.

These people often work hard at repetitious jobs to earn their pay check, and the salesperson needs to have a product which offers real value, or an opportunity for an improved lifestyle for themselves or their children. They often display an inspiring determination to plan for the future, and make sacrifices for worthy goals. They are interested to listen and to learn, and are ready buyers once their needs are met, and value is felt and understood.

11.5.22   Farmers, Landowners

Farmers are traditional thinkers, and their priorities and preferences are deeply entrenched. Independent in their lifestyle, they think in terms of the realities of their environment. If a farmer has made up his mind not to buy until seasonal conditions change, his mind can be closed to both fact and persuasion, discount or premium. A salesperson will have to work hard to change his opinion, as neither a logical nor an emotional approach to the sale is likely to alter his thinking.

In this circumstance the farmer's wife can be your only hope. However, when he believes he can afford your product and he appreciates the advantages of ownership, he is a willing buyer. Farmers are money-conscious even when they have financial security, so the salesperson needs to place strong emphasis on value. The word of a farmer is usually his bond, and he welcomes a salesperson with respect, friendship and loyalty.

11.5.23   Farm Workers

These people need to be led through the demonstration and are usually appreciative listeners as their environment normally offers them little opportunity for important decision-making. The demonstration should proceed slowly and carefully through each feature and related benefit. They usually offer few excuses and ask few questions, but this should not be interpreted as lack of interest.

The figure work needs to be fully but simply communicated. In general, farm workers are happy purchasers, once they see and feel the benefits, and are confident of the payment.

11.5.24   Firemen

Their environment is one of emergency and often danger. In contrast, their off-work time places emphasis on relaxation and pleasure. A product associated with a safety, security, and enjoyment benefit is welcomed. Honest and open to deal with, they tend to be ready buyers of perceived value.

11.5.25   Government Workers, Public Servants

You've guessed it — they're not decision makers! Give a strong positive demonstration with an assumptive attitude. Tailor it to their individual needs, and be responsive to questions and input. These people have a ton of security, but they're often seeking a stimulating interest and are good listeners. Pay them the courtesy of seeking out their needs and listen to their responses. The influence of their environment does not encourage them to act on their own initiative, but it teaches them that every member of a team has an valuable part to perform, so patiently move through the demonstration including every family member, closing as you go. Government employees are encouraging, helpful people and consistent buyers.

11.5.26 Hairdressers, Barbers

These people have distinct personalities offering a variety of idiosyncrasies. Every demonstration is memorable. They are accustomed to listening to many and varied opinions, and this environment nurtures their own! They talk interestingly on a huge range of subjects, and indeed do so regardless of the quality or brevity of your demonstration. The salesperson should concentrate on his listening skills, and yet show flexibility in selecting the time to revert to the sales demonstration.

They like to see value and feel need, and look for quality in everything they buy, and when the time is right they will sign the order ungrudgingly. Close at regular intervals.

11.5.27 Journalists, Reporters

The needs of a news environment are observation and analytical skills, a respect for accuracy, and conversely, creativity. Journalists are trained to take known facts and create something readable and arresting from them. Hardly surprising then, that they approach a sales demonstration with this attitude. They tend to listen with concentration, and then pounce on something seemingly irrelevant or unimportant, and make an issue of it. This tests a salesperson who likes to follow a set demonstration pattern, especially as sometimes it is accompanied by a measure of aggression.

Express appreciation of the points a journalist makes; you can pick up new angles and additional information which can be useful in later demonstrations. If you approach a demonstration to a journalist with an attitude of expectancy of the unusual, you will place yourself in a position to benefit. Ignore objections as long as you can, and close only when tasteful and timely.

Remember that they have a well-developed critical faculty, but that in itself, never made anyone right!

11.5.28 **Judges**

Judges ponder decisions; honor this with deference. As the administrators of justice, would we have them any other way?

Present your product fully and openly, just as the attorney presents his case in court, pausing patiently to allow him to take the lead should he so desire. Permit the product to handle objections as far as possible. Use full closes. Allow him to 'sell' himself, and let *him* tell you — *he invariably does!* Just listen. Smile and be friendly; this is one ingredient of which his work place is devoid. Courts are not places of joy and friendliness, and his daily considerations are solemn. You will find he appreciates this in a salesperson and responds.

Be prepared to return, even though you may feel you have nothing to add; judges often want to 'bring on another witness' or 'consult an expert' before making a decision. Acquiesce.

11.5.29 **Laborers**

These people enjoy sales demonstrations, they like to buy. This doesn't mean a quick demonstration, however, because they like to buy slowly, and won't open their minds to the influence of a salesperson until trust is firmly established. They find repetition reassuring, are interested in all information, and have a respect for knowledge. Closing should be delayed until the product's impact has been grasped. Their children are a source of great pride, and should be involved in the demonstration whenever practical.

11.5.30 **Ministers of Religion**

Even within the same denomination, I have always found marked contrasts of reaction from church leaders. Some respond with spontaneity, and others seem reluctant to indicate interest. They are usually interested in good value and believe they are less able to afford than those in other vocations. Trust can be established by showing a genuine interest in their aims and achievements. An attitude of sincere helpfulness is one to which they are accustomed, and courteously respond. They often react enthusiastically to offers of sales jobs for their congregation, and any sales manager can contribute in this way. Usually they give lots of excuses, but buy on closes if the need is felt strongly enough. Demonstrations to church leaders are more effective in the home than the church environment. They are never stereotyped, but are invariably interesting or rewarding in some unexpected way.

11.5.31 **Nurses, Nurses Aids**

Nurses are 'people' people!

They are traditionally cheerful, responsive and enthusiastic, and always great prospects. Their work environment is one of helping others to look at the optimistic side, often in the face of hopeless situations. They simply are not interested in negatives, and instinctively seek solutions for problems. A salesperson should give a strong positive demonstration, with emphasis on product need and the benefits of ownership, and he will find that many times the prospect himself will find the way to buy! These people are delightful prospects and customers!

11.5.32 **Pensioners**

Pensioners are often a neglected sales arena.

A slow and comprehensive demonstration, combined with a carefully programmed budget plan, not only can result in a sale, but in a much-appreciated sale. Many products on the market which offer pleasure and aid to older people depend on a direct salesperson to make contact and explain the benefit. If offering time payment, a salesperson must be aware of the extent to which his company is able to support the product's purchase, but an increasing number of companies are recognizing the reliability of these sales on time payment. Patience and genuine care should accompany and be communicated during an otherwise standard demonstration.

Treat excuses with the importance normally reserved for objections.

11.5.33 **Policemen**

I have always found policemen considerate prospects and happy customers, but care should be taken to allay any doubt about your credibility which may be an environmental response to a vagrant stranger! You should make an appointment, not call unexpectedly. Policemen, perhaps because they are especially aware of the influence of a home, seem particularly to value home life, and are relaxed and gracious in a home sales demonstration. They need to be led through the demonstration and into buying decisions from closing questions, but they seldom put up much objection to a needed product offering affordable value.

11.5.34 **Politicians**

These are personable people who habitually aim to please their constituents. Once you have circumnavigated their secretaries, the salesperson is given a warm welcome, but not necessarily an easy sale! Possibly because they are accustomed to consulting with other opinions before making decisions, their tendency is to procrastinate and shelve the decision. A strong positive demonstration is required, liberally interspersed with product need and qualified endorsements. Emphasis should be placed on any convenience or timesaving benefit associated with your product. Close determinedly, and use A.E.I.O.U.

11.5.35 **Postmen, Deliverymen, Milkmen**

They run on a well known track in every sense!

They approach new thinking with caution, and break into excuses fairly readily. Their environment exerts little mental pressure, and they are affable, kindly people with a well-developed sense of cheerfulness. Perhaps this comes from constantly greeting people in a friendly way, and an unconfined lifestyle. A salesperson can always establish a common link with a humorous reference to similar hazards faced by both our vocations — making calls, dogs, or falling over bicycles! Give a full explanation of the features and benefits, but be prepared for their sense of fun to distract you from time to time. Don't assume, but close and handle objections with responsive humor.

11.5.36 **Professors, Senior Lecturers**

Academics tend to view sales demonstrations as if from another planet! From lofty intellectual heights they assess the demonstration in a detached fashion, which the salesperson should not endeavor to bridge. When they speak it is as if to a student in class.

Remain on your known track until such a time as you are summoned off it! Intelligence is a gift we should all respect, and with an academic prospect this should be demonstrated by inviting opinion and enquiring about his work. Professors are teachers, their instinct is to impart knowledge; listen and you may well learn. The most he will hope for from a salesperson is an honest, open, preferably brief explanation of your product's features, facts and figures. Provide this to the best of your ability and a sale can result more readily than you may have imagined.

11.5.37   **Restaurateurs, Shopkeepers, Pharmacists**

Make an appointment — these are people who plan and like organization. Their environment demands versatility as it is one of constant important interruption. They are required to slot in and placate many people and you don't want to be regarded as yet another interruption. Your product and time are too precious to be invested casually. Achieve this, and you have an open minded decision-maker who likes to deal with people on an on-going basis. Don't dawdle, get on professionally with a comprehensive sales demonstration. When he buys from you, or even if he doesn't, visit his restaurant or shop whenever in the vicinity. These people know the value of a recommended reputation in business, and if they are grateful to you will provide many quality referrals.

11.5.38   **Salespeople**

My experience has led me to conclude that we salespeople fall into two contrasting categories:
1.   Those who buy readily and constantly, and with pleasure.
2.   Those who seldom buy, and indeed are hard to sell.
     There is no middle group.
Some take the attitude of,
     'Now it's my turn to have the fun of buying.'
They love products of all kinds and eagerly seek their features and desire their benefits.
     The second group adopts the attitude,
     'I'm too knowledgeable to be trapped into buying, it's no good this salesperson thinking he's going to sell me something!'
But the fascinating phenomenon is the fact that a salesperson can change, even regularly, from one attitude to another!
So if you plan to demonstrate to a salesperson, you need to have your antennae out to help you assess the attitude of the prospect on the day of your visit. The first group follows the standard demonstration, but a member of the second group responds best to consultation. Ask for help. He will 'sell' himself, if you communicate the features of the product at a level where the benefits of ownership become apparent.

11.5.39   **Secretaries, Typists**

Easily excited, they approach a sales demonstration with a desire to know, and with a mind open and interested. Their environment tends to make them good planners, and they are most comfortable with a well-organized demonstration. Anything new is greeted with enthusiasm, and the salesperson is assured of a thoroughly enjoyable visit. Cost is a consideration so care should be taken to communicate the options of purchase plans. Close early, close often, and ask for referrals; they are used to putting people in touch with one other.

11.5.40 Small Businessmen/Women

These hard working people like to make decisions in their own time, and on their own terms. They make commitments and follow them through. A demonstration to this group is never dull. In fact it, can be likened to fishing: you hang on to the end of the rod, and wind it in when you can, but you will certainly have to let it out from time to time!

Keep a sense of humor handy.

Give the very top demonstration you have in your repertoire, never encroaching unnecessarily on their time; they appreciate that. These people give life the best they have to give, in the face of triumph or disaster.

See that you do the same, and hang in there!

11.5.41 Social Workers

The work world of a social worker is a giving one. During the warm-up introduction, prior to the start of the demonstration, express a sincere interest in his work, and continue to show it throughout the qualifying period. These people do much good for many people in the community, so take time to give them genuine appreciation. Demonstrate to inform with an attitude of service, taking the leading role from the beginning to end.

11.5.42 Solicitors

Solicitors are naturally conservative, and the salesperson who endeavors to shift their thinking on unsupported sales claims had better come down from his tree!

Their training has ensured a respect and commitment to the known and established, rather than for the innovative. The best way of teaching (and a salesperson teaches about his product) is by stretching people's thinking from the known to the unknown. A salesperson needs to find a starting point, perhaps of an appreciated feature, an understood benefit, or an interest in common, from which to move through the material. Ignore excuses, handle objections openly, and be sensitive to the 'product of the moment'. Solicitors are logical buyers, but sprinkle a little emotion throughout. Across a desk solicitors deal with people all the time and have a genuine concern for the interests of others.

11.5.43　Sports People, Sports Coaches

If anyone ever suggested to you that sports people aren't as intellectually quick as other groups, think again! Their instincts are as fast as their movements. There is a coordination which runs deeper and reaches further than muscle and bone. It extends to total awareness of their environment, and in a sales demonstration that includes you. They are interested but not open-minded. It is just as if they know what works and aren't about to be told! They function in a world of action and reaction. A ball moves as it is hit: you jump the hurdle, lift the weight, knock out the other person, or get knocked out — persuasion plays no part.

Appreciate, therefore, that your demonstration will need to have an elastic quality to enable you to stretch in directions of their choice at times of their choice. They're decision makers, and quick to make judgements; sometimes too quick for their own understanding of the product. Take time to go back over the material, but not too much time. Action is habitual, so their patience level is low. Take an interest in their sports achievements as a common courtesy. Be aware that they can handle tough situations, even rebuffs without changing pace, so make sure you can.

Tenacity is respected.

11.5.44　Teachers, Librarians

Their environment is one of control and authority, and although they are one of the most divergent groups, they tend to bring these characteristics to a sales demonstration.

They are accustomed to commanding attention, so take care not to contradict or override their statements or you are more likely to come away with the dunce's cap than the sale! Elicit their opinion, encourage their participation, and show value and the advantage of ownership. A relaxed, noncontentious atmosphere should be promoted and maintained, as they have little relaxation in the classroom environment, and appreciate the contrast.

Teachers and librarians are buyers of functional value, so explain the features of your products in detail. You will find they understand the 'need' and perceive the benefits quickly, if steered in the right direction.

11.5.45   Waiters, Waitresses, Bartenders

Their environment is one of constant activity and they learn to think and move swiftly. They tackle life with enthusiasm, and often are ambitious for an improved lifestyle. They are optimistic people who usually give you the benefit of a doubt. They fit comfortably into a friendly fast-moving demonstration, which hits the main features hard, but doesn't clog in lateral issues. Close constantly but don't linger if unsuccessful. Keep building momentum to a climax, and ask your closing question strongly.

Usually young people, they are prepared to make decisions involving risk, and often have two sources of income.

11.5.46   Wharf Laborers, Stevedores

This group has the country by the tail, and likes it known! Aggressive in the face of other opinion, disrespectful of authority in any form, a wharfie is inclined to try and intimidate a salesperson to test his mettle. Don't be . . .

Beneath that rough exterior there beats a warm and generous heart. He will reward you with a sale if you come through, awaking in him a need and a want for our product, while projecting the qualities of character he admires. Battle a bit (he often has), and he likes to see a bit of fight in a person. If you're going to get a deposit from him, it will be on his terms. Keep on track if he needles you, and introduce humor whenever you can; he appreciates a laugh.

And, as he will tell you, *it isn't the money*, . . . he could buy and sell the Lord Mayor!

11.6 THIS ABOVE ALL

THIS GREAT PROFESSION OF SALESMANSHIP CONCERNS
TWO GROUPS OF IMPORTANT PEOPLE:

FIRST YOU, THE SALESPERSON.

THEN THE PROSPECT, WHO DEPENDS ON YOU AND
YOUR PRODUCT TO HELP HIM TAKE THAT STEP IN TRUST AND
BECOME THE CUSTOMER.

NO ONE SHOULD EVER FORGET
JUST HOW PRECIOUS THESE TWO GROUPS ARE TO OUR WORLD.

Some years ago I was presented with an Australian award for salesmanship from the then Minister of Employment and Industrial Relations, Mr Tony Street. The inspirational words he spoke at that time I leave with you now, as they apply to thousands of salespeople:

'Thank you, Rosemary, for not just sitting at home, but for going out and helping the wheels of our economy to turn . . .'
I did that? I hadn't thought of it that way . . . *and perhaps you haven't either.*

Salespeople more than any single profession are the custodians of national employment. The more we sell, the more employment we create.

It is my hope that whether you go forth and hold high the banner of salesmanship, blazing untrodden trails and rewriting records, or whether you walk with pride in its shadows, that the choice will have been yours, ...

. . . . . . and that somewhere, sometime, these pages may prove beneficial.

THE END

RECOMMENDED READING

In His Steps, Charles Sheldon: The Zondervan Publishing House, Grand Rapids, Michigan, 1967

Winners & Losers, Sydney Harris: Argus Communications, Niles, Illinois, 1964

How To Be Happy Though Rich, Peter Daniels: Endage Print, Ascot Park, South Australia, 1984

The Magic of Thinking Big, David J. Schwartz: Cornerstone, St. Louis, 1962

See You at the Top, Zig Ziglar: Gretna, La, Pelican, 1975

The One Minute Manager, Kenneth Blanchard, Ph.D., and Spencer Johnson, M.D. : Berkley Books, New York, 1982

How To Give Yourself A Raise in Selling, Howard Bonnell: Frederick Fell Publications, New York, 1980

Winning Strategies In Selling, Jack & Garry Kinder & Roger Staubach: Prentice-Hall, Inc. Englewood Cliffs, N.J., 1981

You Can Too, Mary C. Crowley: Fleming H. Revell Co., Old Tappan, 1976

Be a Winner, Rev. Gordon Moyes: Vital Publications, Sydney, 1982

Live Without Fear, Dr. Andre Davril: Bridge Printery, Sydney, 1973

Mary Kay on People Management, Mary Kay Ash: Warner Books Inc. 1984

Body Language, Dr Joe Braysich: Braysich Enterprises, Perth, W.A. 1979

The Power Of Positive Thinking, Norman Vincent Peale: Fawcett, New York, 1978

How To Master The Art Of Selling, Tom Hopkins: Champion Press, Scottsdale, Arizona, 1980

Body Language, Alan Pease: William Collins, Sydney

Seeds of Greatness, Denis Waitley: Fleming H. Revell Co., Old Tappan, 1983

The Stumpjumpers, Neil Lawrence & Steve Bunk: Hale & Iremonger, Sydney, 1985

Now Is Your Time To Win, Dave Dean: Tyndale House Publishers, Illinois, 1984

Face To Face Selling, Bart Breighner: Arden Glen, Illinois, 1985

Success Through a Positive Mental Attitude, Napoleon Hill & W. Clement Stone: Pocket Books, 1977

The Greatest Miracle in the World, Og Mandino: Bantam, New York, 1977

Salesaction International Pty Ltd

THIS COMPANY CONDUCTS SALES TRAINING SEMINARS INTERNATIONALLY.

THEIR SPEAKERS ACCEPT A LIMITED NUMBER OF PERSONAL SPEAKING ENGAGEMENTS WHEN TIME IS AVAILABLE.

ROSEMARY MOORE'S NEWLY-RECORDED SALES CASSETTES ARE AVAILABLE FROM THE RESPRESENTATIVE OUTLETS LISTED BELOW

FOR INFORMATION, phone or write to

Salesaction International Pty Ltd:

2391 Kennedy Road,	270 Edgecliff Road,	14 Halford Road,
Scarborough,	Woollahra,	Richmond,
Toronto, Ontario, M1T 3T7	Sydney, NSW, 2025	Surrey, TW10 GAP,
CANADA.	AUSTRALIA.	ENGLAND.
Phone: (416) 299-9292	Phone: (02) 389-5613	Phone: (01) 940-2625

YOU CAN
LEARN TO SELL
•Attitude
• Goals
• Approaches
• Qualifying
• Closing
• Handling Objectives
• Rejection and Failure
• Time Management
• Prospecting
• Decision Making
• Sex Differences in Selling
• Handling Grievances and
Controversy
•AUSTRALIAN MADE•

INDEX